MW00489777

HOW THE WEST WAS LOST

BEN RYAN

How the West Was Lost

The Decline of a Myth and the Search for New Stories

HURST & COMPANY, LONDON

First published in the United Kingdom in 2019 by
C. Hurst & Co. (Publishers) Ltd.,
41 Great Russell Street, London, WC1B 3PL

Distributed in the United States, Canada and Latin America by
Oxford University Press, 198 Madison Avenue, New York, NY 10016,
United States of America.

A Cataloguing-in-Publication data record for this book
is available from the British Library.

ISBN: 9781787381933

This book is printed using paper from registered sustainable
and managed sources.

www.hurstpublishers.com

Printed in Great Britain by Bell and Bain Ltd, Glasgow

CONTENTS

CONTENTS

ACKNOWLEDGEMENTS

To paraphrase *The Hitchhiker's Guide to the Galaxy*, the West is big. Really big. Attempting to critique it, and doing full justice to the sheer range of issues that this entails—political, social, historical and philosophical—is probably impossible. Inevitably, some things have not been dealt with in as much depth as they should have been, and I am sure there are plenty of issues that deserved inclusion which have been passed over completely, for which I can only apologise.

Even to cover what is included in this book has required a huge amount of advice and guidance from friends and colleagues. These include Alexander Faludy and Jakub Krupa, who provided essential advice, contacts and material on Central and Eastern Europe, and Izzy Ryan for her advice on tribalism and identity. All of my colleagues at Theos have been wonderful sources of support and wisdom on a range of issues, but particularly Nick Spencer, who also read through drafts and provided detailed comments that have greatly strengthened the book as a whole. I would like to thank Michael Dwyer at Hurst for his enthusiasm for the topic and his colleague Lara Weisweiller-Wu for her hugely helpful and constructive feedback.

I am the child of two academics, and while this has scarred me in all sorts of ways, it has also given me two outstanding histo-

ACKNOWLEDGEMENTS

rians and editors in the family, who each provided excellent advice and criticisms on early drafts.

This book would not have been possible without my wife Camilla, who was the key sounding board for many of my ideas and an invaluable source of support.

Finally, I would like to pay tribute to the late Dr Tony Atcherley, a wonderful family friend, teacher and philosopher on whose advice I read several key books that inspired this one. I would have loved to have been able to discuss its arguments further with him.

FOREWORD

Westerners seem to love the idea that the West is in crisis. Since at least the end of the First World War, writers in every decade have believed that the West is in danger, declining, or even already dead. The immediate aftermath of the First World War prompted a good deal of soul searching and doubt in the progress of the West—most prominently in Oswald Spengler's seminal *Decline of the West*.[1] The French poet and philosopher Paul Valéry and the philosopher Henri Massis represented a parallel French tradition of inter-war existential doubt.[2] The process has continued through to our own times. Even in 2006, at the seeming height of European and Western optimism, Richard Koch and Chris Smith wrote a book entitled *Suicide of the West*.[3] In the 2010s, we have seen various books lamenting the decline of liberal democracy, liberalism itself, Europe, and others.

Though not always recognized as such, this is a profoundly and distinctly Western anxiety. The right-wing British journalist Douglas Murray repeatedly notes in *The Strange Death of Europe* (2017) that Europe is the only continent with the urge to obsess about what it is and what its identity amounts to.[4] He means it as a criticism, and yet this self-interrogation has always been at the heart of European intellectual life, and more broadly the West as a whole. On the other end of the British political spectrum, the same trend is apparent beneath the surface of Afua Hirsch's 2018 autobiographical treatise on racial identity, *Brit(ish)*. She records a comment from her partner who asked, "What kind of black person feels they actually have to write a *book* about being black?"[5]

This is exactly the right question, and the answer must be: the kind of person who has been saturated within a Western intellectual tradition—one that obsesses over its own identity, past and future. The West is nothing if not an intellectual space characterized by constant introspection and an ongoing existential crisis.

This book sits self-consciously within that tradition. As such, one of the questions that plagued me in writing it was whether the current Western crisis, as I perceive it, is in any way special. "Chronocentrism", the charge of seeing things only through the lens of one's own time, is a real challenge. It's impossible to escape the sense that this feels like the end of an era: the end of Western self-confidence and global dominance. The question is whether this is just a temporary blip, the beginning of a long slow decline—the political scientist David Runciman believes that Western democracy is experiencing a mid-life crisis: over the hill but with many years left[6]—or whether we will continue bumbling on, in hope rather than expectation of something getting better.

Whichever of those scenarios proves to be true, this is an era characterized by disappointment, disillusionment and no little anger. The anger is manifesting itself in an increasingly hostile and extreme tone of public debate. To call someone a traitor, a saboteur, accuse them of treason, of being an enemy of the people, or even diabolic would once have been shocking; now it just seems exhaustingly commonplace. Anger is the default of a political sphere gone wrong.

The sense of disappointment and disillusion is felt more by some groups than others—but is certainly a feature of my own generation. I was born in 1990, halfway between the Berlin Wall coming down and the final dissolution of the USSR. The West's last great ideological opponent (or so it was widely thought) had, in a remarkably short space of time, simply ceased to exist. The Cold War was something I learnt about from James Bond films, school history lessons and family stories (both of my parents lived for periods in the Soviet Union), but was not something I had personally experienced. Thatcher and Reagan were semi-mythical heroes or villains, depending on who you spoke to. This was the first—and now probably last—"post-historic" generation, growing up in an atmosphere of supreme confidence in the Western worldview's moral superiority and inevitable victory. The political culture of my youth was the confidence of Blair's New Labour, a promised end to "boom and bust", and a supreme confidence that the middle way was working, and working well.

Even the concept of the West as a geographically limited area looked to be an increasingly absurd anachronism. Japan and South Korea were democratic, capitalist cultures that looked to be blending seamlessly into a broader Western culture—particularly at the youth level where everyone was playing the same video games on the same consoles and increasingly watching the same TV. Has there ever been a phenomenon quite as remarkably capitalist and internationalist, yet as entirely Eastern in provenance, as Pokémon? The long-disparaged "dark continent" of Africa also looked to be riding a wave of Western optimism, defined by Nelson Mandela's presidency in the South and in the North, from the late '90s onwards, by Western powers' rapprochement with Muammar Gaddafi's formerly ostracized Libyan regime. Even Latin America, where every nation barring Costa Rica had had at least one dictator in power during the twentieth century, looked to be establishing a new—and increasingly left-wing—democratic culture. By the time I was in secondary school, not only had most of formerly communist Eastern

Europe been rehabilitated, but we were well on the way to many of those states joining the European Union, itself increasingly confident and assertive.

Of course, this could not last, and the early 2000s saw a series of shocks to the system. Jean-Marie Le Pen's impressive showing in the 2002 French presidential election was an early warning shot that cosmopolitan liberalism was not going to go unchallenged. Austria's far-right Freedom Party had already gone one better and achieved a place in the government from 2000 to 2005—a result met with sanctions from other Western nations, which didn't prevent the same party's return to power in 2017.[7] The greatest blow, of course, was 9/11 and the subsequent War on Terror. This has done more harm to American and Western self-confidence than any other event since Vietnam, or even before. At no point in the Cold War did the communists, existential threat though they were, succeed in killing American civilians on the mainland US with a military strike. Al-Qaeda, in that sense, has proven itself a far more damaging enemy of everyday American life. The ill-fated Iraq War, itself a consequence of the Western response to 9/11, has done incalculable damage to trust in politicians and to public views on the value of foreign intervention.

These developments fundamentally weakened the West. So too towards the end of the 2000s did the global financial crash, a crisis caused by the excesses and failures of our own Western economic system. Simply put, so long as the vast majority of the West's population was getting richer, enjoying increasingly high living standards and feeling safer, the West's economic and political models received a good deal of broadly passive consent. The financial crisis and the rise of terrorism disrupted that sense of security, and passive consent has now turned to doubt or even rejection among large parts of the population. These were not the only reasons for a loss of belief in the West, but they have catalyzed the process of Western decline. Similarly, while this loss of hope in the West is apparent in a whole generation of under-30s, it does not end with them.

How the West Was Lost looks to chart that story: of how the West lost its way, what this has looked like, and how we might save it. Part One looks at the why—at what has happened to the West, which so recently seemed like an invincible force. It argues that the West has lost its sense of positive purpose, the motivating factor or *telos* that gave it such power as a philosophical construct in the past. Without this moral sense of an endpoint, the West has lost momentum. The security and economic crises that once would have seemed mere speedbumps on the road to our destination are now looking far more like a cliff edge.

Obviously, this argument defines the West as a space more intellectual than geographical. Chapter One explores the three pillars of my model of the West: the belief in a moral endpoint; the trio of republican values (liberty, equality, solidarity); and universalism. Each of those features owes a great deal to the West's distinctive Christian intellectualism, explored further in Chapter 2, and were forged together into a recognizably Western identity at some point during the nineteenth century. Each of these foundations of the West as an idea is now in deep crisis.

Part Two looks at how these crises have played out in practice, by exploring a series of groups and nations lost to the West. Chapter 3 looks at the EU, the most ambitious political embodiment of Western idealism, which is now symptomatic of the broader Western decline. Once a project with an imaginative and ambitious moral purpose, the EU today seems past its apex, and appears to have lost sight of any effective endpoint. Most damningly of all, as explored in Chapter 4, it is the nations of Central and Eastern Europe, which most recently and enthusiastically re-joined Europe and the West in the 2000s, who now seem to be leading the charge to dispense with it altogether. Chapter 5 looks at the USA, a nation founded on a constitution imbued with classically Western values, but whose loss of confidence in those same values explains much of its deep-set political and social crisis. Chapter 6 looks at the young who have lost faith in the West and its values, and Chapter 7 at the West's working and lower-middle classes (the "squeezed middle"), who are on the same trajectory. Chapter 8 looks at one microcosm of the West's failure to live out its values: its struggles to develop a response to the challenges posed by migration and, perhaps particularly, by the West's growing Muslim population.

And yet, despite all this, the situation before us is not entirely hopeless. The final part of the book turns to where we might yet see the revival of the West. The West's crisis has been that it has stopped living up to those ideas that truly defined it. The concluding chapters look at ways to rebuild those areas that have been abandoned. Chapter 9 looks at how to restore a common myth and sense of moral purpose. Chapter 10 looks at restoring solidarity, the most forgotten of the three Republican values, and the one most necessary for rebuilding a shared myth.

The West is not in good health, but it remains a model which is not only redeemable, but also still the best hope for a future world order based on admirable moral principles. I am not suggesting that people abandon the West for something else—not yet at least—but that they fight to restore the dream of the West, and to find a new story for the future.

PART ONE

WHAT THE WEST IS

1

WHAT THE WEST IS

Before you can decide on something's good or ill health, you have to be able to define what it is. Unlike a country, or some sort of institutionalized and bordered political entity like the EU, or a trade area like NAFTA, the West is not an entity with fixed borders or an indisputable legal status; it is an idea, an "imagined community". Where its borders lie is a matter of shared cultural and philosophical definitions.

When the political scientist and historian Benedict Anderson first coined the term "imaginary community", he had in mind the status of the nation. For Anderson, the "magic of national-ism is to turn chance into destiny"—in other words, a political construction becomes an identity marker that unites people from different places, classes and religions (with little truly in com-mon), bringing them into a "horizontal fraternity": a single national identity.[1] The West as a concept takes this idea even further—unlike the nation, it has no specifically designated political structures to underpin it, such as a constitution or parliament. It is a purely intellectual construct, a collection of ideals.

Part of the problem with being a collection of ideals is that, more often than not, political practice falls short of those same ideals. No one, least of all me, would claim that there was ever an era in which the West fully lived up to its beliefs. Every nation has dark parts of its history, and the West has often been complicit in crimes against its own principles. This is reality, but the nature of the West is that, even given these failures, the West has always *believed* it was a place of values and morality, on the path to something better.

The other issue with being an intellectual space, rather than something with clear political and geographical boundaries, is that we may not all agree on the cultural and philosophical definitions of the West. Different thinkers have included very different places or societies in their version of the West. In *The Decline of the West* (1918), Oswald Spengler was generally vague on who he had in mind, beyond "West European Americans".[2] He was, however, keen to eliminate Russia from any possible conception of Westernness—this, he explained, was why he preferred the term "West" to "Europe" in defining the cultural phenomenon at hand. A century later, the former *Economist* editor Bill Emmott defines the West in much broader terms: all of Europe, plus North America, Japan and South Korea—essentially, anywhere that combines commitments to liberal democracy and to capitalist economics.[3]

Part of the process, naturally, is a matter of exclusion rather than inclusion. To be the West is to be differentiated from an Other—generally the East, or the Orient. This is an idea with a long history. The Ancient Greeks were prone to contrast their own enlightened, free West with the barbaric and despotic Persian East. That distinction—between a classical West that understood freedom and a despotic East that did not—was used in the twentieth century by the philosopher Isaiah Berlin, in his two conceptions of liberty.[4] The same distinction is found in a host of key European philosophers throughout the intervening period, including Montesquieu, Weber and Marx. Christendom, the ancestor of conceptions of both Europe and the West, was defined in part by its opposition to the threat of "infidel" Turks from the East and South. The age of European empires saw countries like Britain and France interact (sometimes by conquest, sometimes through trade) with various Eastern civilizations, notably China, India and Japan.

The West becomes the West in the nineteenth century. The nascent development of anthropology, and increasing interest in ideas of progress and evolution, led to an intellectual trend that differentiated the supposedly enlightened European mind from backwards or decadent alternatives. The long-term results have been charted by academics such as Edward Said in his work on the concept of Orientalism.[5] The nineteeth century was the point at which we can say the USA had clearly arisen as a stable nation capable of standing up to European powers in its own right. By this time, the values explored below had been crystallized through the Enlightenment and age of revolutions into a clear political framework, expressed in various national constitutions. Of course, most of the features of the West as a political idea predate this period (democracy goes back to the Greeks, *libertas* as a political idea was central to Roman republicanism, and so on), but it was only in the nineteenth century that they truly came together into a recognizable Western whole—something more than just Europe, Christendom or other earlier formulations of difference.

The twentieth century then compounded the idea of the West by providing, in the form of the Iron Curtain, a definitive and, in the case of the Berlin Wall, visible border between the liberal and capitalist West and the communist East. In the early 1990s, after the collapse of this division, Samuel Huntington's famous *Clash of Civilizations* helped feed a durable idea in public debate that the West is a civilization defined in opposition to others—conceivably, violently.[6]

However, it is not quite the case that the West is defined simply by what it is not, and in particular by its hostility to traditional enemies. Certainly that conception of the Other has always helped to focus and crystallize the notion of the West. Yet, what is in some ways surprising about the cosmopolitan West is how little it often really engages intellectually with the worldviews of other peoples. This is a point wonderfully made by Spengler on the narrowness of Western horizons. He looks at the example of Friedrich Nietzsche, an eviscerating critic of so much of Western culture: "Consider the historical horizon of Nietzsche. His conceptions of decadence, militarism, the transvaluation of all values, the will to power, lie deep in the essence of Western civilization". And yet, for Spengler, "he [Nietzsche] never once moved outside his scheme, nor did any other thinker of his time".[7] As we already know, the ongoing existential crisis that characterized the West as an intellectual space is specifically an introspective crisis. This is not to say that there has never been any influence from abroad. The nineteenth-century creation of anthropology and discovery of other ancient texts and cultures did prompt new ideas into the cultural milieu of the West. However, by and large, these were secondary influences, and have not permeated the mainstream of Western thought.

In my model, to be Western is to be defined by three connected ideas, all of which have developed historically through a distinctively Christian, Enlightenment, European intellectual prism:

1. The dream of a moral endpoint, and inevitable progress towards it.
2. The three republican values of the Enlightenment; liberty, equality and fraternity (or, perhaps better, solidarity).

3. Universalism: the belief that the first two features could be fostered in any society of the world.

To be a Western nation is to be committed to those three areas. Critically, however, this is not a simple binary in which a nation, culture or an individual simply is, or is not, committed to the whole. Rather, we would do better to see Westernness as a spectrum on which nations and peoples range. Particular countries can at different times either be considered Western or not, depending on where they are sitting on those three issues. Spain is a good example. Geographically, it sits unambiguously within Western Europe, and though it was not a NATO member until 1982, it was certainly on the Western side during the Cold War, with the conditions of the 1953 Madrid Pact granting Spain military and economic aid from the USA in exchange for use of air and naval bases. However, for the period of Franco's dictatorship (1939–75), Spain was not, in its attitude to those three principles, a clearly Western nation. It became a fully-fledged part of the West only after its rehabilitation following the end of Francoism. In a similar way, much of Central and Eastern Europe could have been considered Western prior to the communist takeover, and ought to be considered so now (though several, as we'll see in Chapter 4, may be on their way out again).

At the time of writing, I would include within the Western world the USA, Canada, Australia, New Zealand and most of Europe, with some notable exceptions—particularly, at present, Russia. Much of Latin America shares a similar intellectual heritage through European and post-Enlightenment notions of politics (Latin America is the place to study for those with an interest in nineteenth- and twentieth-century constitution writing, though few have proven durable). But the twentieth century produced so many dictatorships and reversals, the legacies of which are still being lived out in practice, that Latin America is not there yet. The same is true of South Africa. Japan and South Korea share with the West a commitment to democracy, civil rights and capitalism, and plenty would include them in a definition of the West. I think that case can be made, but those nations have a very different intellectual and philosophical heritage that is notably distinct from the West, and which impacts politics and society to this day. Having defined the West, we can now turn to its current crisis.

* * *

The true basis of the Western crisis can be seen in the dilution of the West's three key pillars, or founding ideas—the combination of suicidal abandonment of itself and cultural amnesia about where it has come from. The remainder of this chapter analyses the state of each pillar in turn.

Firstly, the idea of an ultimate purpose and endpoint, central to the West: the conception of a utopia, and belief in progress towards it. This is a singular characteristic of Western political philosophy and theology, characterized in all its many forms by the idea that the world is changing, progressing era by era towards a superior future. This concept is at the heart of such divergent ideologies as Marxism and neoliberalism. The former believes in the inevitable triumph of the proletariat revolution and the end of capitalism, the latter in the inevitable pursuit of economic growth.

At least until recent decades, much of Western history and philosophy has tended in Spengler's words to be "a metaphysical history; a predetermining history".[8] The West's politics and philosophy have always owed far more than is often acknowledged to the Judaeo-Christian theological idea of "eschatology"—the theology of destiny and the end times. This way of seeing time, as a linear process of successive epochs toward a final state, is absent from Greek philosophy, and largely absent from Eastern philosophy and religion too,[9] but is at the heart of the distinctively Christian contribution to the West.[10] The modern idea of progress, in the philosopher Robert Pippin's words, is "the secularization ... of Christian progress".[11] In other words, Western politics and philosophy have always been about realizing a vision of heaven on earth, whether the Kingdom of God or a non-religious utopia.

The twentieth-century French philosopher Jacques Derrida noted this trend, which connects philosophical thinkers as disparate as Kant, Hegel, Heidegger, Voltaire, Marx and even Nietzsche; Derrida described writing itself as a process towards a "teleo-poetic propulsion of ideas".[12] By this he means that most Western philosophy has not been simply descriptive of the world as philosophers have seen it, but has been designed to propel the West forwards, towards a goal or a vision of a better world. Where that philosophic vision led, politics followed, and we have witnessed a succession of Western-incubated ideas, including the great rival ideologies of liberalism, communism and fascism, but also democracy and the notion of human rights. All are aimed at propelling us a little further on the road to our Western *telos*, or moral endpoint.

What is curious is that Western philosophy, so influential in this driving force, was the first part of the Western edifice to begin to really abandon this key plank in Western identity. Friedrich Nietzsche and Sigmund Freud are only two of the most prominent thinkers who looked to unravel the whole idea of metanarratives and belief in an inevitable and morally desirable endpoint. The focus moved from one of moral progress to one of rupture. Although Nietzsche is arguably most famous for his aphorism that "God is dead", the movement he began was arguably more effective at creating the idea that "humanity is dead"— within that post-modernist philosophical movement, faith in human power to change the world began to unravel. These were early symptoms; the fullness of their predictions and worldviews has only come into focus over time.

However, while Western philosophy has increasingly lost confidence in the idea of progress, to the extent that Pippin describes today's philosophy as one in which a "culture of melancholy, profound, scepticism has become high culture and the dominant academic one",[13] it has taken political and popular culture a long time to catch up. This is due in large part to decades of momentum in which it seemed undeniable that liberalism and the West looked to be going somewhere—even if we were increasingly unsure where the somewhere was, and whether it was even desirable to get there.

Now, though, we have reached the tipping point. There is no clear sense of progress or purpose in Western political culture. The symptoms of this have been playing out for some time—perhaps most obviously in the EU and the USA (see Chapters 3 and 5). The overall trend is one in which the West's political culture is going through the motions: holding elections, talking the talk on human rights and, most importantly, maintaining the economic and political system, but with little genuine vision for a positive future. The most extraordinary example of this was perhaps the Mario Monti government of 2011–13 in Italy. Neither Monti himself, nor any member of his cabinet, was even an MP, and he had never been an elected politician at all; his was a government for which literally nobody had voted, and yet for two years it successfully kept the Italian state in relative equilibrium. This preservation of the status quo did not turn out well: when actually put to the electorate, it was decisively rejected. Monti's coalition won only fourth place, and fewer than half the number of seats won by the emerging Five Star Movement. The subsequent struggles of the successor centrist governments saw a dramatic victory for the populists at the following general election.

Maintaining the system has become the watchword for so much of Western political life. It has lost energy and enthusiasm for aspiring to something more. This, as much as anything, explains the populist upsurge and precipitous decline of the West's traditional ruling political parties—with a partial American exception. Put simply, there is nothing to be excited about, no goal to reach. The vision of Francis Fukuyama, that with the collapse of the Soviet Union we reached the "end of history",[14] was once triumphalist—but from today's standpoint, it seems rather more like an existential threat. At the end of history, is this really all the West had to aspire to?

In the twentieth century, energy could be found to revitalize the system by accomplishing a victory towards the liberal moral endpoint that commanded consensus in the West—particularly through civil rights. In that light, much was accomplished, including first universal male suffrage and then women's rights, the rights of racial minorities (most notably in the USA) and those of LGBT+ people. Each of these movements provided a burst of energy and hope for the system as a whole that progress was being made toward true equality and liberty. However, given the progressive nature of these landmarks, there are few such major developments likely to come in the future. What's more, each successive victory has empowered an ever-smaller segment of society, with a correspondingly smaller energy boost for the Western political movement.

In Europe, rights—including but not limited to voting rights and legal protections—began by benefiting non-aristocrats. Depending on where you were in Europe, this meant that somewhere between 85 and 99.9% of the population gained rights they had not previously held.[15] From there, the West moved to the liberation and establishment of equal rights for women, a process which is still ongoing, but has long been established as a principle—one benefiting about 50% of the population. Then

11

we moved to ethnic minorities, with "minority" being the operative word; in the case of the USA, those who chose to identify as "Black or African American alone" made up 13.4% of the population in 2017, while the total "white alone" proportion is 60.7%.[16] More recently, there has been a focus on LGBT+ rights: fifteen European countries now recognize and perform same-sex marriage, whereas none did in 2000; a further eleven recognize some form of same-sex civil partnerships. Depending on your preferred statistics on LGBT+, they might account for some 2–5% of the population.[17] The current battle is over transgender rights, for which there is little data, but certainly only concerns an even smaller proportion of the population.

All this is not to mention the fact that, in every country of the West, there are residual and exceedingly serious problems with racism, sexism and bigotry directed towards virtually every minority group. This is a double bind for the West. On the one hand, we have now established a minimal legal status for most groups deemed to be in need of it, so there is not much further to go on this particular road to liberal utopia. On the other hand, even with all of this progress, we don't seem to have established a culture in which equality is truly valued, and even the legal status we have set up is under threat in certain parts of the West—in a way, the more nominal progress we make, the harder it is for Westerners to share a belief in it, as the disappointing reality will always show up poorly against the paper equality that we've instituted.

Unless the West can re-establish some form of goal and sense of progress for the future, it is going to continue to lose momentum and supporters; the current trend of maintaining the status quo has left us in true crisis. This is for the simple reason that so much of public life is variable and unpredictable. Economic performance fluctuates, often for reasons beyond any individual government's control. Political personalities and crises also come and go, as do natural disasters, terrorism and other events that can damage public confidence. All that is a given. The challenge is how to maintain confidence in the system and the West as a whole, even when there are major challenges. When in difficult straits, only a greater common purpose, driving us towards a moral endpoint, can continue to motivate people and maintain their faith in the West.

What is interesting is that, while we lose our sense of mission and purpose, the idea that people need this is becoming widely recognized in the West. The problem is that, beyond populist reactionaries, our current political leaders seem unable to provide it. In Western companies, it is now widely understood that employee satisfaction and productivity are higher when staff are motivated by the organization's mission.[18] Management text-books draw on the idea of the hierarchy of needs to show that, though certain employee needs are required to prevent *dis*satis-faction (adequate pay, fair policies), to achieve satisfaction and high performance you need a greater level of belief in the overall direction of travel.[19] The burgeoning research into mental health also increasingly identifies a sense of meaning and purpose as being critical to a healthy life. And yet, despite this growing consensus that such things are critical in personal and profes-sional life, when it comes to public life the ability to articulate a purpose seems largely lacking.

Confidence in the political project of the West has clearly dwindled as a result. In 2013, a majority of Americans believed that the USA was past its peak and getting worse.[20] That trend is apparent across a number of Western countries. Without a sense of moral direction, it is set to continue, and it is potentially destructive to the future of the West. Just as a company whose employees are not motivated will ultimately see dwindling per-formance, no matter how much money is thrown at the problem; just as an individual can have everything but suffer depression without a sense of meaning to their lives; so the West's loss of moral purpose is a critical health issue.

* * *

Perhaps part of the problem is that the building blocks of Western idealism are themselves eroding. If the values underpinning the West's conception of a moral endpoint are not as clear as they once were, this might explain why it has become so difficult for political causes to espouse a way forward. Those values form the second key pillar of Westernness: the great republican ideas of liberty, equality and solidarity.

"*Liberté, Égalité, Fraternité*" was, famously, one of the great slogans of the French Revolution, and was later formalized in the nineteenth century as the motto of the Third Republic, the first French republic to endure (from 1870 until the Nazi invasion and occupation in the 1940s). These three concepts—fraternity we might better think of today by the less gender-specific term of solidarity—have become the foundation of republicanism and modern liberal politics. The Indian constitution of 1950 uses "liberty, equality, fraternity"; the Danish Social Democrats use a very similar formulation, as do the British Liberal Democrats. The idea of these three core values also gave rise to the First Article of the UN Declaration of Human Rights (1948): "All human beings are born free and equal in dignity and rights. They are endowed with reason and conscience and should act towards one another in a spirit of brotherhood."

Even in countries that survived the age of republican revolutions and retain a monarchy have, in practice, adopted the three values into what has become common Western political theory. The UK's constitutional monarchy is a classic example of this trend. Under the Succession to the Crown Act 2013, the UK parliament changed the law of succession to end male-preference primogeniture, whereby sons precede even older daughters when it comes to inheritance. This was greeted at the time as a great triumph of equality—despite the fact that we are still talking about an hereditary process for becoming head of state, a notion about as detached from the republican conception of equality as it is possible to conceive. The UK has absorbed the idea that equality is an essential political and public value, while leaving its particular hereditary institutions in place.

The three concepts were forged in part by the Enlightenment, but also draw on Christian and classical philosophical ancestries that go back throughout European history. The Christian element particularly is often lost in this; as if the European Enlightenment and age of revolution emerged from nothing, and the Christian nature of the societies that conceived the West had no impact on those founding ideas. This will be explored in more depth in the next chapter, but it is worth noting in brief that each of the three republican values are in some ways a development out of Christian anthropology, and in particular the distinctive notion of human dignity. Christianity, unusually among religions, emphasizes personal redemption and salvation; this implies a necessary degree of human freedom, or liberty. The notion of spiritual equality—the breakdown of the distinction between Jew and gentile, and the recognition of equal love in the eyes of God—in turn lends itself to the idea of political equality. Finally, the notion of a relational God, and the demand to love one's neighbour, necessitates the notion of solidarity.

Of course, none of these led immediately or cleanly to republican values, never mind to political and legal structures; nor can we credit Christianity alone with an influence on their formation. Yet, for all that, this intellectual lineage is significant. The novelty that began in the eighteenth century, and proceeded throughout the nineteenth and twentieth, was that the three ideas implicit and developing within so much of political and philosophical thought became the primary basis on which political power could be justified in secular, not Christian, terms. This was the era that established the idea of a people who were sovereign and not merely subjects of rulers. The trend is most famously captured in the American *Declaration of Independence*:

> We hold these truths to be self-evident, that all men are created equal, that they are endowed by their Creator with certain unalienable Rights, that among these are Life, Liberty and the pursuit of Happiness. That to secure these rights, Governments are instituted among Men, deriving their just powers from the consent of the governed, That whenever any Form of Government becomes destructive of these ends, it is the Right of the People to alter or to abolish it, and to institute new Government, laying its foundation on such principles and organizing its powers in such form, as to them shall seem most likely to effect their Safety and Happiness.

Liberty, equality and solidarity have proven, on the whole, to be remarkably durable in the political imagination of the West. And yet, they have also come under strain, with solidarity in particular often discarded from the mix. In part the fault has been with an attitude that seems to hold that the three are really one—or that all Western ideals are essentially the same, and that accomplishing any one of them to their fullest will also accomplish the others. This is a serious error. Each of the values is important, but they are certainly not the same, and in fact an excessive focus on any of the three has the tendency to undermine the other two.

The twentieth century is effectively the history of that excessive focus in practice. It saw a series of ideological constructs come into power that prioritized one value at the expense of the others. Solidarity, taken to its extreme, saw the rise of fascism in Germany and Italy and conservative authoritarianism in Spain and Portugal. Solidarity is an issue of moral and social obligations owed to others within the nation or people. In fascism, a notion of the in-group became so excessive that freedom of the individual became a threat to that togetherness, and so was demolished by authoritarian leaders. Equality became applied only to members of the in-group, with disastrous consequences for minorities and those deemed enemies of the in-group. In Francoism, the results were to prioritize the social bonds of the Church and traditional Spanish values, again at the expense of freedom and equality. Such was the abandonment of the other values of the West that we could see Germany in 1933–45, Italy in 1921–45, Spain in 1936–75 and Portugal in 1926–74 as no longer fully part of the West.

Fascism was, of course, the first great twentieth-century ideology to fall, and until very recently the catastrophic horrors of Nazism had fundamentally compromised the mainstream appeal of nationalism of all sorts. So dramatic, in fact, was the discrediting of nationalism that, as recently as 2006, even the writers Richard Koch and Chris Smith, lamenting a declining West, were nevertheless confident that nationalism was a dead force: "In Europe, toxic nationalism is largely a relic, discredited by the horrors of the two 'European civil wars' and eroded by the success, even if often only grudgingly admitted, of European institutions and identity."[21] This, of course, has changed dramatically in the last decade, not least in Germany itself, where, in the 2017 federal elections, the nationalist Alternative für Deutschland (AfD) won 13% of the vote, giving them the largest number of seats in the Bundestag for a far-right party since the defeat of Nazism.

Equality, meanwhile, was taken to its most significant extreme in the communist takeover of Central and Eastern Europe. Marxism is an ideology incubated and developed in the West, and it shares with other Western ideologies the same commitment to a utopian endpoint (socialism) and to universalism (global class struggle). However, as embodied in the Soviet and Yugoslav regimes and their satellites, this absolutist commitment to equality stripped out all sense of liberty, and sought to destroy alternative forms of identity foundational to solidarity, such as religion or nationhood. Any sense of individual human dignity was sacrificed entirely to the regime. This too was a betrayal of Western values, and nations that had previously been considered to be part of the Western intellectual world (East Germany, Poland, Hungary) were lost to the West until the early 1990s.

The final political collapse of European communism came long after it had failed as a Western government type. The horrors of the famine, the gulags and the violent oppression of opposition discredited Marxism in the same way that the Holocaust had cast a long shadow over nationalism. The Communist Party of Great Britain had two MPs win seats in the 1945 general election and won over 100,000 votes, and won 215 councillors in the following year's local elections, with a membership of some 60,000. As revelations of events beyond the Iron Curtain took their toll, particularly the Soviet response to the 1956 Hungarian uprising, the party declined dramatically. It never had an MP after 1950 and was finally disbanded in 1991.

The fall of both communism and fascism (or conservative authoritarianism) left a single great Western ideology standing: liberalism. This was the context in which Francis Fukuyama famously proclaimed the "end of history" in 1989, meaning the inevitable spread of liberal democracy and capitalism across the globe. A default victor is not the same as a popular victor, however, and the depth of popular commitment to liberalism is not necessarily clear, now or arguably ever. The crisis of liberalism is hard to detect; it has not yet suffered military defeat like fascism, or total internal political collapse like Francoism or communism. Yet it is becoming clear that liberalism is in poor health, visible in the number of books published on the subject in the 2010s, from both the political left and right.[22]

The struggles of liberalism are also evident in Westerners' abandonment of the liberal project. In the USA one in six Americans now believe in army rule as a "good system of government". That's up from just one in sixteen in 1995.[23] The German academic Yascha Mounk has used World Values Survey data to show that, of Americans born in the 1930s, 71% are likely to say that it is "essential" to live in a democracy—perhaps a surprising low figure for people who have lived through both World War Two and the Cold War. Of those born in the 1940s, the equivalent figure is 58%; the 1950s, 57%; the 1960s, 51%; the 1970s, 44%; and finally, of those for which there is good data, just 29% of those born in the 1980s believe it is essential to live in a democracy.[24] Equivalent trends are evident across most of Western Europe—though not, interestingly, to the same extent in much of Central and Eastern Europe. Chapter 7 will explore this generation gap when it comes to faith in the West, but these figures clearly show change over time.

In fact, not only are Westerners losing confidence, they are actively becoming less liberal. Fifty per cent of the UK population are now reportedly likely to support a strongman leader, up from 25 per cent in 1999. Poland, Hungary and arguably the USA already seem to have acted on that willingness with their votes. A quarter of American millennials think democracy is a bad system of government and 44 per cent would back a strongman.[25] These beliefs are also being borne out in practice: the Freedom House annual report on worldwide freedom and democracy found that 2018 marked a decade of consecutive years in which the world as a whole became less free, including the USA and other former paragons of democracy.[26]

The sins of liberalism that have led to this crisis are much harder to identify than those of communism or fascism. There is no equivalence, moral or otherwise, with the Holocaust or Stalin's purges. Yet, Western liberalism is suffering in a sense from the same malaise as its competitor ideologies. By over-committing to just one of the republican values—liberty—it has come to undermine the other two, and ultimately betray itself.

The first consequence of this is in fact closely related to the loss of a utopian endpoint. Today's liberalism owes a particular debt to Isaiah Berlin's notion of "negative liberty"—"freedom from" the interference from others, rather than "freedom to" act freely. What has been lost, though, is the sense of purpose: of what to do with that freedom. We see this in particular in debates on freedom of speech. There are many across the political spectrum—from the liberal American journalist Anthony Lewis and gay rights activist Peter Tatchell to the conservative philosopher Roger Scruton and the controversial popular intellectual Jordan Peterson—who have demanded freedom of speech as a near absolute value, including the necessary freedom to offend others. For some people, the right to offend has become the same thing as the necessity to do so, and any criticism of causing offence amounts to undue censorship. But the origins of free speech within liberalism were around the search for truth, not the ability to offend for its own sake. The difference between the right to say something, and the just purpose of doing so, has been eroded. There is some irony that it is precisely freedom of speech and freedom of the market that have come to empower the peddlers of "fake news"[27] who undermine both the value of truth and public confidence in institutions. The commitment to freedom has opened the door to those who deliberately abuse it, threatening the system as a whole.

At the same time, there is a second liberal trend which has had the opposite effect: one which demands total conformity, in the name of liberal equality. This battle has played out particularly on university campuses in the UK, Canada and the USA, where speakers have been disinvited, no-platformed or otherwise prevented from speaking on the grounds that they hold views which are deemed to be unacceptable in the public square. In the UK the most prominent examples have included the feminist Germaine Greer, who was blocked from several university campuses due to alleged transphobic views. In the British political sphere, a more striking example was the fate of Tim Farron, the former leader of the Liberal Democrats, who eventually felt compelled to step down after being unable to formulate a sufficiently liberal answer, as an evangelical Christian, as to whether he thought gay sex was a sin. It was not enough to say that, as a liberal, he believed in voting for people's rights, even if he did not accept their behaviour. His actions were not enough—his thoughts needed to be wholly "on message" as well. We have somehow arrived at a scenario in which liberal democracy has lost its sense of purpose, yet its defenders have become ever more assertive advocates, acting blindly to its detriment.

A second failing of liberalism has been the consequences of excessive individualism. There is a balance to be struck here. Soviet Russia killed individualism entirely, in a manner that denied any individual agency or dignity. Christianity, as the historian Larry Siedentop has demonstrated,[28] has had an enormous intellectual bearing on the idea of the individual. However, within Christian anthropology, humans are not simply atomized individuals who operate alone. Rather, they are necessarily relational beings: operating in families and social bonds. To its critics, the logic of liberalism has always been to dissolve those social bonds, making the individual a totally independent autonomous unit.[29] Many now argue that the result has been a crisis in which people are divorced from all collective forms of identity, such as the nation, religion, family, or any other "tribal" identity. Legitimate identity becomes a matter of rational individualism, with anything else an irrational and therefore illegitimate model; or, worse, an example of unacceptable racist, sexist or otherwise bigoted rejection of others.

This creates a problem for liberal politics, because—much to the confusion and surprise of many analysts—these identity markers have not gone away. In truth, Westerners—as much as any other humans—do not think of themselves simply as rational individual actors, but as part of bigger, collective identities. Placing such a focus on individual liberation and the autonomous individual as the key societal unit has blinded much of the West's political thinkers to the enduring importance of these identity markers. In other words, losing sight of solidarity as a key value has unbalanced the system. Following political upheavals in the 2010s, there is now an increasing recognition of this effect. The British political theorist David Goodhart created a stir in 2017 with his book *The Road to Somewhere*.[30] In it he argued that the UK, and to an extent the broader West, had become divided between "Anywheres" and "Somewheres". Anywheres tend to be younger, university-educated, urban, socially liberal (though, for Goodhart, politically illiberal—in the mould of the conformists discussed above), and comfortable living anywhere without putting down deep roots. They make up about 20 per cent of the UK population. Somewheres, by contrast, are rooted in a particular community, tend not to be university-educated, and—though they are more socially liberal than is often imagined on many issues—hold other factors such as duty, patriotism and religion to be sacred. For Goodhart, this divide explains the current British political malaise. If true, it also demonstrates the particular challenge of liberalism's failure: it has succeeded in convincing one portion of the population, but has alienated another.

The academic and lawyer Amy Chua has explored a similar trend in the USA, arguing that for decades US policymakers have underplayed the importance of tribal identity, particularly concerning racial and religious group markers.[31] Race is particularly interesting in this context. For many in the West, the ideal seems for some time to have been the idea of "colour blindness"—i.e. affecting not to "see" race, and thus not to place any importance on it. This is a logical consequence of a trend that sees people simply as individuals, combined with a well-meaning attempt from many liberal-minded people to downplay racial differences, as an antidote to racist overplaying of such differences.

At the same time, as Afua Hirsch has explored in her autobiographical memoir on race and identity in Britain, the effect of this colour blindness is actually to write people's identity out of the story.[32] To be a British Ghanaian, or an American Vietnamese, or a Dutch Surinamese is special to people; they do not want that aspect of their identity discounted and dismissed. At any rate, racism remains an everyday reality for many, as endless statistics from across the West can attest, on anything from the likelihood of being arrested or incarcerated, being overlooked for jobs, the state taking children from their parents, and a host of other issues where race is an indicator. Refusing to acknowledge the importance of race in our society does not help the victims of these problems; it hampers our ability to address them.

A final symptom of today's Western liberalism crisis has been the evolution of its economic model. The definition of "neoliberal economics", and even the idea that such a thing exists, is thoroughly contested. Yet, however we quibble with particular definitions, it seems undeniable that from the 1980s there was a change to the economic model of much of the West—certainly the USA and UK, but also within the EU (see Chapter 3). Again, this is related to prioritizing liberty far above the other two republican values. However, in this case it is not about the liberty of individuals per se, but rather the idea of an entirely free market, one that enjoys fully the idea of Berlin's negative liberty—freedom from intervention.

That, at least, is the myth. In practice the free market model takes enormous levels of state intervention to maintain. Yet it is illustrative of the abuse of liberty that a notion originally applied to individual citizens, with other values serving as checks and balances, has become strangely de-humanized—applied to markets and even companies, as the value that overrides all others. This is perhaps best encapsulated in the work of the Nobel Prize-winning economist Milton Friedman, whose work—especially the suitably titled *Freedom and Capitalism*—made freedom of the market and political freedom essentially linked, with the former necessary for the latter.

Nowhere has this trend been more apparent that in the USA, where the near ubiquitous belief in the market as a moral force for good has been united with the idea that a company can be a person, with an individual's rights. This dystopian vision has effectively been given legal status in the USA. With the infamous Supreme Court ruling *Citizens United vs Federal Election Commission*, it has been established since 2010 that companies have a right to free speech, which can be imperilled by political campaign funding limits.[33] A 2014 case went further still, ruling that even for-profit organizations can, on grounds of religious conscience, refuse to comply with federal mandates that their healthcare insurance cover birth control.[34] Corporations are now people, at least in some circumstances; and they are people who demand liberty from any government interference, no matter the demands and contributions of wider society.

So we are in a state of liberal mission creep, with more and more parts of public life effectively invaded by the market. This is recognized by the philosopher Michael Sandel, who has for years lamented the constant spread of the market into new areas.[35] It points to a broader Western problem: the transition of the market and economics from a means into an end, one in which economics is the primary criterion for assessing political success and value. Eternal growth is the ultimate political goal. This can be seen not least in the changing status of foreign ministers and finance ministers since the 1980s, with the top finance job ever more prominent and the country's top diplomat diminishing in importance. The destructive consequences of this changed economic focus have been particularly clear in the fate of the EU, an issue discussed in more detail in Chapter 3.

* * *

After the utopian endpoint and the three republican values, the last major pillar of Western identity has been the idea of universalism. By this I mean that, although every part of the world has its philosophies, politics and ideas, a distinctive feature of the West and its antecedents ("Europe" and "Christendom") is the sense that our philosophies and politics are not simply for us— they are not parochial concerns, but rather universally applicable, in every human setting.

Here, again, it is possible to detect a Christian intellectual heritage. Christianity was unusual among ancient religions for not being tied to any particular people, but instead being explicitly universalist and evangelistic. We see this in the deliberate attempts to export and imbed Christianity in European imperial colonies, and in the West's attempt to export its notions of government. Throughout the twentieth century, we saw it in the expansion of the Cold War from an initial ideological conflict between the USA/Western Europe and the USSR/Eastern Europe into an ideological and military conflict which engulfed the whole world, with West and East bankrolling regimes on every continent in their own image, or at least interest. The Truman Doctrine, which began as American resistance to communist takeovers in Greece and Turkey, became an all-encompassing global mission to intervene and establish Western-style (or at least Western-allied) governance. Nomadic Mongolia suddenly became a communist country, in total defiance of any Marxist historical doctrine, with a school, museum and theatre for every town—only rarely a permanent designation throughout Mongolian history—built from identical components.

Democracy, capitalism, even models of education and industrialization have been exported by the West, both as a matter of policy and in the expectation that all such projects are not only superior to alternative ways of doing things, but also based on such self-evident values that they are universally applicable. Perhaps the most obvious example of the way in which Western values have been universalized and then exported is the Universal Declaration of Human Rights, adopted by the UN in 1948.

The value of human rights, like all Western values, has not always been enacted in practice. On campaign, Napoleon's troops carried with them across Europe a copy of the 1804 Civil Code—a new constitutional document guaranteeing a more modern set of legal rights before the law, and a fine example of universalism in principle. The idea was that Napoleonic soldiers would be bringing with them the light of modern civilization. The fact that their campaigns had a reputation for rape, pillage and ruthless repression was an irony apparently lost on the emperor, in a manner somewhat typical of the West, which has always been stronger on principle than on living its commitments in practice. But even if it has fallen desperately short in the application of its values, this attachment to their principle shows how strongly the West has always believed them to be both universal and important.

The West is turning inwards. Since the debacle of the Iraq War, which did enormous damage to the credibility of international intervention, the West has been far less intent than it once was on spreading its values. Instead it has begun to settle for firming up its own borders, to prevent the barbarians from getting in. One prominent example is Donald Trump and his ridiculous "travel ban" policy, preventing people from a few supposedly dangerous (and Islamic) places from reaching the USA. In truth, though, Trump's isolationism is only one symptom of a much broader trend. Western countries have spent the past decade ramping up opposition to migration, increasing external barriers, and passing internal legislation to force greater levels of assimilation than was previously required. It's true that this policy shift is linked to an understandable response to a changing global migration picture, but that doesn't change the fact that approaches to integration and migration have become more and more hostile across the West, even in countries facing a mounting demographic crisis, such as Germany and most of Central and Eastern Europe.

France is typical of this trend. The French are overwhelmingly supportive of *laïcité*, their own distinctive brand of secularism. Indeed, according to a 2015 poll by IFOP (Institut français d'opinion publique), 46% of French adults believe that *laïcité* is the most important republican principle—ahead of universal suffrage (36%) and freedom of association (8%). Nearly three quarters, 71%, put secularism in the top two republican principles.[36] Yet this supposedly neutral approach to religion is increasingly being weaponized as a means of forcing assimilation. This has been shown at some length by the American journalist Sasha Polakow-Suransky in *Go Back to Where You Came From*. He looks at the West's growing hostility to migrants and increasing illiberal—anti-Western—set of assimilation policies.[37] He notes the hypocrisy of French campaigners calling for a ban on Muslim women wearing a burkini or insisting on serving pork in schools, while also calling for nativity scenes in all public buildings and even for an increase in state funding of churches to prevent them being turned into mosques. Supposedly in the name of secularism, churches are to be funded by the state. In one particularly revealing exchange with the French philosopher Alain Finkielkraut, Polakow-Suransky manages to get to the heart of the matter, with Finkielkraut conceding that he doesn't actually care if *laïcité* is truly neutral; he wants it used to force assimilation, not liberal neutrality.

In a host of other Western countries, including the Netherlands, Italy, Austria and Australia, migration restrictions have been drastically ramped up in the 2010s, and anti-migrant parties and factions have significantly increased their popular support. At various points over this decade, European governments—including ones that were previously relatively stable, like Germany—have been brought to the verge of collapse over the issue of how best to control migration and assimilate or integrate migrants. The point behind this trend is easy enough to understand. The West feels vulnerable, and many feel that outsiders are the force that will undermine it. Immigration is, of course, a factor in this. It is easy enough to commit to universal values which are being exported elsewhere, as has been the case for Europe since at least the fifteenth century. The difference now is that the rest of the world is coming "here", far more than Westerners are going "there". This tension is inadvertently captured by the right-wing British commentator Douglas Murray: "we [Europeans] cannot become Indian or Chinese. And yet we are expected to believe that anyone in the world can move to Europe and become European".[38]

What Murray perhaps does not appreciate is that this belief in universalism is fundamental to the West. Yet he is also correct, insofar as he is, himself, part of a new trend: one that rejects the West's universalist heritage and seeks to preserve a nostalgic—and at least partly fictional—vision of the "pure" West as was. Murray thinks he is defending the West, but in fact he is helping to undermine it, by breaking with a key value that has defined who we are.

* * *

It is easy to believe that our own era, and own crisis, is something worse and more fatal than any that has preceded it. Likewise, one can easily seem to be exaggerating the scale of the problem. Western nations are still more Western in their commitment to its three critical features than other nations—moral progress, republican values and universalism are better supported in the West than anywhere else. If it's so bad here, the argument goes, why don't we leave and go to North Korea, or Iran, or Saudi Arabia? Of course this retort is absurd, since it could be used to deflect or deny internal criticism of any sort, and shut down the instinct to reform things for the better. Aside from anything else, this is a particularly dangerous proposition when one of the fundamental pillars of Westernness is precisely a belief in moral progress—we are, by nature, in constant search of self-improvement. Turning away from criticism not only shuts down debate, but goes against the very purpose of the West. Nevertheless, such arguments serve as a reminder of perspective: the West remains more Western than anywhere else.

As we've established, being Western is not a binary "in or out" calculation, and nor is support of any of the West's three crucial ideas. Rather, "Westernness" should be seen as a spectrum, and one which is seeing most of the West sliding backwards—becoming less Western. The decline of universalism leaves the West ever more insular. The diminishing commitment to moral progress leaves the West without a clear purpose, crippling any momentum and making us vulnerable when crises emerge—economic, military, environmental—since citizens have no goal to inspire them to persevere through the hard times. Finally, the misuse of the three great republican values leaves the West unbalanced, with solidarity suffering most markedly, though it is still much discussed. As far back as the early 1990s, the French philosopher Jean-François Lyotard noted: "Contemporary society no longer speaks of fraternity at all, whether Christian or republican. It only speaks of the sharing of the wealth and benefits of 'development'. Anything is permissible, within the limits of what is defined as distributive justice. We owe nothing other than services, and only among ourselves. We are socio-economic partners in a very large business, that of development."[39]

The more these three trends continue, the less Western we become, and the deeper the intellectual crisis that confronts us. This is a theoretical argument, but the practical fruits of the crisis are becoming more apparent with each passing day. Each chapter of Part Two will look at a particular way in which this is playing out in practice across the West. Before turning to those examples of how the West was lost, the next chapter completes our overview of what it is that has been lost, by considering the particular role that religion has had in this process—both positive and negative.

2

WHAT'S BEEN LOST

There is a perception among many in the West that the role of religion is rather like that of the appendix in the human body. Certainly it had a purpose once, as part of our evolution, but today its purpose is unclear, and on the whole it can be happily ignored—except on those occasions when it erupts in a manner highly dangerous to the body as a whole.

Most would accept, as a matter of historical fact, that religion has had a role in shaping our history and culture. Quite how much importance it is afforded in shaping the modern world is contested but at least some historic influence tends to be accepted. As for contemporary relevance, however, religion is often relegated to status as a quaint but rather peculiar private practice, considered important for providing some social services, with a role in promoting or hindering social cohesion, and—most notably in public discourse—considered to be a security threat. The latter, of course, particularly concerns fears about Islamist extremism.

How these issues play out in practice does vary significantly from country to country. In Italy, for example, the Catholic

Church runs some 11,000 educational facilities and 5,000 hospitals,[1] giving Christian churches a far greater social significance than in somewhere like Sweden, where they are less important in the public sector. Overall, though, the Church remains a significant provider of public services, at least to some degree, across the West, even in legally secular nations such as France and the USA. In fact in the USA the Catholic Church runs more than 10 per cent of hospitals, a proportion which seems to be growing.[2] The involvement of organized religion in social cohesion varies to some extent according to how diverse a country has become. The UK government considers religion to be an important factor, and recognizes the role of religious leaders and communities in building cohesion.[3] The UK's minority faiths made up about 8 per cent of the population in the 2011 census.[4] Data is harder to acquire in France, due to the French state's ongoing, *laïcité*-related refusal to collect data on religious affiliation, but it is probable that the Muslim population is near 10 per cent.[5] By contrast, only about 0.75 per cent of Finns are from "other religions" besides Christianity.[6]

On the other hand, the significant fear about Islam and Islamism in today's West is present regardless of the reality of religious diversity. In the UK, a ComRes survey found that a majority of the British believed Islam was not compatible with British values; only 28 per cent believed it was.[7] Across the West people are likely to drastically over-estimate the proportion of their population that is Muslim.[8] The rhetoric against Islam as an anti-Western force is a feature of a number of populist political parties, including Geert Wilders' Dutch Freedom Party, Marine Le Pen's French National Rally (formerly known as the National Front), and Hungarian Prime Minister Victor Orbán's Fidesz, to name but a few.

To some extent, the perceived threat of Islam is changing the wider picture on religion in the West, but overall it is still a story of religion's declining importance and relevance in public discourse. This is having a broader impact than is perhaps often recognized. It is impossible to truly analyze the changing nature of the idea of the West without considering the fate of religion, and specifically Christianity, within that story.

This chapter looks first at the evidence for religion's decline in the West—even in the USA, which is widely regarded as a deeply religious country. Second, it looks at the ways in which religion is developing a double-edged sword when it comes to questions of identity. On the one hand, religion is increasingly used as a tool by the West's (particularly right-wing) populists, enlisted as an ally against both Islam(ism) and liberalism. On the other, religion also serves as a bulwark against those forces, as an essential plank in the identity of the West. Those who wish to sideline religion or any talk of religious identity may undercut the populist threat—though it seems more likely that this would encourage it—but in doing so may risk losing a key ally in the fight against elements who would use and abuse this one aspect of the West's identity by pretending that it is the whole. Finally, the chapter explores the real extent to which religion serves as the basis for that identity, and the weakness of the rival values epidemic that has arisen in its place.

* * *

For those who regret the decline of Western religion, the best that can be said is that it's not yet as bad as many people thought it would be. In 1968 the sociologist Peter Berger was by no means alone in believing that "By the twenty-first century, religious believers [were] likely to be found only in small sects, huddled together to resist a worldwide secular culture".[9] This, as Berger himself recognized in the late 1990s, has not quite happened, even in secular Europe; and worldwide the population of the religious is increasing dramatically.[10] The change, of course, is that while the global Christian population has greatly increased, this trend has happened almost entirely outside of Europe. In 1910, two thirds of Christians were in Europe and just 1.4% in Sub-Saharan Africa. In 2010, the European population made up just 26% of all Christians, while Sub-Saharan Africans made up 24%.[11]

Though Berger's prediction may have been excessive, religion in the West is unquestionably seeing a decline in the number of people who call themselves religious, who believe in God, and who attend religious services. This trend is apparent across any number of Western countries, but a few examples bring home the shift. In the UK the British Social Attitudes survey showed for the first time in 2017 that more than 50% of the UK population considered themselves to have "no religion". In 1983 the same survey had shown that the "non-religious" population was only 31% of the total. In the same period, the number of self-professing Anglicans has halved, from 40% of the population to 20%.[12] This is a marker of affiliation: of what people consider themselves to be. It is an important measure, but arguably partially masks the reality of religious decline. If we look at what these self-describing Christians actually do about their faith, the reality looks bleaker still for the Church. One recent study claimed that only 4% of professing Christians are regular churchgoers.[13]

Polls in France exhibit a greater level of variability, with one recent poll by the Pew Forum suggesting the majority of the French (64%) still consider themselves Christian,[14] while one from 2012 suggested that only 37% thought of themselves as religious at all.[15] This is illustrative of some of the issues in gathering accurate data on religious affiliation, but comparison of polls over time indicates that, wherever France is today on religion, it is a less religious country than it was a generation ago—potentially dramatically so.

Looking at France may seem a cheap shot—it is, after all, a famously secular country. Similarly, exhibiting religious decline in the Netherlands or Scandinavia would probably not cause any surprises. These are countries that have long been known to be largely secular (although many of the Scandinavian states join the UK in retaining an established Church). What is perhaps more noteworthy is that even the West's supposed religious bastions are seeing sharp declines in their Christian populations. Take, for example, the Republic of Ireland, a country renowned for its affiliation with the Roman Catholic Church. Between the 2011 and 2016 censuses, the "no religion" proportion of the population grew by 74 per cent,[16] and the Church has been left on the sidelines as the country voted against its wishes, first for gay marriage in 2015 and then for the legalization of abortion in 2018. Though 78 per cent of the Irish remain Catholic, a high proportion by European standards, the recent decline is noticeable and significant.

The public perception of the USA is of a deeply religious country. Despite its secular constitution, few nation-states have embodied such a consistently proactive Christian identity. Take, for example, the commonplace signoff in American political speeches, "God bless America"—a line that few European leaders would ever utter. In American political leadership, a failure to be seen as religious is deemed disadvantageous. Among members of Congress (the class elected in 2017), 91 per cent define themselves as Christians, a virtually identical proportion to that of the 1960s. Only one member out of 535—Rep. Kyrsten Sinema, a Democrat from Arizona—defines herself as non-religious.[17]

Yet, despite all that, even the religious landscape of the USA is rapidly changing. The non-religious now make up some 24% of the American population, but among the 18–29-year-olds that number increases to 38%.[18] White Evangelical Protestants are in particular decline. Today they make up 17% of the population, down from 23% in 2006, with white Catholics and white mainline Protestant churches declining at only a marginally slower rate.[19] In other words, for all the noisy Christian rhetoric, the USA is now on the same trajectory as Europe. The British sociologist Grace Davie's *Europe: the Exceptional Case* argued in 2002 that European secularism and non-religious trends were unique in the modern world, and could today be seen as applying to the West more broadly.[20] The West is becoming less and less religious; the rest of the world—with a few exceptions, including Japan—is not.

We should not, however, take this trend to mean that the West has become a consistently rational, secular and atheistic culture. The assumption that non-religion is the same as humanist secularism not only is wrong (as shall be argued below), but masks a fundamentally problematic element in our present Western society. The issue is not, necessarily, that we are losing the specific values structure of Judeo-Christianity; the reason this is helping to pitch the West into crisis is that we are not seeing its replacement with another, including secular humanism. Instead, the systematic values structure on which the idea of the West was built has given way to a chaotic, shifting mass of subjectively constructed personal faith positions. According to the World Values Survey, 27.3 per cent of Americans would call themselves "Not a Religious Person", but only 4.4 per cent call themselves an "atheist".[21] So what has happened to the other 22.9 per cent?

In the UK, more than three quarters of the population—including 61% of the non-religious—believe that "there are things in life that we simply cannot explain through science or any other means".[22] But the same poll found that only 25% of the non-religious agreed with the statement that "humans are purely material beings with no spiritual element". Astonishingly, 8% of the non-religious claimed that they, or someone they knew, had experienced a miracle. Hardly a rational, secularized people, then.

What we are seeing is the breakdown of shared value and belief structures in favour of a far more individualized, subjectively constructed approach. Perhaps the most typical development in this trend has been the growth in popularity of "mindfulness". With origins in Buddhist meditation, mindfulness has been appropriated in the West in such a way as to strip any religious or philosophical content out of those practices, leaving something palatable and useful in dealing with stressful twenty-first professions, without any of the messy spiritual dimension. In this, mindfulness is a classic example of a broader Western trend: appropriating the aspects of historic traditions that suit some "useful" contemporary purpose, while stripping them of their historic and original cultural significance.

This poses a challenge in how we conceive of Western identity. Until very recently, it could be said with some confidence that Christianity was a critical aspect of the West's identity and meaning. Simply, the default identity was Christian. In 2018, however, the majority identity position in Canada, France, Austria, Spain, Switzerland, Germany, the UK, Ireland, Denmark, Sweden, Australia, the Netherlands and the Czech Republic was to be non-religious or atheist.[23] The replacement of this collective identity marker with the more individualized and subjectively constructed identities of the twenty-first-century West is more significant than is often recognized, as we will see below.

Religion and Western identity today: the double-edged sword

The role of religion in Western identity had been in decline for some decades. One distinction of the 2010s in particular is that that trend is now being weaponized. Across the West, "Christian values" are being portrayed by a growing number of political actors as under attack and in need of robust political, legal and cultural defence.

That, in and of itself, would be nothing new if it were being said only by religious actors. There has always, for instance, been a strain of that thought in Catholic Europe; the most marked example is perhaps the 1864 *Syllabus of Errors*, a document attached to a papal encyclical (or circular) that laid out the errors of the modern world. It condemned ideas including the opinion that "The Roman Pontiff can, and ought to, reconcile himself, and come to terms with progress, liberalism and modern civilization."[24] Similar motifs have existed throughout the West for decades. They have been espoused by very disparate conservative religious actors: one example is the so-called "Religious Right", a largely Evangelical movement that grew in prominence from the 1970s through to the 2000s in the course of America's "culture wars"; another is Poland's conservative Catholic radio station Radio Maryja, under the leadership of a radically conservative Catholic priest Father Tadeusz Rydzyk.

Beyond those who held religious values, however, this cause had been fading throughout the twentieth century—and since, as we have shown, Christianity and religion itself has been in decline across the West throughout the century, this amounts to an overall decline in acknowledgement of Christianity as an integral part of Western culture. This was seen in the EU's much-discussed decision in 2003 to omit any mention of Christianity as a European value in the preamble to the (ultimately aborted) European constitution. At the time this provoked a reasonably prominent public dispute, with Pope John Paul II lobbying hard for an explicit mention of Christianity's unique contribution to Europe. The idea was supported by various politicians from Catholic countries, notably Spain and the Pope's native Poland, but also by a number of Christian democrats and Christian socialists across Europe and, interestingly, particularly from

Romania.[25] It was opposed by socialists, greens, liberal democrats and secularists, particularly from France. Former French president Valéry Giscard d'Estaing, who presided over the convention tasked with drawing up the constitution, had little patience for the idea: his own narrative of European history made no mention of Christianity, skipping straight from Antiquity to the Enlightenment.[26]

The inclusion of Christianity in the preamble was ultimately voted down; instead the compromise was for a rather vague and non-committal mention of "cultural, religious and humanist inheritance". The international relations expert Scott Thomas cites this conclusion as evidence that secularists have comprehensively "won the day" in defining European values.[27] It was a moment symptomatic of a broader trend of amnesia about the basis of our Western culture and values structures (see below). And yet, fifteen years later, we find a host of political figures whose religious faith is not much apparent, but who have latched onto the idea that Christianity is a critical aspect of Western culture, in need of robust defence. George W. Bush certainly believed this, but he is himself, of course, a deeply religious man. The curiosity of this development is that the political flag-bearers for the new movement are not especially pious. One of the first major Western politicians to embody this trend was French President Nicolas Sarkozy (2007–12). Sarkozy has described his own faith as "episodic",[28] a view his critics would presumably endorse given his very public divorces and affairs and love of the good life, which brought him the nickname "President Bling-Bling".

Yet Sarkozy, more than any other French president, has done more to push back against *laïcité* and insist that religion is at the root of French culture. In a 2007 speech in Rome, he outraged many French intellectuals by arguing that "In the transmission of values, and in learning the difference between right and wrong, the schoolteacher will never be able to replace the priest or the pastor".[29] He also criticized *laïcité* as having caused suffering in France. Critics, such as Jean Baubérot, a historian and sociologist of religion and secularism, have claimed that Sarkozy was conducting "a neo-clerical effort to relink religion and politics and for the instrumentalization of religion by politicians".[30] The Christian Democrat politician François Bayrou attacked Sarkozy's speech on the grounds that "it makes the religious question partisan. And it works! He made the ... speech not by conviction, but for the political mobilization of Catholicism".[31] These criticisms may be a touch harsh, since there is evidence to suggest both that these views were sincerely and deeply held by Sarkozy, and that they wouldn't have done him much good as a political ploy, being thoroughly unpopular with the pro-*laïcité* electorate. But in some ways Sarkozy can be seen as the prototype for a decade of "populist" politicians with little previous personal record of piety beginning to weaponize religion in public discourse.

The populist right has been particularly keen on this tactic, leading to notable electoral success in those parts of Central and Eastern Europe with more religious populations, especially Hungary and Poland (see Chapter 4). However, it has been a growing trend across the West. We have already seen examples of French campaigners, perhaps taking their cue from Sarkozy's presidency, fighting for essentially anti-Muslim state measures on the grounds of *laïcité* at the same time as supporting specifically Christian actions by the Republic (see Chapter 1). This lobby is particularly, though not exclusively, connected to Le Pen's National Front/National Rally. Le Pen, like Sarkozy before her, has attracted some public scepticism for her professed Catholicism, given that there is little evidence of her regularly attending church, and plenty of her being daggers drawn with the hierarchy on the issue of migration. She herself embodies the contradiction within this supposed French pro-secularism, simultaneously posing as a proudly Christian politician and as a profound supporter of excluding religion from public life. She is also, somewhat paradoxically, and to the chagrin of many more conservative Catholic voices, a very public defender of gay marriage.

Those more Catholic-focused policies—putting nativity scenes in schools and so on—have been popular with traditionalist Catholic voters, but also carry broader appeal, insofar as they use Christianity to exclude those who are considered non-Western, particularly Muslims. They tie into what Marion Maréchal Le Pen (Marie Le Pen's niece, and a senior party figure in her own right) calls "France's status as the first daughter of the Church".[32] The sociologist Rogers Brubaker has characterized this stance as "a *Christianism*—not a substantive Christianity ... It's a secularized Christianity as culture ... It's a matter of belonging rather than believing." He further describes the attitude as being one in which "*We* are Christians precisely because *they* are Muslims. Otherwise, we are not Christian in any substantive sense."[33]

Similar trends have been apparent in other countries. After decades in which the German CSU party was criticized for losing its religion and suppressing its Christian origins, suddenly—and only, critics say, to head off election losses to the far right—CSU leaders have been campaigning for the introduction of crucifixes into state schools in Bavaria. It's a tactic used by anti-establishment right-wing parties in a number of countries. In Italy, Lega Nord—a right-wing populist party usually known in English as the League—has campaigned for obligatory crucifixes in all public buildings, including schools, ports and prisons. Matteo Salvini, Italy's deputy prime minister since 2018 and the party's leader, has made a point of holding a rosary during speeches—despite vociferous criticism from the Church. Salvini does, it seems, attend mass—though he was publicly a neo-pagan for many years—but his party's record on relations with the Church, in common with a number of populist parties, is a curious one, oscillating between rampant anti-clericalism and claims to Catholic authenticity.

The story repeats itself across Europe, with parties including the German Alternative für Deutschland (AfD), who have referred to their role in defence of the "Christian Occident";[34] the Dutch Freedom Party; the Flemish Vlaams Belang (Flemish Interest); and a number of parties in Poland, Hungary, Slovakia and elsewhere. All have, at one point or another, laid claim to being the party of Christian values, particularly in opposition to Islam. As with so many other issues, though, it is Donald Trump who steals the headlines. There is nothing about the history or lifestyle of the American president to suggest any sort of deep or meaningful religious faith, and plenty to suggest quite the opposite.[35] Despite this, white Evangelicals have overwhelmingly voted for him, with the explicit backing of community leaders such as Jerry Fallwell Jr, Franklin Graham and Robert Jeffress. Trump has been painted as the champion of a Christian America, or at least a white Christian America—black Evangelicals and Hispanic Catholics voted overwhelmingly the other way—and he won the presidency in large part due to high turnout among white Christian voters.

And yet, despite all the evidence of right-wing populists weaponizing religion (and specifically Christianity), the flip side of religion's current role in the West is that it seems to provide some "immunization" against right-wing populist politics. In countries with functional Christian political parties, church-going Christians do not tend to abandon those parties, and so are simply not available to the far right. This would apply, for example, in the Netherlands, Belgium, Germany and Scandinavia, where church-going correlates with the tendency not to vote for the populist right. Statistically, this effect is significant: active Christians are disproportionately likely in such countries to resist the overtures of the far right. In those counties where there are no Christian political parties, such as the UK and USA, the effect is significantly reduced or even, by some estimates, non-existent.[36] It is also important to note that this applies to specifically church-going Christians. Germany, for example, has a growing far right that seems to appeal particularly to nominal Christians—those who identify as such, but do not ever attend church.

Much also depends on the particular history of religion and its association with the national culture in question. In countries in which religion is closely associated with conservative notions of national identity—such as Scandinavian Lutheranism or Italian Catholicism—there is some evidence that the right-wing popu-lists can tap into religious identity to gain support (though again, actually going to church seems to reduce that effect). However, if particular Christian denominations are not associated with national identity, then religion can act as a really significant bar-rier to support for nationalist policies. Catholicism, for example, can drive support for nationalist parties in Italy, but serves as a major block to the same trend in Protestant countries like the USA, Germany and the UK, where it has little association with historic notions of national identity.

Finally, and crucially, the actual role of churches has a signifi-cant impact on whether religion helps or hinders Western popu-lists. Where churches have been public and vocal in their opposi-tion to right-wing populism—as in France and Germany, where the churches have been vociferous in their criticism of such groups over at least the past 20–30 years—church attendance is strongly correlated with not voting for such parties. Indeed, in countries with vocally anti-populist churches, that effect seems to extend even to non-practising Christians.[37] Moreover, there's evidence that vocal church opposition can even make right-wing populists more reluctant to instrumentalize religion. A few spo-radic efforts aside, the UK's foremost populist right-wing party,

UKIP, has made little systematic attempt to position itself as the party of Christian values. It has been theorized that this may be linked to the fact that, in recent decades, the Church of England and the Catholic Church in England and Wales have both been prominent and consistent in their support for refugees and sympathy towards migrants more generally.[38]

Christianity, then, provides a double-edged sword when it comes to contemporary challenges in Western identity politics: used and abused by the populist right to suit a nationalist agenda, particularly as a stick with which to beat Muslims, yet at the same time a bulwark against the electoral success of such parties. The sadness is that the reason the populist right has been able, with mixed success, to co-opt religion at all, into their particular reactionary vision of Western identity, is that they have been aided and abetted in this process by mainstream Western culture, which has spent the past few decades, either through amnesia or active whitewashing, attempting to erase the relevance of Christianity from the foundations of Western identity.

The branch we're sitting on

You could argue that Europe really saw the shattering of its universal intellectual and identity heritage with the Reformation, long before the West existed. That was the point at which Christendom, the sense of a space united with a truly common religious and intellectual tradition, "broke". There is something to this argument, and it is true that in some ways Catholic and Protestant Europe would develop quite distinct political and social models, the legacies of which are still seen today. For example, across Europe Catholics have been shown to be consistently more in favour of European integration (see Chapter 3). However, the legacy of Christianity remained shared across the denominational divide(s), and acted as a key differentiator against non-Christian, "Other" civilizations, against which the West was defined. Christianity, even if seemingly irrevocably divided itself, remained a unifying source of identity, and intellectual heritage, until comparatively recently.

Today, that would no longer seem to be the case to anywhere near the same extent, certainly in much of the public imagination. One example of how things have changed is the Fox News trope, echoed in various other Western right-wing media sources, of the "war on Christmas". Each year, journalists are tasked with finding egregious and bizarre accounts of towns, local governments, businesses and others who have supposedly removed Christianity from Christmas, or suppressed the notion of Christmas entirely. By and large, the trope is total nonsense—a ridiculous forcing of the culture wars for easy media outrage. However, I suspect that the reason it proliferates as a myth is because it does have a ring of truth to it; a sense that, nowadays, the polite establishment view is to be faintly (or even thoroughly) embarrassed that Christianity is a part of our culture, or even a fear that talking about Christianity is offensive to those of other religions and should, therefore, be discouraged.

Sometimes there is a sort of amnesia about the role of Christianity in the formation of our Western culture. At other times it is more like a whitewash. In 2014 the then British prime minister David Cameron declared that he considered the UK to be a "Christian country".[39] This provoked an immediate response from a list of academics and celebrities, gathered by the British Humanist Association, who wrote a letter to *The Telegraph* declaring that they

> object[ed] to [Cameron's] characterisation of Britain as a "Christian country" and the negative consequences for politics and society that this engenders ... At a social level, Britain has been shaped for the better by many pre-Christian, non-Christian, and post-Christian forces. We are a plural society with citizens with a range of perspectives, and we are a largely non-religious society.[40]

Such complaints are deliberately obtuse. While it is obviously true that the UK population is not now, and never was, universally Christian—and, equally obviously, that there was a world before Christianity in what is now the UK—the idea that this makes Christianity just one influence among many is clearly nonsense. Culturally, legally, philosophically, the UK and the West have been forged in a distinctively Christian milieu. Because the West is a set of ideas, and a shared myth, this means that it is defined by that milieu.

To recognise this is not Christian over-claiming; it is simply a recognition of who we are and what has shaped our intellectual horizons. Or, as Jean-Paul Sartre—famously no fan of Christianity—observed:

> we are all still Christians today; the most radical unbelief is Christian atheism, an atheism that despite its destructive power preserves guiding schemes—very few for thought, more for the imagination, most for the sensibility, whose source lies in the centuries of Christianity to which we are heirs, like it or not.[41]

We find a similar observation in Nietzschean thought—not least in the very same famous passage of *The Gay Science* in which a madman declares that "God is dead". The audience for Nietzsche's madman is instructive—he first goes to those who do not believe in God, and it is to them that he declares:

> We have killed him—you and I. All of us are his murderers. But how did we do this? How could we drink up the sea? Who gave us the sponge to wipe away the entire horizon? What were we doing when we unchained this earth from its sun? Whither is it moving now? Whither are we moving? Away from all suns? Are we not plunging continually? Backward, sideward, forward, in all directions? Is there still any up or down? Are we not straying, as through an infinite nothing? Do we not feel the breath of empty space? Has it not become colder? Is not night continually closing in on us? Do we not need to light lanterns in the morning? Do we hear nothing as yet of

the noise of the gravediggers who are burying God? Do we smell nothing as yet of the divine decomposition? Gods, too, decompose. God is dead. God remains dead. And we have killed him.[42]

The madman's warning to the atheists is precisely that the culture we take for granted is built on religion—it is nothing short of our horizon, the making of our collective Western identity. Stripping out God from that identity is not just a matter of a change in people's private beliefs; it is inherently linked to the whole intellectual and moral basis of the West. The French Jewish philosopher Emmanuel Levinas sums this up in the pithy formulation that Europe—though we might expand it to the West more broadly—is defined by "the Bible and the Greeks": the fusion of Greek philosophy and Judaeo-Christian religion.[43]

Nietzsche and Sartre would have been first in line to note that this does not prove the truth of Christianity as a religion. However, they clearly understood that the amnesia or whitewashing of Christianity weakens the basis for many of our intellectual, political and social assumptions. Human rights make for a classic case in point. The UN Declaration was greatly shaped by Catholic theological principles introduced by Jacques Maritain, the father of the human rights movement and an expert in Catholic theology and philosophy, as well as by the work of the Protestant World Council of Churches.[44] Today the declaration is recognized simply as a secular document, and functions as such. Yet it provokes an important question: why are humans special, and what implies that they ought to be imbued with rights?

For Maritain and the World Council of Churches, the answer to that question was obvious. Human dignity is owed to each human by virtue of their being made in God's image. A long Christian heritage underpins the development of rights, including the sixteenth-century Spanish Dominican Bartolomé de las Casas, who was the first to define American Indians as human beings and to demand better treatment for them from Spanish colonists. Within the development of our conception of human rights, the intellectual roots are deeply embedded in Christianity. It is a similar story in a host of other areas which we take for granted. Even those with non-Christian origins have been mediated through a Christian lens within a Western context.

In 1994 the sociologist Grace Davie wrote the seminal *Religion in Britain Since 1945: Believing Without Belonging*.[45] She introduced the idea that religion could be assessed according to two indicators: believing and belonging. Religious beliefs (people's spirituality and ideas about the divine) have held up much better than active membership of religious organizations. Accordingly, Davie suggested that Britain was moving towards a state of "believing but not belonging"—or, in terms which have become more and more popular in recent years, the British people have come to embody the idea of "spiritual but not religious". I would like to suggest that, while this trend remains true of individuals, the big change has been on the opposite trajectory. We have already looked at this in right-wing populism's interaction with religion. The West is increasingly characterized culturally by belonging to and having been shaped by a Christian heritage, at the same time as increasingly losing any belief structures to underpin that culture. For a long time, that trend has held true. The result of the growing amnesia and whitewashing is that those roots are being pulled out.

To which it might well be asked: so what? Post-modernism is about rupture from the past; just because those ideas helped shaped something historically does not mean that they are inherently worth keeping. And yet, the point—as made by another (this time contemporary) atheist philosopher, John Gray—is that all the underpinnings we take for granted are being hollowed out. They rely essentially not only on faith as such, but on an implicit sense of moral purpose toward an endpoint that is foundational to Christianity, but absent from contemporary discourse. Or, in Gray's words: "decoupling the universal claims of liberalism from monotheism is easier said than done. Secular liberals believe history is moving in the direction of their values. Yet without a guiding providence of the sort imagined by monotheists, history has no direction."[46]

The loss of a sense of moral progress and of its universalism, as argued in Chapter 1, is proving devastating for the West as an intellectual idea. The relationship of that loss to the decline of religion is perhaps only just becoming fully clear at the end of the 2010s.

The Western values epidemic

It is not that the West of today is without values. On the contrary, what we are witnessing is an epidemic of suggested values, of varying degrees of vapidity. Every corporation, charity and, increasingly, government and political party, feels the need to define its "values". In 2015 Lucy Kellaway noted in the *Financial Times* that only seventeen of the UK's top 100 companies did not feel the need to define and list corporate values.[47] She also found that precious few people, even at managerial level, could tell you what those values actually were. Provocatively, she noted that over the past ten years the seventeen "valueless" companies had outperformed the others in the FTSE 100 Index by about 70 per cent.

According to a report from the financial PR company Maitland, by far the most commonly defined values for businesses are "integrity", "respect" and "innovation".[48] Others that seem to crop up regularly are "ethical" (usually as loosely defined as possible) and "sustainability"—including, with a certain chutzpah, Volkswagen, whose serial attempts to defraud emissions tests suggest that this was rarely more than a paper value.

I am yet to find the company that lists its key value as "maximization of profits at all costs", though I can identify plenty for which that would be an entirely honest assessment of their business practices.

It is a similar story in the political realm. There is plenty of talk of values, but little evidence of much depth to the discussion. One classic example was a moment in 2014 when the Luxembourger Jean-Claude Juncker was selected by the European People's Party as their *Spitzenkandidat*—their preferred candidate to become president of the European Commission. The European People's Party is the largest party in the European Parliament, and the successor to the grouping of Christian Democrat parties instrumental in shaping the early European project of the 1950s.[49] Those parties had had a very real and powerful conception of the values and morality of international politics (see Chapter 3). It was, accordingly, a deep disappointment to see Juncker, in his victory speech, reduce the whole of the European project's values and identity to the single line "We are a community based on rights".[50] Can the European Union's vision really be reduced from all the ambitions of its founders—its economics, its commitment to peace and so on—to an entity whose primary purpose is around the rights of individuals?

Juncker's failure to suggest a powerful purpose for his party's European vision is illustrative of the struggle of so much of the contemporary West. Rights are, of course, important. But there is an apparent difficulty in suggesting any sort of ambitious future mission or sense of purpose, beyond moderately refining what we have already largely accomplished. This same problem has been shown again and again in elections of the 2010s. There were many causes of the 2016 Brexit referendum result, but arguably the most significant was the lamentable failure of the Remain camp to come up with a truly convincing story of why being part of the European Union mattered, and of where the

EU was going. Instead the Remain case was twofold: that Europe was in most people's best economic interests, and that to be on the Leave side was to align yourself with racists, xenophobes and right-wing lunatics.

The US presidential election later that year followed a similar script. To back Clinton was depicted by her campaign as the responsible choice; to back Trump was to support a misogynist, racist and, in Clinton's ill-advised metaphor, join the "basket of deplorables".[51] The same fault lines have defined elections in France, Italy, Spain, the Netherlands, Sweden and elsewhere. Sometimes this tactic has worked; in 2017 Emmanuel Macron won the French presidency against the extremes of Marine Le Pen, although he himself was running as an anti-establishment candidate, with a new party and a manifesto promising radical change. More often, asking voters to play it safe has failed. What is telling in all these cases is that the "establishment", as it is now so often characterized—rarely with much clarity as to what that means—has been woefully lacking in any true vision for the future. There is no teleology, no sense of moral purpose or progress. Electorates have been encouraged simply to stay the course, but it is no longer clear whether the course is set to anywhere that anyone really wants to go. We have a great many political values, and no shortage of people claiming to stand for them, against an onslaught from those who are threats to them. Dozens of Democrats and politicians from around the globe have accused Trump of undermining common values—Macron went so far as to imply it in a speech before Congress[52]—but few seem able to truly articulate any sort of compelling alternative vision. Ultimately, that's why, despite the misogyny, racism and rank ineptitude, he is the president, and Clinton is not.

It would be ludicrous to claim that there would have been no populist uprising without the decline of religion. However, looking around at the West's political leaders, it is hard to escape the impression that, while talk of values is ubiquitous, it is becoming more difficult to articulate any meaningful sense of what those values mean. There is less and less faith in the idea that history can be moved in a more positive direction, or that there is any set of genuinely shared moral values bringing Westerners together. The whole schema of Western progress was based intellectually on what the philosopher might call a "Christian-ized" understanding of history, progress and values. Without that underpinning, it can be little surprise to see the listing and waning of a common Western dream.

* * *

There is nothing new in saying that religion in the West is in decline, and has been for decades. The question is whether this matters. Evidently there are those who believe it does, or at least are prepared to make use of it to further a broader ethno-nation-alist agenda. We have seen that this instrumentalized use of religion, and particularly using Christianity as a stick with which to beat Islam, is a feature of a number of political movements across the West. What is perhaps new in the 2010s is that they are being allowed to run the field—at least partly because no one else seems to be putting forward a compelling narrative of shared values, or a plan for where the West is heading.

The decline of religion matters for that narrative because, until relatively recently, Christianity has always served in the West as an assumed—often unsaid, but no less real—underpinning values structure uniting society. Sartre's claim that "we are all Christians", whether religious or not, was true. However, as suc-cessive generations of decline have built on top of each other, even those fundamental assumptions have become increasingly hol-lowed out. If Christianity had been replaced by some sort of comprehensive atheist humanist belief system, this might have been different. But that has simply not happened. The fact that governments and political parties (and corporations) speak about values far more than they used to is not a sign that we have a society genuinely built on something in common, but quite the opposite. It is a sign of the lingering fear that, actually, the emperor has no clothes—that there is no truly shared set of collective French, British, American, Swedish, or Western values.

Faced with this situation, it is little wonder that there is such a struggle to define any moral endpoint for the West, or to have confidence in the universalism of our chosen values. There is less and less on which to base such a unified vision. But without finding a new one, the West's crisis is unlikely to abate at any point soon, regardless of whether the West's economy can be belatedly rebooted. We may be able to understand the origins of the crisis of the West, but it is already deep-rooted—as we will see in the examples of the following chapters.

PART TWO

HOW THE WEST WAS LOST

3

THE FADING OF THE EUROPEAN PROJECT

Few institutions better embody the crisis facing the West than the EU. The European project began with huge ambitions, an unshakeable belief in its own morality, values and universal applicability, and a determination to expand. In that sense, it was a profoundly Western political construction. Like the West more broadly, there was a period of profound optimism in which it seemed like progress was inevitable, and, also like the West more broadly, in 2019 that period of optimism is finished. In fact, it now seems clear that—barring an enormous and currently unforeseeable change in fortunes—the EU has already passed its peak, and is now faced with a question of how far it can prevent its fall from the heights of status it reached in the mid-2000s. There remains the real possibility of a sudden and catastrophic disintegration—a "bank run", in the analogy of the Bulgarian political scientist Ivan Krastev.[1]

The heart of the EU crisis is not economic, though that is obviously an issue. Nor is the much-discussed democratic deficit, although that is in some ways symptomatic of the broader crisis. The real problem is that the EU, in common with the broader

Western malaise, has lost its sense of moral purpose. In making itself nothing more than a project of economic expedience for member states, it has inadvertently cut out its whole basis for existence. The tragedy of the European project is that it did originally have a powerful dream, and a very clear idealistic moral goal, but it has managed to abandon that sense of purpose.

Directly contrary to what many of its critics in the UK believe, the EU is not an economic partnership that has been politicized. It has always had economics at its heart, but previously these policies and structures were in service to a greater political and moral vision. In shedding that vision, the decline of the EU has been almost wholly self-inflicted, and entirely in keeping with the more general loss of Western idealism. This chapter charts the history of the European project—from its 1950s dream of a new, moral approach to international politics, through the peak optimism of the early 2000s, to the decline of the 2010s, which had many warning signs, but which has been confirmed most prominently by the 2016 Brexit vote.

The founding dream

Despite what many critics claim, the origins of the European project were not socialist. True, the Belgian socialist Paul-Henri Spaak played a key role in the early process, but by and large integration was more concerned with opposing socialism than with supporting it. The Italian and West German governments of the 1950s were militantly opposed to the risk of socialism spreading. The Cold War created a context in which American, West German, Italian and indeed Vatican support for European integration rested on the assumed need to reinforce the Western bloc against a perceived socialist enemy. This did not prevent socialist support in some countries for integration—especially on matters such as living standards for workers—but, given the broader geopolitical context of the time, it would be very strange to see it as a primarily socialist initiative.

Nor was the project led by American intervention, as others have been keen to argue.[2] European integration was, of course, vociferously supported by the USA. Tying into the Marshall Plan and the Truman doctrine of containment, European integration was seen as another means of creating a strong Western bloc against Soviet aggression in Europe. Simone de Beauvoir perhaps best encapsulated the view that American influence was the basis of European integration, arguing that the whole concept of "Europe" was a myth of the USA, designed to restore Germany as a counterweight to the USSR.[3] However, while the USA desired European integration, it had little influence in practice over how that took place. In fact, the evidence consistently points to the creative activity of Europeans in conceiving the nature of integration. Jean Monnet, the French diplomat credited as one of the great architects of the European project, noted in 1950 that a dynamic and constructive solution proposed by France was necessary to prevent the USA from re-arming Germany without any concern for French wishes.[4] American records similarly reflect a belief that the establishment of the European Coal and Steel Community was a remarkable innovation initiated within Europe and according to European priorities.[5]

The true foundation of the European project lay in Europe's political traditions of Christian democracy. This was particularly associated in the 1930s and 1940s with Catholic politicians and a centrist ideology forged in close connection with developments in Catholic Social Thought. In this light, the historian Wolfram Kaiser has noted the role of the Nouvelles Équipes Internationales (NEI) and Geneva Circle of Christian Democrats.[6] These were discussion forums that operated from the 1930s onwards, bringing together key Catholic political figures from across the continent. Among the most prominent fruits of these connections was the embryonic idea for the European Coal and Steel Community. The eventual formal proposal for this came from the French foreign minister (and Christian Democrat) Robert Schuman, but the idea had long been familiar to West German Chancellor Konrad Adenauer and other key players in European politics, since it had often been discussed in NEI and Geneva Circle meetings even before the Second World War.

Integration was greatly facilitated by such connections—for example, through Josef Müller, who served as a link between the German CSU and French MRP Christian Democrat parties, and who met with Pope Pius XII, Italian Prime Minister Alcide De Gasperi and Schuman between 1945 and 1946. This network allowed for a common, pan-European ideology to form between Catholic politicians. Following the war, Christian Democrat parties won a series of critical elections, and were the single most dominant force in 1950s politics in all six original member states of the European project: Italy, West Germany, Luxembourg, the Netherlands, Belgium and France—though their success was short-lived in the latter.

* * *

The ideology that came to define the European project, driven by this Christian democrat mindset, had three strands to it, each strongly resonant with Catholic political thought and Western universalism: solidarity, subsidiarity and a moral vision for a new multinational politics.

"Europe will not be made all at once or according to a single plan. It will be built through concrete achievements which first create a de facto solidarity."[7] So says the Schuman Declaration, delivered in May 1950 as the starting gun for European integration, which ultimately culminated in the 1951 Treaty of Paris and its establishment of the European Coal and Steel Community. Solidarity, a key theme throughout the early European project, drew closely on a tradition of Catholic social teaching—the

Catholic doctrines on human dignity and common good in society. For the European project, solidarity had two primary aspects: the securing of peace between nations, and solidarity between classes.

Peace between nations, particularly France and Germany, was an obvious need after two world wars. The failure to maintain peace for even a generation after the First World War, and the scale of military and civilian death in the Second World War, made this an absolute priority. Early European integration not only attempted to ensure peace, but rather more radically to prevent independent militarization altogether. In Schuman's words, "the solidarity in production thus established will make it plain that any war between France and Germany becomes not merely unthinkable, but materially impossible".[8] In other words, the European Coal and Steel Community forced a pooling of sovereignty in the two industries necessary for arming a military, thus preventing Germany from rapidly outstripping the French industrial sector.

The early treaties are also notable for their commitment to prosperity, not of national governments, but of ordinary people. The commitment was explicitly to "the equalization and improvement of the living conditions of workers in [the coal and steel] industries."[9] This commitment, also applied to member-state citizens more broadly, is referred to extensively in both the Treaty of Paris and the 1957 Treaty of Rome, which founded the EU. See, for example, Articles 2–3 of both treaties, and Article 117 of Rome, which declares that "Member states agree upon the need to promote improved working conditions and an improved standard of living for workers".[10] In short, when it came to the European project's founding value of solidarity, economics was a tool towards a higher, moral and political end, not the other way around.

* * *

Subsidiarity, according to the EU's official glossary, is a concept seeking

> to ensure that decisions are taken as closely as possible to the citizen and that constant checks are made to verify that [such] action at EU level is justified in light of the possibilities available at national, regional or local level.
>
> Specifically, it is the principle whereby the EU does not take action (except in the areas that fall within its exclusive competence), unless it is more effective than action taken at national, regional or local level.[11]

Here again we can see in the European project the wider Western values discussed in Part One. For one thing, subsidiarity clearly relates to the idea of liberty, insofar as it is a concept designed to limit excessive centralized control. For another, its emphasis on strong and empowered localized communities feeds into the idea of solidarity.

It is equally clear that subsidiarity was an idea of Christian background, having been lifted consciously from the 1931 papal encyclical *Quadragesimo anno*. The decision to use it as a key concept in the European project was originally suggested at a 1953 NEI congress in Tours, which brought together Christian democrats from across Western Europe; the French politician Pierre-Henri Teitgen suggested it, based on his reading of the encyclical. Critically, not only was subsidiarity seen as an issue of governance, but one of justice. Indeed, in *Quadragesimo anno* Pope Pius XI summarized the concept in those terms: "it is an injustice and at the same time a grave evil and disturbance of right order to assign to a greater and higher association what lesser and subordinate organizations can do."[12] This is tied into a broader conception of how society should function. As an ideology, Christian democracy emphasized "personalism"—the idea that all people are fundamentally relational and tied to others. In other words, humans are not atomized individuals, but essentially bound into social structures, and particularly families. Subsidiarity's emphasis on supporting families and local communities while resisting centralized power is equally critical to the models of Christian democracy and European integration.

* * *

The West German chancellor Konrad Adenauer stated in the Bundestag in 1952 that he felt all six governments involved in the early European project "realise ... that the political goal, the political meaning of the European Coal and Steel Community, is infinitely larger than its economic purpose."[13] This is often missed today, when the EU is considered by many to be little more than a tool for economic performance. The American author James Kirchick has described Europe as a "negative creation", despite its utopian trappings—as something only really defined in order to prevent conflict and hold back the communist East.[14] This is unduly cynical. The early project aspired to far more than peace, but rather dreamed of a moral, universalist political project that would go beyond the errors of the past. The international relations expert Scott Thomas is closer to the mark when he refers to the early European project as an act of "theo-political imagination".[15] It was never designed to be merely a single market, or a customs union, or any other sort of economic club. The hope was of something far more than that.

Reading the Schuman Declaration, you might note that the European project has never deigned to place a geographical limitation on its definition. Quite the reverse—this text founding the Coal and Steal Community explicitly names as "one of its essential tasks ... the development of the African continent." It dreamed of uniting all countries into a single moral mission, "the leaven from which may grow a wider and deeper community between countries long opposed to one another by sanguinary divisions." The early European project, then, was a typical

Western political project. It had an explicit moral goal: the creation of a better world order of politics. It was heavily influenced by Christian political theology, indeed far more consciously so than most Western political projects, and it was imbued with a sort of universalism and claim to superiority over what had come before (in other words, a sense of moral progress). The influence of Christian democracy in the 1950s left a durable ideological legacy which has been surprisingly adaptable and enterprising at incorporating both Anglo-American economic liberalism and socialist social market concerns.

Why does it matter that we pin down these origins of the European project? Because, as we've already seen, we've now lost touch with those founding values, and it's not hard to argue that the current state of the EU has been one casualty among many. After all, for a long time the European project seemed to be on the verge of breaking through as a world superpower.

The high-water mark of the European dream

It is easy to forget, given the politics of our own age, quite how recently the EU was considered to be not only succeeding, but well on the road to challenging the USA as the world's pre-eminent power. In the mid-2000s, a string of publications earnestly anticipated that the future of geopolitics would be defined by the EU. In 2005 the British political scientist Mark Leonard wrote *Why Europe Will Run the 21st Century*, arguing that Europe more than America would be effective in spreading their shared values of democracy, and in defining the future of international politics.[16] In 2004 the American economist and social thinker Jeremy Rifkin wrote *The European Dream: How Europe's Vision of the Future is Quietly Eclipsing the American Dream*, which similarly argued that Europe's particular values, in finding a new way of combining capitalism and civil society, would win out as the definitive model for the twenty-first century.[17] Both built on the early 1990s idea of the British historian Alan Milward, who credited European integration with saving the nation-state.[18]

These optimistic views were not without critics at the time, but what seems remarkable now is that they were written at all. Such views could be contested, but were not considered implausible reflections on Europe's future. Indeed, why should they have been? In the current climate it is difficult to remember quite how justified European triumphalism looked. Germany and France had been reconciled—a possibility considered slight in the late 1940s and early 1950s. Spain and Portugal had been rehabilitated from their recent authoritarian past. From 1957 to 2005, the European project presided over an economic miracle and an astonishing rise in living conditions, resuscitating even the comparatively backward economies of the Republic of Ireland and Greece. Most ambitiously of all, by the end of 2004 the EU had expanded to encompass eight former Communist Bloc countries; Romania and Bulgaria followed in 2007, and Croatia in 2013. It cannot be a coincidence that our current age is the longest period of peace in Western Europe on record—a fact recognized by the Nobel Peace Prize committee in 2012.

The failings of the Eurocrisis can easily distract us from this astonishing achievement: that so many European countries have voluntarily ceded aspects of their own power and sovereignty to be part of the European project. It should not be understated even now. Yet, even then, this victorious expansion was masking the warning signs of Europe's impending crisis. Somewhere between its postwar origins and the mid-2000s, the EU began to lose sight of its mission. It lost its sense of moral purpose, and yet could not see how this would cause the entire project to unravel. One of the great ironies of Europe's condition today is that the EU leadership remains within the idealistic Western mindset that progress is inevitable—and that, therefore, the solution to all the EU's ills is simply "more Europe". Holding on to this belief, Europe's leaders cannot see or acknowledge that they have lost sight of what idealism was really about. Without a genuine, shared sense of moral purpose and progress, the EU's centralizing tendency loses all legitimacy in the eyes of its citizens.

This irony became apparent to me at a 2013 conference hosted by the Berggruen Institute on Governance in Paris on "Europe, les prochaines étapes" (Europe: The Next Steps). The conference had a remarkable roster of speakers including the then French president François Hollande, the Spanish prime minister Mariano Rajoy, the future French president Emmanuel Macron, his rival for the presidency and former prime minister François Fillon, the former Italian prime minister Mario Monti, the WTO director and former French prime minister Pascal Lamy, the then president of the European Parliament Martin Schulz, the former Spanish prime minister Felipe González, and Jacques Delors, the former president of the European Commission.

What it did not have were any major figures from the UK, or anyone from a country east of Germany. Panels discussed business, economics and how to reform democratic instruments within the EU. None considered seriously the likelihood of Brexit, or even mentioned the incipient populist backlashes against the EU that were even then beginning to enter public consciousness. No one thought to consider what Central and Eastern Europe might have to say on the future of the union. All the crises that now threaten the EU were entirely absent from the agenda of 2013, in part because there seemed to be a collective disbelief that any country, having joined the EU, could ever really intend to leave; that a member-state might suddenly depart from the path towards an ever more liberal, tolerant, democratic and European future.

The Polish political scientist Jan Zielonka has summarized this irony by observing that, while there are any number of academic theories of European integration, there are virtually none of European disintegration.[19] The very idea of reversal is alien in a Western philosophic mindset, and we are now seeing this denial unfold in practice, in the EU's floundering attempts to come to terms with the various existential challenges it is facing.

Where Europe lost its way

It is perfectly obvious to everyone that the EU is currently in deep crisis, and that the optimism of the mid-2000s has severely waned. What is less evident is the cause of this crisis. There are still plenty of people for whom the solution is fundamentally economic. In this line of argument, what the EU needs is to revive its economic growth, which would restore confidence and head off the reactionary populist revolt. The European Commission president Jean-Claude Juncker's 2017 State of the Union speech reflected this optimistic picture, arguing that the EU's improving unemployment figures and positive economic growth—higher than the USA's—showed that the EU was "bouncing back".[20]

While good economic performance will certainly help to prolong the EU and to offset some of the populist backlash, it is naive in the extreme to think that this is enough. If the EU is entirely reliant on popular support for economic success, then the problem lies dormant, ready to rear its head every time there's a downturn in fortunes—as we saw after the financial crisis. As the philosopher Jürgen Habermas has observed: "In its current form the European Union owes its existence to the efforts of political elites who could count on the passive consent of their more or less indifferent populations as long as the peoples could regard the Union as being in their economic interests."[21] This circular reality has now been exposed. The EU is not currently weak because of economic turmoil. It is fundamentally weak, because it no longer has a raison d'être beyond economic expedience.

For the same reason, the overlapping group of analysts who see the future of the EU as dependent on a resolution of its so-called "democratic deficit" are also kidding themselves. Such an analysis has held that democracy is a means of creating unity. On the contrary, an increasing body of evidence reveals that, where there is polarization and division—as there surely is in Europe—democracy serves to exacerbate divisions, not overcome them.[22] Democracy in and of itself is not enough. Unless there is a common goal giving meaning to that democracy, then having more elections will only serve to stoke existing tensions, opening the door to exploitation of the system by populists with no genuine interest in pursuing positive ends.

The true crisis is neither specifically economic or democratic—it is in the loss of the EU's fundamental moral mission. The cohesive identity and ideology based on clear moral criteria that was evident in the origins of the European project has become hollowed out, and this is only proven further by commentators' focus on the EU's economic role or performance, or indeed their identification of democracy as a value in itself, rather than a system with which to achieve values. I argued above that the early European project was built on commitments to solidarity and subsidiarity, and a desire for a new moral politics. To see how the EU lost its vision, we need only return to how well those three principles are embodied today.

* * *

As we've seen, solidarity was conceived in the early European project with two primary domains: peace between nations, and peace within societies, particularly as concerned the rights and living conditions of workers. On both these counts, the EU of recent years has fallen short of its original ideals.

On peace, though we can recognize the significance of prolonged peace in Western Europe (where the founding member-states are situated), the EU has proven impotent at preventing European conflicts more widely. Three times in the past thirty years, the European project has had the opportunity to intervene as a moral force for peace on its own continent, and each time it has fallen short. In 1992–5, it stood on the sidelines as disintegration in the Balkans culminated in the Bosnian genocide. The failure was repeated a few years later in Kosovo, where—despite the promptings of Prime Minister Tony Blair—the EU failed to coordinate a response and left the task of European security to NATO. Since 2014, economic sanctions do not seem to be having much effect in checking Russia's annexation of Crimea and ongoing war in Eastern Ukraine.

There were no easy solutions to any of these conflicts, but the failure to be seen as an active agent must be considered a betrayal of the European project's commitment to peace. For Estonians and Poles looking nervously at their eastern borders, can there be any meaningful confidence that, in the event of Russian aggression, their EU partners will rally to their defence? Beyond that, there must be a recognition that supporting peace is about more than defence or even preventing armed conflict. True peace advocacy is about creating conditions conducive to peaceful cooperation. In this light, the turn towards authoritarian governments in several Central and Eastern European countries is a worrying trend for the future of peace—for example, the ambitions of parts of the Hungarian right to see a restored Greater Hungary, which would include parts of modern-day Ukraine and Romania. The EU seems almost entirely impotent to address this threat.

This is dealt with in more depth in the next chapter, but it is worth noting at this point that part of the EU's failure to respond is precisely tied to a Western belief in progress. The EU sets robust criteria for the state of constitutions, civil liberties and separation of powers in nations applying to join the EU. Once they have joined, however, there seems to be no effective procedure to enforce those standards. The expectation of the Western mindset is that, having joined the West, a nation will continue on the path towards becoming ever more Western. There is simply no Western way to respond to events that contradict this expectation.

* * *

When it comes to living and working conditions, the situation is even worse than that of peace in Europe—not only is the EU falling short of its ideals, but it may be actively undermining them.

Western Europe saw an economic miracle and dramatic increases in living conditions from the 1950s through the 1990s, and particularly during the period until the mid-1970s known as the *trente glorieuses*, which saw dramatic advances in reconstructed Western Europe. The European project's commitment to a social market that enforced rights for workers and consumers was instrumental in that process. However, since the beginning of the Eurozone crisis, it has been evident that working rights and living conditions have come a distant second to sovereign debt and GDP as an institutional priority.

At one stage, the determination to protect the Euro and maximize economic performance led to enforced austerity measures that reportedly left almost 45 per cent of Greek pensioners below the poverty line.[23] The European project was once seen as a world leader in proving that economic success and a welfare state were not only compatible, but mutually reinforcing. Now, the EU is itself one of the biggest causes of strain on European welfare states.[24] No one disputes that reforms were desperately needed to alleviate the financial crisis. However, it seems undeniable that the priority was given to salving the wounds of the market first, over and above the commitment to standards of living and workers' rights. The economics that was seen by Schuman as the means to achieve solidarity has become more important than solidarity.

In this context, we have to talk about EU migration. Free movement has long been seen as critical to the European economy, but it has had two significant damaging effects on solidarity. First, in much of Eastern Europe, free movement has seen a drastic brain drain and population depletion towards the EU's West. Romania lost 50% of its doctors in 2009–15.[25] The effect this will have on living standards, Romanians' perceptions of the EU and of their fellow citizens is obvious; in 2017, 10% of the population reported going without healthcare. Further south, in the last quarter-century around 10% of Bulgarians have left their country, and the population is expected to have shrunk by 27% by 2050.[26] It is not hard to see why Bulgarians might fear the erosion of their national identity. Meanwhile, in Northern and Western Europe, free movement has led to significant net immigration. In strictly economic terms, this has been broadly beneficial. However, it has also prompted significant levels of popular resentment, undermining solidarity in some states. Brexit, though its causes are complex, is the highest-profile example of this reaction.[27]

Few people genuinely want to see all migration stopped, and many see at least some types of migrants as making a major contribution to society, or deserving of our protection. A 2018 YouGov poll found that a significant majority of the UK (71 per cent) felt either that we should allow in more people with high levels of education and skills, or that the current level was about right. Only 5 per cent believed we should not allow this group at all. People paying to study at British universities and wealthy people looking to invest also received favourable ratings, and only a third of the British wanted to see a reduction in, or a ban, on refugees. The most popular group were those seeking to work in the National Health Service.[28]

However, overall the British still felt that migration levels in the past ten years had been too high, with 63 per cent giving this answer, while only 4 per cent felt it had been too low. It is quite clear that this is an issue of solidarity which has not been sufficiently addressed. Internal European migration is a fine idea for increasing solidarity in principle, but only if it can be delivered in a way that neither systematically undermines poorer countries in Eastern and Southern Europe, nor undermines social cohesion in the North and West. As it stands, the current situation seems to be a barrier to European and national solidarity, not a benefit to it.

* * *

As with solidarity, the original European commitment to subsidiarity seems to have become muted over time. To reiterate, subsidiarity is the idea that the EU should intervene only where doing so is more effective than leaving action to national, regional or local actors. Of course, this is to some extent a matter of interpretation, and people's idea of the most effective level for intervention varies according to political taste. What is perhaps striking is that even committed Europhiles have come to concede that the principle is not being sufficiently applied. Jean-Claude Juncker, now the president of the European Commission, warned the European parliament in 2014 that

> Since the Maastricht Treaty [furthering European integration in 1992], we have been talking about the correct application of the subsidiarity principle. What we are doing, however, is not sufficient. Our speeches last longer than our efforts to make real headway in reducing red tape, and to ensure that the European Commission— and the European Union—concerns itself with the really major European issues instead of interfering from all angles in every detail of people's lives.[29]

The myths about EU legislation on bendy bananas or the colour of passports may be absurd and regularly debunked, but they hint at something that the fact-checkers haven't been able to dis-prove—a general perception that the EU does too much, that it intervenes in matters that ought to have been left to national parliaments.

This itself is linked to the failure to find a meaningful goal that resonates with citizens. The EU has allowed itself to become an organization whose support from citizens is guaranteed only so long as it brings economic benefits. If that is all that citizens believe the EU is for, it is unsurprising if they see it regularly exceeding its remit. Perhaps because of this, in combination with the recent financial crisis, we are seeing mounting levels of dis-trust in European institutions. In 2015 the academics Sara Hobolt and Olaf Cramme demonstrated that more Europeans now distrusted the EU than trusted it. A large number of European citizens had come to see the EU as a threat, not a saviour: 83% in Greece, 47% in Spain and 34% in Italy saw the EU as posing a major threat to their economies.[30]

As far back as 2000, while others were overcome with European optimism, the political philosopher Larry Siedentop identified the undermining of subsidiarity by an EU deemed to be moving too fast, too soon:

> Some European nations continue to speak a "purer" language of federalism, notably the Germans and the Dutch. But that language no longer carries conviction throughout Europe, where public opin-ion, dazed by the speed with which monetary union is being imposed, and uncertain about its implications, has a growing sense that the elites of Europe have left public opinion far behind ... In their pronouncements the elites of Europe have fallen victims to the tyranny of economic language at the expense of political values such as the dispersal of power and democratic accountability.[31]

Never was this clearer than in the 2005 failure to pass a European Constitution. The proposed constitution (technically the "Treaty establishing a Constitution for Europe") seemed in many ways to be on a firm footing. It was generated after a lengthy consultation process which involved NGOs, publicly available discussions, and debate under the Convention on the Future of Europe, presided over by the former French president Valéry Giscard d'Estaing. It identified a clear intention and direction of travel for Europe, and—by committing to a social market, subsidiarity and a charter of fundamental rights—paid homage to the moral and intellectual foundations on which the European project had been built.

However, it also moved beyond what Europe's citizens were ready for, as evidenced by its failure and abandonment after lost referendums on its ratification in the Netherlands and France— two of the most pro-European nations in the EU, and both founder members of the European project. Rather than learn the lessons of this defeat, and reflect upon how better to create a motivated European public that would back a bold EU future, the decision was instead taken to repackage the constitution into a series of major reforms. It was no longer presented as a genuine constitution in the name of European citizens (a good idea, whose time had not yet come), but as the 2009 Treaty of Lisbon (a bad idea, which further damaged the EU's credibility as an organization committed to subsidiarity).[32]

When Adenauer told the Bundestag that the European project had a purpose that far exceeded its economic ends, he was entirely serious. The early European project was indeed an effort to redefine politics, using economic tools to accomplish a morally grounded political end. If Angela Merkel were to make the same speech today, it is not at all clear that she would be telling the truth. What has underpinned the shift in solidarity and subsidiarity is that, first, the EU has lost the ability to articulate a moral endpoint that resonates with its citizens; and, second, that the economic means of the 1950s have become the political ends of the 2010s. When faced with the financial crisis, the EU's first response was not solidarity—meaningful support for those countries most affected, or protection of living conditions in the worst-hit economies—nor did it respond with subsidiarity—on the contrary, the centre dictated economic and domestic policy to Greece and others. Instead, the first instinct and driving goal was to preserve the market. The populist Greek leader Alexis Tsipras, watching the EU's brutal approach to the Greek situation, summarized his take on it before coming to power: "In the years since 1989, the morality of the economy has fully prevailed over the ethics of politics and democracy ... Today our task is to restore the dominance of political and social moral values, as oppose to the logic of profit."[33]

Such a view might be expected from the left-wing leader of Greece, but it is interesting to note Angela Merkel's speech in 2012, in which she declared that "it's our obligation today to do what has been neglected, to break the vicious cycle of generating ever more debt and breaking the rules", and that Germany was convinced that "Europe is our destiny and our future. If the Euro fails, Europe fails".[34] In this and other speeches, Merkel has laid out the new orthodoxy for the EU's approach to the crisis. The priority is first and foremost to save the currency and reduce sovereign debt—regardless of the extent to which such measures undermine solidarity or living rights.

This is a paradox for the EU of the twenty-first century. On the one hand, the only way it has been able to preserve its popularity (or at least acceptance) in most Western member states has been to make its case as a body that is simply good for national economics. On the other hand, the move toward being nothing more than an economic entity has itself made the development of any aspiration to greater goals impossible. Ordinary people do not feel loyalty or commitment to economic tools for their own ideological sake. So it should have come as no surprise that the economic crash saw a sharp rise in support for Eurosceptic parties; if loyalty is based on economic performance, then poor economic performance will see people abandon the EU completely.

* * *

In February 2018, Boris Johnson made a key speech on the future relationship of the UK and Brexit, in which he referred to the EU as a "teleological construction"—a body aimed at realizing a moral goal.[35] He was both right and wrong. Had he said it in 1958, he would have been entirely correct: the early European project was absolutely committed to a moral utopia and was designed to accomplish a new politics that could lead to it. In 2018, however, he was only half right. The EU does still believe in itself as a project with moral purpose, and so has never come to terms with the idea that progress is not inevitable. In this worldview, once a nation is fit to join the great moral crusade that is Europe, it will only ever become more liberal, more social, more committed to human rights and more European—or Western. There was never any consideration of the possibilities currently being engineered by political movements in Hungary, Poland and the Czech Republic, where constitutional gains are being reversed and hard nationalist governments hold sway. The EU's belief in its own inevitable moral progress has left it blindsided to those shifts—as, to some extent, was the Remain camp in the Brexit debate. This is a serious problem, which the EU is struggling to confront.

However, Johnson was also wrong about the EU as a teleological construction today. The EU's contemporary malaise has arisen because it has stopped believing in itself as an institution with a moral purpose. Whilst it still believes in a sort of inevitable progress once member states join, the EU's greatest failing is that it has abandoned the dream of its founders. That bold moral mission—based on peace, solidarity, subsidiarity and a new politics—has become more and more muted over time. In its place, the EU has become technocratic—a "technocratic hegemony" in the words of Jürgen Habermas[36]—and ever more focused exclusively on narrow economic goals. The commitment to the common good has become more of a commitment to sovereign debt.

In fairness to Europe's leaders, this existential crisis has not gone entirely unremarked. In a powerful address to the European Parliament in 2010, Jacques Delors, one architect of the modern European project and a former president of the European Commission (1985–95), warned that Europe was floundering, and needed a "soul" with which to confront the combination of individualism, globalization and lack of interest from national governments.[37] However, recognition that the crisis exists does not amount to a proper response to it. In the words of the Bulgarian political scientist Ivan Krastev, "It is a moment when political leaders and ordinary citizens alike are torn between hectic activity and fatalistic passivity, a moment when what was until now unthinkable—the disintegration of the union—begins to be perceived as inevitable."[38]

In this sense, the EU—always a fundamentally Western organization, in terms of its philosophical outlook—is the institutional embodiment of the West's broader crisis. Belief in the idealistic promises of the past seems to have faded, and without that endpoint to sustain the project, the entire edifice is in danger of collapse. At the very least, the EU has passed its peak. In the long run Brexit will hurt the EU more than it hurts the UK, not economically but because it marks a critical break in the history of the European project. Not only is the UK the first country to leave the European Union—a circumstance that shouldn't be possible on the road to an ever closer, more European continent—but its departure punctures the EU's founding dream of serving as a new model of global politics. If even nations of longstanding and uninterrupted Westernness like the UK have lost faith in the European project, then there is surely little hope for more fragile, more erratic or more recent members of the club.

4

BROKEN PROMISES
AND SHATTERED DREAMS

HOW THE NEW WESTERNERS LOST FAITH

Timing is everything. Had this book been written in the mid-2000s, this particular chapter would almost certainly not have been included. Indeed, as the British historian Timothy Garton Ash wrote in the *New York Review of Books*, "Had I been cryogenically frozen in January 2005, I would have gone to my provisional rest as a happy European. With the enlargement of the European Union to include many post-Communist democracies, the 1989 'return to Europe' dream of my Central European friends was coming true."[1]

In 1985, few would have confidently predicted that the entire communist apparatus would disintegrate within five years. Absolutely no one would have predicted that, by 2007, three post-Soviet states (Latvia, Estonia and Lithuania), six post-communist states (Czech Republic, Slovakia, Poland, Hungary, Romania and Bulgaria), and post-Yugoslav Slovenia would all be independent states, free of communist control, and would voluntarily join a European Union. Even by 2010, EU enlargement, despite much scepticism, seemed to have gone remarkably smoothly. Just as post-authoritarian Spain and Portugal had been successfully rehabilitated into the West with their 1986 accession into the European Economic Community, much of what had once been considered lost in Central and Eastern Europe seemed finally to have been recovered for the West.

However, writing in 2019, optimism is noticeably thin on the ground. A number of the new Westerners—those who came back to Europe in the mid-2000s—now seem to be hovering back on the threshold. The Polish political scientist Jan Zielonka has described today's Europe as "a déjà vu in reverse order"—in a mirror reflection of the end of communism, liberal democracy, far from spreading out across the world, now finds itself in full retreat.[2]

This chapter charts that transition, looking first at the success story of post-communist rehabilitation and then at how this crisis and reversal has set in across a number of states in Central, Eastern and Southern Europe. Crucially, it concludes that the failure is not simply a matter of domestic reversals in these individual states, but is related to the collective failure of the West. A failure to recognize this and win back the wavering new Westerners is ultimately a mortal risk to the West as a whole.

Back to Europe

Anne Applebaum, the American-Polish journalist and historian, recalls that in the late 1980s Poles spoke frequently of a desire "to be normal".[3] Normal meant Western and European, with all the trappings: a capitalist economy, democracy, a free press, and so on. When the communist collapse came, the trajectories of so many newly liberated nations were strikingly similar. A few struggled on for a while, attempting to deliver a softer socialism, but most attempted a remarkably rapid shift towards a capitalist market economy and democracy. Those that joined the EU followed a particularly similar model, because they followed the EU accession criteria. Arguably, this would later become one of the challenges to Westernness in these states, as the process of deriving democratic and legal norms was outsourced to the EU process, rather than being allowed to emerge organically within the states themselves.[4]

The drive to be "normal" and "Western" was a strong one, and in this, the era of Western liberal triumphalism characterized by Fukuyama's famous proclamation of the end of history, there seemed to be no alternative offering available. A generation of European leaders, perhaps most prominently led by the Czech leader Václav Havel, embodied a trend of being "more Western than the Westerners", and of seeking to establish nations in that image.

The hope was to bury the very concept of Eastern Europe, and swiftly. "Eastern Europe", as Applebaum is keen to remind people, is a political, not a geographical, term.[5] While many of the nations in the EU are of course east of Europe's centre, the term is never applied, for example, to Greece, Sweden or Finland, never mind Cyprus. Instead, the term was and remains a political tag for the part of the continent that fell under communist control—the part that ceased, in our model, to be Western, and so needed a new designation. Such nations had nothing else in common; there is no linguistic, ethnic or historical unity to what became Eastern Europe in the 1940s. The 1990s and 2000s were the era of transition from being part of "Eastern Europe" to rejoining "the West". The key actor in this transition was the institutional framework of the EU. Joining the EU was not just an economically savvy thing to do, but a mark of return to the West, expressed in institutional form.

There was precedent for this process. In the 1980s, the former Western states coming out of an authoritarian regime and pariah status were Spain and Portugal. In the 1950s, it was West Germany and Italy. European integration has been a key tool in Western efforts to rehabilitate and develop both new and returning Western nations. Spain, in fact, became the model for EU enlargement in 2004, including the accession criteria and efforts to establish a backstop defending against democratic backsliding—a process which, as we shall see, has not been very successful the second time around. The 1980s Iberian enlargement of the EEC followed a very similar narrative to the post-communist one, including the desire to recover a perceived "natural Europeanness"—in this view, the authoritarian period was simply an unfortunate blip in the progressive Western narrative.[6]

The same was true of the idea of the Balkans. Unlike "Eastern Europe", the Balkans is a geographical, not merely a political, invention, but if anything as a term it is used even more pejoratively. The Balkans is Europe's own dark mirror, an idea onto which Europe projects all of its own worst failings: rampant nationalism, internecine conflict, a failure to learn from history and a constant failure to prevent violence and mass murder. The Balkans are represented in popular discourse as a place of constant ethnic conflict, warring fiefdoms, corruption, economic backwardness and hopelessness. It was known as such in the late nineteenth century, when the region was ignored and left underdeveloped by both the Ottoman and Austro-Hungarian Empires; recent history has done little to dispel the prejudices.

It is not surprising, then, that rejoining the West, in joining the EU, has been linked to an explicit rejection of the Balkans. In 2005, as Croatia moved closer to EU accession, "Bye Bye Balkans" was the headline of *Novi List*, the country's oldest daily newspaper and a staple of liberal anti-Balkan prejudice.[7] This was just one in a series of Croatian articles and pieces that talked openly of leaving the Balkans behind. It was also the narrative pushed by many of Croatia's leading politicians, notably Ante

Gotovina—depending on one's perspective, either a war criminal (convicted in The Hague and then acquitted) or a national hero. In 2012 Gotovina gave a speech advocating EU accession, with a key message that "The war belongs in the past, let's turn to the future!"[8] Returning to the West is a commitment to moving on from the past, to rejecting it as an "abnormality" interrupting inevitable and universal moral progress; and to moving instead towards the end goal of that progress, the Western values of freedom, equality and solidarity. This theme—of the West and the EU as a "normal" future that permits past messiness to be left behind—had currency across the "new West" until quite recently. For these newcomers—or prodigal returnees—Westernness really did stand for something.

It still does, up to a point. Despite the migrant crisis, Brexit, the downturn in the EU's economic performance and the democratic reversals in Hungary and elsewhere, at the time of writing there are four Balkan nations with official candidacy for EU membership (Serbia, Macedonia, Albania and Montenegro), and two more are formally recognized as potential candidates, actively seeking that status (Kosovo and Bosnia and Herzegovina). In some ways, this should not be a surprise. After all, the overall transition for "Eastern Europe" from the early 1990s to today has been remarkable, and these nations aspiring to (re)join the West have been there to witness it, against the odds. There was serious scepticism in 1990 that it would be possible.

Cynics doubted, for example, that Poland—with a patchy history of pre-war democracy, and a number of bloated, inefficient industries—would really prove to be a safe, sustainable capitalist democracy.[9] Yet, as Yascha Mounk argues, until at least 2005 it was an enormous Western and European success story. In 1990–2005, the government changed hands in free and fair elections five times, while GDP increased sixfold, far exceeding the threshold beyond which no democracy has ever reverted to authoritarianism. In the same period, civil society organizations appeared to flourish, including an active and independent media that held the government to account.[10] When Poland co-hosted the European Football Championship in 2012, it prompted a glowing write-up from *Der Spiegel*, entitled "The Miracle Next Door: Poland Emerges as a Central European Powerhouse". The article went on to note that not only was Poland one of the West's few great success stories since 1990, experiencing an economic boom in defiance of the overall sluggish European economy, but it was also increasingly liberal, gay-friendly, entrepreneurial and "future-orientated".[11]

Poland became a model of democratic consolidation and a posterchild for the EU's work rehabilitating Eastern Europe. Current European Council president Donald Tusk (Polish prime minister 2007–14) and his foreign minister Radosław Sikorski were two of the EU's most prominent backers, and for a period it seemed likely, even inevitable, that Poland would become a major force in EU politics, to rival France, Germany and the UK. Poland was the flag bearer, but it was far from unique in "former Eastern Europe" in terms of its economic performance and seemingly durable democratic and civil society structures. To a greater or lesser degree, positive stories could be told in every one of the new EU member states of 2004.

* * *

The successes of this period, from 1990 until the late 2000s, are frequently dismissed these days. It is now common to encounter cynical accusations that former Eastern European states' commitment to the West was never more than skin-deep. The American journalist James Kirchick, for example, is typical of the trend when he suggests that "To Easterners desperate to crawl out from under the thumb of a four-decade-long communist subjugation, the primary motivation for re-joining

Europe was to get rich fast, not to acquire the socially liberal values of the Dutch."[12]

Certainly, the fact that the EU has been pivotal to propping up the economy in many of the newer members is a big part of its appeal. Billions of pounds in EU structural and cohesion funds have been paid to develop the economies of poorer member states, quite apart from the economic gains of the single market. Further, it is true that there has been a degree of asymmetry in what the longer-standing EU15 and the "class of 2004" have wanted from the European project in the fifteen years since the enlargement. But this goes beyond economics. If the newer member states are united by one thing, it is astonishingly low levels of trust in politicians. Whether it was forty years of communist propaganda failing to match reality, or the rampant corruption of the 1990s and 2000s, faith in politicians is far lower than in Western Europe.[13] For Jan Zielonka, this goes some way to explaining why so many Poles seem blasé and unconcerned about the "post-truth" tendencies of populist politicians: they assume that all politicians lie as a matter of course, and for them the only relevant question is whether "he is *my* liar or *your* liar".[14] In this context, the EU is seen as a bulwark against corruption, a check and balance on the failings of national politics— a noticeably different take from, say, Brexit Britain, where it is EU bureaucrats who are the corrupt chancers.

Cynicism about the sincerity of the newer EU member states ignores the deep-felt desire to be normal; the redemption and restoration story of returning to Europe and the West. It matters to these nations—or, at least, mattered—to leave behind Eastern Europe and the lost decades of status. Elites in Central, Eastern and Southern Europe have bought as much as anyone else into the "no alternative", end-of-history narrative that sees Western liberal democracy and late-twentieth-century capitalism as both inevitable and desirable. Believing in that founding myth brought them, at least temporarily, huge economic and democratic gains. These came in the face of a fair few sceptics arguing that the 2004 enlargement was too big and came before those countries were ready.

One of the great theorists of liberalism and Europe, Ralf Dahrendorf, warned that transitioning from communism to a market economy was likely to entail huge amounts of pain as well as gain: guaranteed jobs and welfare systems propped up by an unsustainable communist system would have to be demolished. He feared that democracy could not survive this pain; that it would leave post-communist nations easy prey for populists and revisionists, who would claim that everything had been better under the old system.[15] Until very recently, it seemed as though Europe had managed to defy those warnings, and was seeing simultaneous democratic consolidation and economic advancement. Even in 2019, despite the political chaos, former Eastern Europe is doing rather well economically, certainly in comparison to Southern European nations like Italy, Spain and Greece. Unemployment is low, and growth is relatively steady.[16] If it were all about the money, there would be less cause for pessimism.

But even at the height of the success story, there were warnings emerging, not least during Hungary's first Orbán government in 1998–2002. The issue, in fact, was never primarily economic, but a matter of belonging and direction. Simply put, the tension is over what a "return to Europe" and to the West actually meant. It is unfortunate that the mid-2000s, just as Eastern Europe was being brought back into the fold, coincided with the West losing sight of what it represented. As we've seen, the Western commitment to itself—as on the move to somewhere better, with a commitment to freedom, equality, solidarity and universalism—has been waning. This has come exactly at the point when a strong sense of identity and moral leadership was most needed, during the economic crash, the migration crisis and an era of increasing fears over terrorism. With that emerging vacuum on one side, an alternative vision has been given increasingly free rein, just as Dahrendorf predicted. But the populism that has emerged has not been a left-wing call to return to communism. Instead, the narrative of return to the West now gaining traction across the "new West" involves the rediscovery of the captive nation, and the chance to re-establish strong national identities that were suppressed for decades or longer.

The Baltic states had been part of the USSR since 1940. Poland and Hungary had been great European kingdoms subject to decades of foreign control and humiliation. Many of the newly independent Balkan states, after the violent break-up of Yugoslavia, were effectively experiencing independence as nations for the first time. Bulgaria was an independent kingdom in 1908–46, a brief national moment between Ottoman and Soviet domination. It is unsurprising, then, that a yearning for a strong national identity has been underway in the "new West" since before 1990. Indeed, in what the Polish philosopher Bronisław Baczko has called the "exploding historical memory", the Polish Solidarity movement fought its battle with the communist leadership in part as a war of "true" national history versus propaganda, revisiting such episodes as the Polish–Soviet war, and the Katyń massacre.[17] History became a political and moral battlefield, and the historic nation a key facet of the movement for a return to the West. This was necessarily a double-edged sword: recalling a nascent national history helped to undermine communism, but it could equally well empower an anti-Western, or anti-EU, nationalism.

The question of return, therefore, is not a simple one. Were these nations returning to a European West—progressive, democratic and on the road to some new vision of European modernity, as Havel had dreamed? Or were they, conversely, resetting the clock back to the moment of their lost sovereignty in the

1940s or earlier, in order to mark their own particular path, distinct from the West? In fact, even this dichotomy does not quite do justice to the complexity of the identity question. Interwar Poland was relatively cosmopolitan and diverse. Communism, of course, was a deliberately cosmopolitan ideology that suppressed national identity. It's true that the Poland of 1990, through to today, is one of Europe's most ethnically homogeneous, but even so the nostalgic vision of a "pure" Poland that ethno-nationalists wish to "return to", often saturated with Christian symbolism, is a nation that did not exist in 1939—if, indeed, if ever truly existed.[18] Despite its fallacy, this is a powerful alternative model to the early 2000s' optimistic cosmopolitanism—calling for a return not to the West, but to an earlier model of Christendom in which homogeneous nation-states were protected from outsiders. This idea of "return from", rather than to, the West is becoming increasingly popular as the Western vision fades.

The tipping point: the loss of the new Westerners

Across former Eastern Europe, the extraordinary process of rapid Westernization in the 1990s–2000s is being unravelled. The trend is particularly pronounced in Hungary and Poland, but is growing elsewhere too. The Washington-based think tank Freedom House produce an annual index scoring states worldwide on their level of freedom; it looks at such categories as freedom of the press and democratic liberties. In recent years, this index has made grim reading for supporters of Western freedom: worldwide, we have been witnessing a democratic recession. This process has been particularly marked in Hungary, with the country's status downgraded from "Free" to "Partly free". This is on the basis of observations that the democratic process is now unduly managed by the government, and stacked against opposition parties; and that the press and judiciary are excessively controlled by the executive. In other words, Freedom House is warning of an authoritarian slide in Hungary.[19]

The prime minister, Viktor Orbán, has made no secret of this trend, nor of the appeal he sees in establishing an "illiberal democracy"—although he has retreated from that branding a little in recent years, at least before international audiences.[20] Orbán first became prime minister in 1998–2002, but it is in the 2010s that he has managed to radically reshape Hungary. Key to his programme was a landslide win in 2010 that gave his Fidesz party a supermajority in parliament (around two thirds of the deputies, based on 52.73 per cent of the popular vote). With this supermajority, Orbán has been able to drive through constitutional reforms at breakneck speed, with minimal legal or parliamentary oversight. In the journalist Paul Lendvai's words, this has amounted to Orbán "almost effortlessly put[ting] in place, without any resistance worthy of the name, a skilfully veiled authoritarian system".[21]

The changes have included an effective end to any separation of powers, with the courts stuffed with political appointments. The constitutional court has been largely neutered as a force. The chief prosecutor, Péter Polt, is an old Orbán ally, married to the head of human resources at the national bank; Polt is on the board of two foundations holding accounts at the same bank, which have been accused of channelling money to Orbán and his allies' business interests.[22] The media is no longer free, exhibiting significant bias towards the government, with Fidesz supporting media heads rewarded with significant advertising revenues, and devoting wildly disproportionate coverage to the government.[23] The liberal newspaper *Népszabadság*, which had been notably critical of the government, found itself forcibly bought out by a foreign firm with links to the regime; it was then summarily closed. The electoral system has been overhauled to virtually guarantee the continued dominance of the ruling party. The independent intergovernmental Organization for Security and Co-operation in Europe condemned the 2014 elections on the basis that Fidesz had a significant undue advantage—including a biased media landscape, an election framework established without opposition consultation, and a general failure to separate the Fidesz party from the state.[24]

Orbán, for his part, has come to resemble less a democratically elected Western leader and more a mafia godfather, dispensing favours and protection in exchange for absolute loyalty.[25] Friends and allies have received prominent governmental and public positions; the prime minister's home village of Felcsut, population 1,800, has a shiny new football stadium; his family seem to have profited remarkably from his premiership. By any reasonable measure of objectivity, Hungary is no longer a truly free democratic state, but an autocratic one using the vestiges of liberal democracy to lend itself credibility in the eyes of an international audience. If freedom is one of the markers of Westernness, then Hungary is retreating fast.

Though the EU belatedly seems to be waking up to the fact that it has been helping to incubate an authoritarian regime, its responses to date have been weak. Orbán, meanwhile, is becoming bolder. At the time of writing, new proposed laws seek to criminalize doctors who treat illegal migrants, and to punish charities that look to help migrants applying for citizenship if the application turns out to be unsuccessful. The Central European University, the jewel of Hungary's higher education system, drew students from across the world—as of 2017, it has been driven out of the country. While the UK's Conservative politicians have become ever more agitated about free speech in British universities, their party voted in the European Parliament against censuring Orbán and Fidesz—a rank betrayal of any true commitment to that cause, one not committed by any other governing conservative party.[26]

Depressingly, however, looking at our definition of Westernness from Chapter 1, liberty is not the only Western value where Hungary seems to be backsliding. On equality, too, the Orbán regime appears to have put the country in reverse. Overall, Hungary's economy has been improving for some years—it weathered the financial crash relatively well, in comparison to Southern Europe—but its true performance has been distorted by very significant EU investment, of up to 5 per cent of GDP. Without this, the Hungarian economy would effectively be stagnant. Worse, the gains are increasingly limited to particular pockets of Hungarian society. While those in Orbán's inner circle are becoming enormously rich, the economist Tamás Mellár estimates that the poverty of the lowest third has reached unprecedented levels. He describes Hungary as "a nation of 3 million beggars".[27] Inequality in land ownership and healthcare is widening.

Of the breakdown in Hungary's commitment to universal values, much has been written. Orbán has been a leading figure in refusing to accept non-Christian refugees, demanding a reduction in migration on the grounds both that those seeking asylum are fundamentally different from his own people, and that Hungary is, by nature, European yet also at odds with the rest of Europe on this question. In a blistering speech to the European Parliament, Orbán noted that "we [Hungary] think differently about Europe's Christian character, and the role of nations and national cultures; we interpret the essence and mission of the family in different ways; and we have diametrically opposed views on migration".[28] That much is probably true. It is striking that Orbán has, particularly in recent years, branded himself as a Christian democrat—though his understanding of Christian democracy is, indeed, diametrically opposed to the anti-nationalism of the 1950s Christian democrats so instrumental in designing the European project. Orbán's model is of the anti-Western "Christianism" explored in Chapter 2. His Christian identity is a fundamentally negative creed, built on the idea of excluding others—particularly Muslims.

This brings us to the final, sad failing of the Western project in Hungary: the abuse of solidarity. As explored in Chapter 1, the twentieth century was a tale of the West's great ideologies consuming themselves through a failure to balance the three republican values. Fascism, an ideology that prized solidarity high above liberty and equality, destroyed the promise of the West by promoting the solidarity of the in-group (the pure nation) while demolishing freedom and trammelling upon minority groups. Hungary is not a fascist state, despite all the problems described above. However, it is exhibiting a worrying trend towards a pure nation narrative, against an increasingly marginalized minority. In Hungary, that means migrants, Muslims, and Jews. Both Fidesz and its rival, the far-right Jobbik party, have engaged in the targeting of these minorities. George Soros, the Hungarian-American billionaire who has devoted a fortune to strengthening education, democracy and civil society in Hungary—and whose foundation funded Orbán's studies at Oxford—has been branded an enemy of the people. Orbán's rhetoric against Jews in general evokes some of Europe's ugliest past failings. In one speech, for example, he told an audience:

> we must fight against an opponent which is different from us. Their faces are not visible, but are hidden from view; they do not fight directly, but by stealth; they are not honourable, but unprincipled; they are not national, but international; they do not believe in work, but speculate with money; they have no homeland, but feel that the whole world is theirs. They are not generous, but vengeful, and always attack the heart—especially if it is red, white and green [the Hungarian flag].[29]

He did not use the word "Jew". He didn't have to. The tropes were obvious to anyone with ears to hear. In the same way, to most Western audiences Orbán's employment of the term

"Christian National Idea" may seem an innocuous, if slightly anachronistic, Christian democrat term; but in Hungary it evokes the language of Admiral Horthy's fascist regime, which rounded up Hungary's Jews both before and during the Nazi occupation—a historical fact that the Orbán regime has invested significant financial and cultural capital in denying.

* * *

If Hungary is the ignominious leader in the race to leave the West, then Poland—once the posterchild of post-communist democratic consolidation and economic success—is not far behind. Poland's situation is not yet as extreme, but given how high expectations had risen by the early 2010s, the transition has in some ways been even more disappointing. The sense of shock and incomprehension was captured by the Polish liberal intellectual Adam Michnik, who had been a prominent dissident under communism. After a victory for the nationalist Law and Justice party (PiS), Michnik gave a despairing interview, commenting, "Sometimes a beautiful woman loses her mind and goes to bed with a bastard".[30] It's a line deeply patronizing to both women and Polish voters, and somewhat short of enlightened contemporary liberalism in its own right—but it does capture a snapshot of the angry helplessness among a liberal elite that has lost power, and currently has absolutely no expectation of winning it back.

The PiS' model is in many ways identical to Orbán's in Hungary, though without quite the same cult of personality— the party is chaired by its co-founder Jarosław Kaczyński, a backbencher widely perceived as the *éminence grise* of the system, leaving the presidency and premiership to protégés. When Kaczyński's business dealings came under scrutiny, it was revealed that in 2015 the government had appointed Ernest Bejda, a former PiS parliamentary candidate, as head of the anti-corruption bureau. The courts have been systematically targeted to under-mine the separation of powers and the strength of the judiciary. The constitutional tribunal, the highest court in the land, has been brought under executive control through an increased num-ber of judges on the bench, and the rushing through of nomina-tions for party loyalists. Its powers, as in Hungary, have been systematically stripped back, while the parliament has become more and more powerful. In a series of sweeping reforms, the government has lowered the compulsory retirement age for judges in order to remove a generation of experienced judges who might have opposed it, while simultaneously allowing the president to prolong Supreme Court judges' mandate to keep supporters in post long after they should have been removed.

Also mirroring events in Hungary has been the Polish gov-ernment's clampdown on the media, with government funds used to spread propaganda and limit opposition.[31] The state broadcaster is now effectively an arm of the government. Private companies have lost advertising contracts, and, again as in Hungary, liberal media operations have found themselves bought out by corporations with links to the government. Prominent political opposition figures have been marked out as enemies. Even Lech Wałęsa, hero of Polish nationalism and the Solidarity movement that brought about the end of commu-nism, has been increasingly whitewashed from recent history. The PiS was partly founded by the Kaczyński twins as a deliber-ate rebuke to Wałęsa's pro-European, pro-Western sympathies. Always a party somewhat given to conspiracy theory, it has turned against Wałęsa in particular, with accusations that he was an agent of the communist secret police all along. "We are sure he was a Communist conspirator," said Tomasz Sakiewicz, editor of the magazine *Gazeta Polska* and a close ally of Jarosław Kaczyński. "He was playing for the other side. Who is Lech Wałęsa really? I'm afraid he didn't know either."[32]

All of this has prompted consternation in the EU and the Council of Europe, an international human rights and pro-democracy organization. The Venice Commission, the Council's advisory body, stated in 2016 that the "rule of law is in danger ... so are democracy and human rights".[33] The European Commission, after two years of monitoring and warnings, finally launched unprecedented disciplinary measures against Poland in late 2017, invoking Article 7, which could include the suspension of Poland's voting rights in EU institutions. Measures against Hungary followed in September 2018. Neither case is yet resolved at the time of writing, prompting the Commission to take a more radical step: proposing new legislation that may link future EU funding to upholding the rule of law.

Along with the decline in legal, media and democratic freedom, solidarity is also fading, as in Hungary; and again it is migrants, particularly Muslim refugees and Jews, who are bearing the brunt of hostility. Following the Hungarian model, the Polish government has been rewriting history, making it illegal to suggest any Polish complicity in the running of concentration camps or the rounding up of Jews during the Second World War. The anti-migrant rhetoric is particularly focused on the alleged failure of multiculturalism in Western Europe, and on the threat posed by Muslim refugees. Poland harbours some of the strongest anti-Muslim sentiment in Europe. More than 70% of Poles fear that refugees will increase the likelihood of terrorism— higher than any European nation except, predictably, Hungary (76%). Even more, 75%, are worried that refugees will take their jobs and social security.[34] These fears have been fanned by the government. Recently, they appointed Adam Andruszkiewicz as a junior minister responsible for policing hate speech online, despite complaints from Jewish groups and video footage of him calling migrants "a disease" and making homophobic remarks in public speeches.[35] This is not an isolated appointment, but a mark of the party's and the government's willingness to tolerate and promote marginalization of minority groups.

As in Hungary, the Polish government has emphasized its Christian heritage as a point behind its policies. Poland certainly has a notably strong Catholic identity and relationship with the Church. John Paul II's prominent opposition to communism, status as the first Polish pope and relationship with the Solidarity movement helped cement that connection in the 1990s. The PiS government has pushed it further, most notably with a Mass that crowned Jesus as king of Poland—an event attended by the nation's president, several leading parliamentarians and the Catholic bishops. The real question is how far this relationship can be used to justify policies designed to exclude minorities from participation in Poland's national story. We will come back to this in Part Three.

Poland and Hungary have been sister nations in this process of de-Westernization. They are also two of the so-called Visegrád Group (or V4), with the Czech Republic and Slovakia, which has become a bulwark of anti-liberal, nationalist resistance to the EU. The group has been critical of and resistant to attempts to redistribute refugees across the EU. Each member country has, to a greater or lesser degree, been on a similar journey of right-wing populist government. Interestingly, the leadership of the V4 has been increasingly appealing to right-wing populists in other Western nations. It enjoys strong support, for example, from such politicians in Bavaria and Austria—to the extent that the FPÖ has publicly toyed with the idea of Austria joining the group.

* * *

Where Hungary and Poland are leading, others are following. Populist nationalist parties are growing in strength across much of Eastern and Central Europe. In Croatia, the EU's newest member, the speeches about turning to the future and leaving the Balkans behind cannot disguise the fact that much of the political elite is the same nationalist elite that fought in the Yugoslav wars. A new right-wing populist party called Živi zid (Living Wall) has arisen, promising a strident return to Christian moral values along the same lines as Fidesz and PiS and rapidly gaining ground. Since 2016 it has had eight deputies in parliament. As in much of former Eastern Europe, there have been significant economic gains in Croatia since EU accession, but these have been largely concentrated in a few better-off regions. Inequality is taking its toll on the credibility of the Western dream. In the Baltic states, there is a notable growth in parties defined largely by their ethnic identity.[36] In Latvia, the greatest vote share in the 2018 parliamentary election went to Harmony, a Russian-ethnic party with close ties to Putin's regime, which won just short of 20 per cent of votes. In Estonia, several seats in parliament are occupied by the Conservative People's Party of Estonia, founded in 2012 as an ethno-nationalist ethnic-Estonian party, known for its torchlit processions. It is expected to make further gains at the next election, and in 2018 it was the country's only political party to have a growing membership.

In late 2017 the Czech Republic elected the eccentric billionaire Andrej Babiš as prime minister, despite what was then an open criminal investigation for alleged fraud. Babiš is unpredictable, an ideological hodgepodge who is generally perceived as pro-European but also clearly represents an anti-establishment vote. Indeed, his election was marked by the successful performance of such candidates across the board. Apart from Babiš' own ANO, the next three largest parties in parliamentary representation were the SPD (far-right Czech nationalists), the Czech Pirate Party (a direct democracy movement founded as a student movement) and the ODS, a conservative party previously quite close ideologically to the British Conservatives, but with an increasingly hard line against migrants and multiculturalism.

Evidently Czech voters are disillusioned with the models of democracy and capitalism put before them.

The list could go on and on. In the Western Balkans—those states that had once been part of Yugoslavia—the political scientist Jasmin Mujanović has summarized a litany of dismal recent developments: "The most dangerous myth of contemporary Western Balkans politics, and the most popular in Brussels and Washington, is that the present combination of democratic backsliding, anaemic economic growth, and geopolitical flux can persist indefinitely in some kind of stable form".[37] He has it right, and is not alone in the observation that what we are seeing is not as simple as failings in individual countries. The trend is in large part the fault of the West as a whole, which has absolved itself of responsibility for promoting and protecting its own values. The New Westerners of the 1990s and 2000s are in danger of being lost again, and instead of fighting to reverse that process, too much of the West is turning inwards, ignoring the rising chaos.

What next?

The story of the new Westerners, as told in this chapter, is a tragedy: from the triumphalism of the 2000s to the gathering threat of disintegration today. It would be a mistake to think that this is the natural outcome for fundamentally corrupt and hopeless regions that were ill-suited to Western values. Firstly, it is the communist history of these countries, often involuntary, that has left them vulnerable to a global weakening of Westernness. Secondly, what's going wrong is a failing not of these countries but of the whole West, and one of its own making. As the Bulgarian political scientist Ivan Krastev puts it, "if disintegration does happen, it will be not because the periphery has run away but because the center ... has revolted."[38]

BROKEN PROMISES AND SHATTERED DREAMS

There are three ways in which the West has failed the new Westerners. First, the loss of moral direction, which has caused promises to look empty and fatuous at a time when vision was most needed, in a difficult socioeconomic climate. Second, the failure to properly envisage solidarity and identity, which has opened the door for those who abuse identity to anti-Western ends. Finally, the West has turned inwards, becoming simply defensive rather than seeking to enact more change elsewhere. In its efforts at damage limitation, it is betraying itself, and ultimately causing more harm than good.

* * *

"Democracy has won; the free market has won. But what in the wake of this great ideological victory is today the substance of our beliefs? To what is the human being in the democratic West now truly committed? ... I think this emptiness, this potential emptiness, if not yet the reality, is dangerous."[39]

So said the Polish-born American diplomat Zbigniew Brzezinski, in a 1990 lecture at Georgetown University. The question he asked has become the great challenge for the West. In the 1990s and 2000s, it felt like there was a momentum and a dream for the new Westerners: to make up for lost time and be restored to the West as "normal"—encompassing democracy, a functioning economy and membership of Western clubs like the EU, the Council of Europe and NATO. Having by and large accomplished those aims, however, the new Westerners found themselves in a Europe and a West that wasn't actually sure what road it was on.

This was particularly true of the EU, once the quintessential political expression of Western values, now stuck viewing itself primarily as an economic body and acting accordingly. Problematically, this loss of a greater moral vision in favour of a narrow economic programme coincided with the financial crash—

and, unsurprisingly, the economic crisis undercut the EU's legitimacy, fast. Moreover, it is becoming clear that the economic gains for the "class of 2004" have been concentrated and not shared, amidst rampant inequality. Too many have not seen the benefits that were promised with a return to the West. As we have seen in other chapters, this trend has emerged across the West. But when looking at post-communist Europe, the consequences are more obvious and more dangerous. Some Western nations may be able to draw on deep reservoirs of historically accrued cultural or political capital to retain their faith in Western idealism, despite recent failures and difficulties. For nations that have only relatively recently regained that same status, it is far easier to backslide and be lost to the West. Unless we re-establish a moral mission and endpoint, the rapid unravelling and disintegration of the progress made since 1990 will continue.

Hungary and Poland may be two prominent examples of national identity and solidarity being abused, with an ugly nationalism employed to the exclusion of minorities—but they are far from unique in the West. The backlash against globalization and the reality of twenty-first-century migration patterns, allied with a broader breakdown in community and identity, has been going on everywhere. The stakes are simply higher in Central and Eastern Europe, precisely because their nationhood is often more fragile. Many are nations that have not existed long and have endured external occupation or oppression. This creates a particularly sharp sensitivity to having identity threatened or undermined, and makes for a greater level of vulnerability to those who would exploit that sensitivity.

This, as Mujanović notes, has very much been the history of the West Balkans. National elites have no interest in overcoming nationalisms and hatred of their neighbour, because playing one off against another is precisely the process that keeps them in power.[40] The West's complicity in allowing the region's break-up into ever smaller, more homogeneous communities does little to solve underlying tensions, and everything to prop up local potentates for whom national and ethnic identity is the throne on which they sit. Fragile nationhood certainly underpins much of Orbán's appeal in Hungary. One of his first major reforms since returning to power in 2014 was to establish a day of national solidarity, marking the anniversary of the hated 1920 Treaty of Trianon that gave away two thirds of Hungary's territory and 40 per cent of its population to neighbouring countries. That slight has been exploited by Orbán, and by his further-right rival party Jobbik, again and again. Doing so taps into a deep-seated Hungarian national identity trope of abandonment and betrayal. The nineteenth-century Hungarian poet Sándor Petőfi said, "We are the most forsaken of all the people on the earth"—and that was before decades of communist oppression.[41]

The phenomenon of the fragile nation has perhaps best been captured by the Czech writer Milan Kundera, who described Central Europe as a family of small nations, where "the small nation is one whose very existence may be put in question at any moment; a small nation can disappear and it knows it".[42] This may seem a curious paradox: how can both nationalism and the sense of a fragile nation be strong? Yet, in fact, it is precisely when an identity is most under threat that support for it becomes most noisy and desperate. The virulent nationalisms emerging in so much of Central, Southern and Eastern Europe are a response to fear that those nations are eroding—not a sign of national confidence.

Demographically, if nothing else, this fear is not irrational. One uniting feature of all the new Western nations that have joined the EU is depopulation. In 2000–17 Latvia lost more than 18% of its population, and the national birth-rate is now a major political issue featuring in the manifestos of almost all political parties.[43] Lithuania is not far behind. As we saw earlier, Bulgaria has lost

10% of its population in the past twenty-five years, and it is expected to shrink 27% by 2050.[44] By some calculations, Bulgaria's is the fastest shrinking population of any country on Earth. Romania has shrunk by almost 20% since the end of communism.[45] Croatia, Poland, Hungary, Serbia—across former Eastern Europe these nations are shrinking, or at best stagnant, as in the Czech Republic and Slovenia. In the long run, this will have devastating economic effects, particularly since it is particularly the emigration of younger people driving the depopulation.

The most profound impact of all will not be economic, but the challenge to fragile nationhood. For nations only recently restored to independence, this threat is existential. It is not an idle fear that nations—their languages and cultures, which have often been repressed under foreign occupation or ethno-nationalist dictatorships—could simply vanish, particularly if the population is diminishing. Without the West or the EU providing a strong sense of moral purpose and progress, too many émigrés have no hope that their own nation is on a path to somewhere better, or that they will benefit from staying, and so they leave. The ones left behind are those who are more emotionally invested in their national culture, or who lack the means to leave. For the ethno-nationalist populist right, this is a perfect storm in terms of a shifting electorate, and the longer it goes on, the more extreme the scenario is likely to become.

The likes of Viktor Orbán have identified something crucial that too many in the West have failed to recognize. Identity still matters, particularly those cultural bonds provided by religion and nation. In Eastern Europe, this is more obvious precisely because the sense of nationhood is more precarious. If we cannot recapture a way of embracing that solidarity, without compromising the notions of freedom or equality, we will not be able to kick-start the stalled progress of the West.

* * *

BROKEN PROMISES AND SHATTERED DREAMS

One of the saddest aspects of the story of how the new Westerners are drifting away is how little the rest of the West seems to care, and how little it has done to prevent it. Viktor Orbán's Fidesz is still part of the European People's Party bloc in the European Parliament, despite calls for its expulsion. Too many conservative parties in Europe have provided cover for that increasingly autocratic regime. EU efforts to rein in Poland and Hungary have, as yet, had seemingly no impact. How sincere can our commitment be to the rule of law and democracy if we are not able to bring ourselves to do anything effective to defend those commitments within the EU?

Worse still has been the failure of the West to work towards helping the West Balkans on the path to the West. Jasmin Mujanović writes, "Ironically, they [the West] abandon the Balkans in order to preserve the edifice of liberal democracy within the European core, thereby embracing an inherently illiberal binary and zero-sum conception of the world. Democracy and liberalism are in the new calculus finite resources to be rationed and preserved for the Western heartland."[46] Because intervention and development in the Balkans is hard work, and because too many Western governments are struggling with economic and political issues at home, they have absolved themselves of the responsibility to contribute. For the past twenty years, the only guarantors of peace and security in the Balkans have been the USA, the UK and Germany. In the Trump administration—and actually even before then, under Obama—the USA has been turning inwards, limiting its foreign policy work to the Middle East and abandoning the cause of the West in Europe. What the UK will do after Brexit is anyone's guess, but few would predict that it will be taking a more prominent position in Balkan politics. That leaves only Germany, propping up a region where the wounds of recent genocides and wars are barely bandaged, and could burst open at any point.

This is a betrayal of past promises, and of the West's commitment to its values. It is also mirrored in the broader lack of enthusiasm for spreading the West further. The West, as we explored in Chapter 1, inherited from Christianity an evangelistic fervour. It believes in universal values, and in both the possibility and moral value of spreading them. If it is going to fail to do so even in Europe, that is a dark sign for the future of Western values. The European model of building Westernness has been consistent since the effort to rehabilitate fascist Italy and Germany in the 1950s: setting up institutions and rules to enforce commitment to an underlying value system. However, we must ask whether there needs to be more work on cultivating the values, and less focus on maintaining the institutions. At present, the defensiveness of the West—relying on institutions and failing to fight to spread and maintain values—is a self-destructive cycle. It is hard to claim a moral high ground while not doing anything to suggest that you take those morals seriously.

The European project, despite its name, was never really meant to be limited to Europe. Its founders hoped that it would become a truly global model of governance. If those countries and institutions that have been at the heart of the European dream decide that it isn't worth pursuing, then the entire project's aspirations are undermined. For the EU, as for the West, a hopeful future demands that the most powerful nations buy into the dream at least as much as the least powerful. On that note, the next chapter turns to the USA: the country most obviously founded on Western idealism and values, and still the most powerful Western military and economic force—but also, like the EU, apparently falling out of love with itself.

5

AMERICA AFTER THE END OF HISTORY

FROM TRIUMPH TO TRUMP

Watching from the UK, the Trump phenomenon that began during the 2016 Republican primaries was a source of amusement—a bizarre stunt from a man best known on these shores as a B-list celebrity with some comically extreme views. As time went on and Trump won the Republican nomination, amusement turned to incredulity. As he gathered momentum and ultimately won the presidency that November, the incredulity turned to shock. George W. Bush perhaps captured the zeitgeist of the European and establishment American mindset in his widely quoted aside at the Trump inauguration ceremony, describing it as "some weird shit".

This is not a chapter about Donald Trump. It would have been easy to make it so. Whole libraries could be filled with complaints about the president's blatant misogyny, racism, and constant unrepentant dishonesty. The consequences of his domestic and foreign policy may be felt for many years. But it is too soon to know that for sure, and at any rate to focus on the individual is the mistake that critics have kept making since the beginning of his political rise. In terms of big ideas, ideologies, or the philosophy of the West, Trump is not a remotely interesting individual. He has no coherent personal ideology, or indeed consistent ideas of any sort. He is a brand based on winning, and little more than that. The interesting thing about the Trump administration is not the man, but the circumstances that have made him so successful: the transformation of the USA from the symbol of an utterly dominant and triumphant West, to a country that seems to be revelling in victim status and suffering an existential crisis.

Trump's famous motto "Make America Great Again" is a truly remarkable sign of how the USA has changed. The key word here is "again"—suggesting, presumably, that America is not great now. Indeed, the whole Trump programme speaks to an America presented as the victim of globalization, abused as the world's piggybank, beset by waves of unworthy immigrants, attacked by Muslim terrorists, and losing jobs to foreign nations. Compare this with the astonishing optimism and triumphalism of Francis Fukuyama's famous thesis on the end of history in the late 1980s. The USA of the early '90s had seen the average family's household wealth double between 1945 and 1965, and again between 1965 and 1985. The Cold War was over. Capitalism and liberal democracy were not only working, but were proven winners, and the rest of the world was falling into step. There were problems, of course—and, particularly on the right, naysayers warning of an American slide into decadence—but the overwhelming atmosphere was of confidence and US dominance.

In Chapter 1, I laid out the idea of the West as a cultural project, defined by a great moral endpoint in turn defined by commitment to and progress towards universalism and the three republican values. I also suggested that a nation's Westernness was not so much a binary as a spectrum. I would suggest that the American commitment to those ideals has been diminishing in the new millennium: America is becoming less Western. This chapter charts what I mean by this. It looks at the way in which America has gone backwards in each marker of Western identity, and at the USA's apparent retreat from Western idealism.

Before we begin, it is worth justifying for a moment why the USA is the only country in this book to get its own chapter. The answer is twofold. The first reason is that, in many ways, the USA is the West in microcosm. In Amy Chua's terminology, it is a "super-group": an almost uniquely diverse nation-state whose identity is, at least in principle, not primarily ethnic but cultural— a "tribe of tribes".[1] What made an American was not some blood-based Americanness, but commitment to the dream of America as the "land of the free". No nation in history has been founded on such a strongly Western ideological basis. Its *Declaration of Independence* famously tells us that "We hold these truths to be self-evident, that all men are created equal, that they are endowed by their Creator with certain unalienable Rights, that among these are Life, Liberty and the pursuit of Happiness." In other words, much like the EU, the USA was a nation with a moral purpose, founded on freedom, equality and brotherhood—a set of universal values that could unite disparate former identities and overcome ethnic or religious differences. That, at least, is the myth of American identity, as summed up in the poem on the base of the Statue of Liberty, Emma Lazarus' *The New Colossus*:

> "Keep, ancient lands, your storied pomp!" cries she
> With silent lips. "Give me your tired, your poor,
> Your huddled masses yearning to breathe free"

This was an explicit comment on America as a place transcending former European identities in favour of a commitment to liberty. Just as post-communist states with a fragile nationhood and a history of interrupted Westernness are vulnerable to a crisis of the West, the same is true at the other end of the spectrum: America is a nation of unbroken Westernness, founded on and defined entirely by that cultural construction. The stakes for the West are higher nowhere else. This is also true because, since the 1950s, the USA has been the unrivalled primary force in the West—militarily, economically and culturally. We need a full chapter to consider its plight because it has been the West's flag-bearer. Its future will necessarily impact everyone else.

Failure one: universalism and America after 9/11

When looking at causes for the change in American self-confidence and triumphalism, it is impossible to avoid the pivotal importance of 9/11. Osama bin Laden succeeded where fifty-odd years of Cold War had failed: successful execution of a strike on the American mainland, resulting in the deaths of almost 3,000 people and the destruction of a symbol of confident America that was both iconic and quintessentially capitalist, the World Trade Center. The USA plunged into the War on Terror, its sense of safety and inevitable worldwide dominance shattered. The consequences of 9/11, and of the Bush administration's response, matter in all sorts of ways. Domestically, the clampdown on civil liberties and dramatic growth of state surveillance was, and is, a riposte to a liberal public square. The use of drones for killing targets abroad, torture and extra-judicial rendition, and the infamous Guantanamo Bay—all in breach of previous legal norms—have left a long and difficult legacy. This inheritance we must also place at the door of Bush's successor, Barack Obama. For all his attempts to shift US foreign policy towards diplomacy over military intervention, Obama ultimately kept in place and indeed expanded upon virtually all of Bush's foreign and anti-terror policies, including ramping up the use of drone killings.

But what does any of this have to do with commitment to universalism? One result of the excesses of the Bush and Obama regimes, and perhaps particularly the failures in Iraq—especially the dishonesty over WMD—has been an increased insularity and fatigue with internationalism in the USA. The leader of the free world has drawn back into ever tighter, more secure borders, and is increasingly opting out of international commitments and forums.[2] The response to 9/11 has led to a discrediting of America's role internationally and wariness on the part of American citizens themselves to back such foreign intervention or engagement. Trump's threats to withdraw from NATO, his battles with the G7 leaders and China over trade tariffs, his withdrawal from the Paris Agreement on climate change, his changes to the terms of international trade agreements, his proposed wall along the Mexican border, his so-called Muslim travel ban and plenty of other examples are just the culmination of this process. Trump didn't start the trend of retreat from the world stage, but he has upped the ante considerably.

Trump promised to put America first, and so to turn inwards, rejecting international trade or environment deals that did not necessarily primarily benefit the USA. In that, he is doing nothing particularly new: for many years a whole series of American presidents have ignored international bodies and treaties, other than the US-dominated NATO. To some extent, Trump is only pulling the American political establishment back to the standard position of the American electorate. Samuel Huntington looked at polling between 1978 and 1998 which suggested that the public was always considerably less enthused than its political leaders about US intervention abroad. Leaders were almost universally pro-international intervention, while among the electorate only a small majority wanted the same.[3] The exception to that rule was any intervention directed against a specific threat. There was a surge for support after 9/11 for foreign invasions, for instance.[4]

The other huge, and intimately connected, reversal on universalism has been sparked by the treatment of Islam in a post-9/11 world. Trump's travel ban does not exist in a vacuum, and it is telling that it was effectively stopped not by government or Congress, but only through the courts. Opinion polls show that Americans are highly divided on the ban. Forty-two per cent of Americans feel that Islam is incompatible with American values.[5] Research in 2016 found that 47 per cent of Republicans and 34 per cent of Democrats believe some or half of the Muslims in the USA to be anti-American.[6] The threat of violent Islamist extremism has undermined confidence in the inevitable triumph of Western democratic liberalism, and this insecurity has lashed out against ordinary Muslims.

Failure two: toxic liberty

No idea is so associated with American self-identity as freedom. It calls itself the "land of the free". Among its most prominent symbols are the Statue of Liberty and the Liberty Bell. Its origin myth revolves around pilgrims fleeing religious persecution in favour of freedom. Of every aspect of Western identity, then, you would expect liberty to be the strongest in the USA. But this is not the case; American liberty has gone wrong.

For one thing, since 9/11 there has been systematic growth of the domestic intelligence agencies and rising strength in surveillance powers. More broadly, the powers of the police and justice services have become extraordinary for a liberal democracy. No country on Earth imprisons a higher proportion of its own citizens than the USA, not even famed totalitarian states. In 2016, almost 2.2 million Americans were behind bars.[7] Were that population a city, it would be the fifth largest in the country. America, incredibly, accounts for almost 20% of the world's prison population.[8] Its police forces are also far more heavily militarized than elsewhere in the West, and seem to be escalating something of an arms war. As of 2015, almost 90% of American cities with populations above 50,000 had SWAT teams—a 400%

increase since the mid-1980s.[9] There is limited evidence that this militarization of the police has had any positive impact on citizen safety or violent crime reduction, and plentiful evidence of an enormous increase in policing costs and diminishing urban trust in the police.[10] Reporting of "justifiable homicides" is voluntary and only accounts for those shot dead while committing a crime, but even so the FBI reports that US police commit over 400 per year. In 2014, the USA saw 458 police killings; the UK and Japanese police had no such killings, and Germany had eight.[11] Rarely is an increasingly empowered security service and militarized police force associated with an increasingly free society.

There is a much broader and more challenging trend, however, when it comes to America and liberty. In Chapter 1 I argued that the three great republican values (liberty, equality, solidarity) needed to be kept in necessary balance, and history has shown that maximizing one will not deliver the other two. I further argued that liberalism, the ideology most embodying the value of liberty, has begun failing for this reason: freedom has been prioritized to such an extent that equality and solidarity have been hurt. The American system has lived this liberal excessivism and self-destruction to a greater degree than perhaps any other in the West.

In the 1964 presidential election campaign, the Republican candidate Barry Goldwater famously declared, "I would remind you that extremism in the defense of liberty is no vice." Goldwater, considered an extremist fiscal conservative at the time, won just six states in a landslide loss against Lyndon B. Johnson; he lost the Electoral College by 486 votes to 52. With the benefit of hindsight, though, we might think that Goldwater was just ahead of his time. Since the end of the Cold War, extremist visions of liberty have become an American pastime. Patrick Deneen is one of a number of recent authors, particularly on the political right, who have identified this sickness within the American model of liberalism. His *Why Liberalism Failed* identifies the essence of the problem: too much liberalism becomes destructive of society.[12] Its logic—to promote the rational individual as the key unit in society—disempowers all intermediary institutions and forms of belonging, and, ironically, empowers the state. The more individual freedoms such as speech and association are treated as more important than institutional or collective groups, the more the state is required to intervene to enforce those rights. The more the state intervenes, the more non-state institutions suffer, and the more individuals need the state to support their freedoms.

For Deneen, liberalism's success "generates titanic inequality, enforces uniformity and homogeneity, fosters material and spiritual degradation, and undermines freedom".[13] This has also been recognized by Amy Chua, who notes in *Political Tribes* that the individualism created by this liberal system has killed off meaningful group identities: "domestically US elites either don't care or are oblivious to group identities that matter most to large segments of Americans".[14] This touches on what Deneen and many other American critics of liberalism have failed to recognize: that the problem is not simply a specific fault of liberalism, but a deeper issue in the balance between liberty, equality and solidarity. Deneen argues that part of the solution is to try and preserve the good parts of liberalism while removing the parts that are flawed. There he is not dissimilar to today's socialists, who continue to hold on to the belief that socialism has never been properly tried. But it has been tried, and it has failed, for much the same reasons that contemporary American liberalism is failing. It had no sufficient balance between the three republican values.

This is seen even more clearly when we look at how the idea of liberty has been applied to the American economy. Since the 1980s the rise of neoliberal economics has been unstoppable in

American public life. This is an application of "freedom" entirely unlike what came before, now applied not just to people but to corporations and markets. Building on the work of Nobel prize-winning economists like Milton Friedman and James M. Buchanan, American public economics has increasingly thought of freedom as primarily concerning free business and defence of property rights, to the expense of all other aspects of government activity. Friedman's most famous book, *Capitalism and Freedom* (1962), presents human liberation and the freedom of the market as two sides of the same coin—indeed, for Friedman, political freedom is predicated upon economic freedom.[15] Buchanan's model added a further dimension: the idea that politicians and bureaucrats act primarily in their own self-interest, and that self-interest rarely leads to the best policy outcomes. Dividing people into tax producers and tax consumers, he calls for radical spending cuts and heavy limitations on what public money can be spent on.

Earlier Republican economists were critical of excessive spending, but recognized the importance of the state in providing key public goods and services, notably in education. Since the end of the Cold War, and in particular acceleration since the turn of the century, the Republican party has taken a more extreme approach to public spending. In this new settlement, the champions have been the likes of Scott Walker, governor of Wisconsin (2011–19), who succeeded in essentially abolishing collective bargaining and labour unions, while presiding over quite astonishing cuts, particularly in education and pensions. Drawing on Friedman's model, the role of government has been reduced to law and order and protection of property rights. The irony is that these Republican champions of market and corporate freedom do not truly want a limited state. They want a thoroughly activist state—just one that defends their own particular political interests and supports the free market, which requires constant state intervention. Walker is a classic example: his huge programme of legislation to counteract union power needed significant political interference, to secure a very particular model of freedom.

We can gain further insight into this strange new approach to freedom from the Heritage Foundation's annual Index of Economic Freedom. The conservative think tank's criteria for ranking nations are based on Adam Smith's mantra: "basic institutions that protect the liberty of individuals to pursue their own economic interests result in greater prosperity for the larger society".[16] The index regularly scores Hong Kong and Singapore very highly (in 2019, at numbers one and two). Currently the UAE is ninth.[17] Yet these rankings, while illustrative of good news for business, bear little relation to the sort of freedom envisaged by America's founding fathers. Neither Hong Kong nor Singapore are remotely free societies, regardless of how appealing they may be for enterprise.

The real consequence of this creeping change in the definition of freedom has been an ever greater corporate takeover of American public life. This has not been beneficial to individual freedom or equality, and in some cases has actively done enormous damage to American society. One classic example has been the reckless abuse of public land and resources by major corporations. Arlie Russell Hochschild's *Strangers in their Own Land* (2016) explores Louisiana, a resolutely Republican state where the electorate is anti-big government, pro-business, pro-oil and anti-environmental regulation. And yet, in what Hochschild called "the great paradox", this is an area horrendously damaged by large companies who care nothing for the local residents. Whole habitats and communities have been wiped out by corporate negligence, and the state has the worst health in the USA, with life expectancy fully ten years behind Connecticut. In some areas this is due to obscenely high rates of cancer, linked to local industry.[18]

But, as Hochschild has illustrated, citizens do not blame businesses. In fact, they are supportive of industries and of the jobs they bring. Beyond that, what chance do local people or politicians have at holding corporations to account, when the financial deck is stacked against them? Compensation is constantly denied, and the local state legislature is in thrall to business, the only force promising jobs and bankrolling political campaigns. A string of Republican politicians, at both state and federal level, have made central to their work the fight to demolish or at least restrict the Environmental Protection Agency, held responsible for reining in the most egregious excesses of companies when they impact upon public health. Lest we forget, it was only a generation or two ago that this body was introduced by a Republican president—Nixon, in 1970—yet the world has changed. Freedom of corporations now outranks public wellbeing and the freedom of individuals to enjoy public land.

The corporate takeover of US politics has been remarkable. In Chapter 1, I mentioned the astonishing 2010 Supreme Court decision in *Citizens United vs Federal Election Commission*, which ruled that political spending is a form of free speech, and so corporate campaign donors are protected under the First Amendment as if they were individuals. What freedom do ordinary citizens have in the political realm, if their voice must compete against America's biggest corporate funders? This, at least, is not a strictly partisan issue: a majority of both Republican and Democrat voters think that big money in politics needs to be confronted.[19] One of Trump's most popular campaign tactics with voters was the claim that, because he was rich he could not be bought by corporate interests, unlike everyone else in Washington. This message resonated well with people on both sides of the traditional political divide.

If this chapter has so far been particularly critical of Republicans, we can remedy that by looking at the 2016 presidential election, when the corruption of a bipartisan system with far too much corporate power was on stark display. The Clinton campaign took a reported $1.7 million in donations from employees and registered lobbyists of the fossil fuel industry.[20] Greenpeace estimated the total support from the industry, if you include investment in super PACs, was over $6.9 million.[21] Clinton's consistent support of so-called philanthro-capitalism (letting billionaires sort out the world's problems, in partnership with government) has left her constantly open to charges of a far-too-cosy relationship with the super-rich.[22] Infamously, both Clinton and Barack Obama have taken huge fees from Goldman Sachs for speeches on Wall Street. Goldman Sachs and the fossil fuel industry have also done remarkably well out of the Trump presidency—the cabinet is dominated by men who are former employees of one or the other—which leads us to the inescapable conclusion that these corporate giants stood to gain regardless of who won the election.

We can also see the consequences of "the new freedom" in the privatization of so much American public service provision—not necessarily for the better. Education is a good example. A majority of states have significantly cut education budgets since 2008, in some cases drastically; in Oklahoma, for example, education spending per pupil in 2017 was 28.2 per cent lower than in 2008.[23] Private education, meanwhile, is enjoying a financial windfall, despite little evidence that it provides any improvement in standards, and some that it actively harms them.[24] The net impact on equality is obvious. Bill Emmott, former editor of *The Economist* and no enemy of business or privatization, has noted that the USA is now the only country in the West—and one of only three in the developed world, with Israel and Turkey—in which there is more public spending on education for richer pupils than for poorer ones.[25]

Corporate involvement in prisons shows a similar story. The US Justice Department has reported private prisons to be consistently more violent than those still run by the state.[26] In a 2016 memo from Deputy Attorney General Sally Yates, the Justice Department also noted that private prisons "compare poorly" to state facilities: they provide no substantial reduction in costs for the state, and significantly less educational and rehabilitative support for prisoners.[27] The government pays private prisons $23,000 per prisoner per year; one of the biggest providers, CoreCivic, had a revenue of $1.8 billion in 2017, mostly from US tax dollars.[28] Public land is yet another example. The Department of the Interior is responsible for the management of the USA's national parks and conservation areas. In 2018 an investigation by *The Guardian* and *Pacific Standard* magazine revealed that the Trump administration, particularly Secretary of the Interior Ryan Zinke (who has since resigned), had "favored corporate and conservative calls" in scheduling and correspondence, in order "to prioritize resource extraction at the expense of conservation, while consistently delivering on industry desires—despite sometimes running afoul of conflict of interest rules."[29] This included evidence of industry over-influence on gas regulations and mining.

Corporate America, in the name of freedom, is now running public life in the USA. While that might suit their own liberty, the impacts on everyone else are decidedly negative. We ought to heed the warnings of political philosopher Michael Sandel, who has noted the ever greater expansion of the market into parts of public life in which it has no history or place, and provides no moral good.[30]

Failure three: equality—has the emperor got any clothes on?

In August 2016 Colin Kaepernick, a moderate star in the USA's National Football League, kicked off a remarkable public battle. In protest at the killing of unarmed black men by police,

Kaepernick—then a quarterback for the San Francisco 49ers—refused to stand for the pre-game national anthem. His protest went national, with a series of black players choosing to kneel instead. The effect was nuclear, sparking a prodigious media and online war fuelled in part by the outrage of conservative commentators and politicians. Among them was the then presidential candidate Donald Trump, for whom this would become a *cause célèbre* that he continues to fight several years later. Videos of fans burning Kaepernick's jersey went viral, and he claimed in a now settled lawsuit that the protest had led to him being blackballed by the whole league—he has been without a team since 2016.

Kaepernick's protest was powerful and controversial. In refusing to stand for an anthem or salute a flag, he was suggesting that the emperor had no clothes—that the USA, claiming to be a nation of equality and freedom for all, was less than it promised; that it was failing its black citizens. Critics lambasted him for failing to respect those who had died serving the USA; his supporters pointed out that, by Kaepernick's argument, it was the contemporary USA itself that had dishonoured that sacrifice, by failing to live up to all that it claims to stand for. The anger around the issue has been remarkable. Kaepernick's protest spoke to a black community furious at their apparent lack of value in American public life. The specific trigger was a string of police shootings of black males. In 2015, black people were killed by police at twice the rate of other racial groups, despite representing just 2 per cent of the American population and being more likely than whites to be unarmed.[31] Blacks and Hispanics are over 50 per cent more likely than whites to experience some form of force in their interactions with police.[32] Black Americans are also disproportionately likely to be imprisoned: five times more likely than whites, and almost six times higher for drug-related offences.[33] According to one estimate, the USA imprisons a larger percentage of its black population than South Africa did at the height of Apartheid.[34]

When this racial injustice before the law is added to complaints about economic exclusion, bias in the labour market, political gerrymandering to subvert black voting and a host of other complaints, it is no wonder that—decades after the civil rights era victories—43 per cent of black Americans are sceptical that the USA can ever give them truly equal rights.[35] Somehow, though, more than 50 per cent of white Americans believe that "whites have replaced blacks as the primary victims of discrimination",[36] and Hispanic Americans have seen candidate Trump weaponizing Hispanic immigration and branding all Mexican migrants as rapists. The resurgence of neo-Nazi, KKK-linked and alt-right groups has led to widespread concerns in the Jewish and black communities. Whoever is right in this culture war, what is absolutely undeniable in 2019 is that Americans do not believe the cause of equality is working, and everyone feels like their group is a victim.

Nor is it all about race. The Trump presidential campaign brought issues of gender equality into the spotlight, not least the leaked tape recordings of Trump boasting about "grabbing women by the pussy" and his suggestion that the news anchor Megyn Kelly was menstruating. A study by Pew found that 22 per cent of employed women had experienced sexual harassment in the workplace, and 42 per cent reported experience of gender discrimination in the workplace. A majority of American women (almost six in ten) say that the country has not gone far enough in giving women equal rights to men.[37] In 2017 the hashtag #MeToo started to trend on Twitter. Its origins went much further back, but this was the point at which its public profile exploded, sparked by the allegations that the Hollywood producer Harvey Weinstein had been sexually harassing and abusing actresses over several decades. Social media users picked up the hashtag both as an act of solidarity with Weinstein's victims and to highlight their own lived experience, showing that Weinstein was not an isolated or extreme case, but part of a broader culture of normalized sexual harassment and abuse, common across society. Less than twenty-four hours after the actress Alyssa Milano used the hashtag on 15 October 2017, it had been used by more than 4.7 million Facebook users in over 12 million posts.[38]

The campaign was powerful precisely because it held up a mirror to society, demonstrating the prevalence of an under-discussed issue to reveal that the West was falling grossly short of its commitment to equality. The issue of gender equality, of course, goes well beyond assault and harassment. The Republicans have as many men called John in the US Senate as they do women, despite only 3.3 per cent of the male population being called John and 50 per cent of the population being women. Nor is this simply a Republican problem: there are more Democrat governors called John than there are women. There are also as many CEOs of Fortune 500 companies called James as there are women.[39]

However, perhaps the starkest American example is economic inequality. Between 1947 and 1975, family income increased dramatically, but at roughly the same level on both ends of the income scale. Families in the bottom 20% saw their income grow by 90%, a very similar rate to that of families in the top 5% (86%). Since 1975, however, it has been a dramatically different story, with the bottom 20% remaining basically stagnant (3.7% growth over the whole period of 1975–2010), and the top 5% gaining by more than 57%.[40] Real wages of American men educated to high school level have fallen 40% since 1970, and the entire bottom 90% of earners have seen wages flatline since 1980.[41] At the top of the heap, meanwhile, the CEO of a manufacturing business could expect to earn twenty-four times more than the average production worker in 1965; today they earn 185 times more.[42] This is not simply the consequence of a natural American affection for low taxation. On the contrary, as the economist Thomas Piketty has argued,

Between 1930 and 1980, the rate applied on the highest incomes was on average 81% in the United States, and the rate applied to the highest inherited estates was 74%. Clearly this did not destroy American capitalism, far from it. It made it more egalitarian and more productive, at a time when the United States had not forgotten that it was their level of educational advancement and their investment in training and skills that was the backbone of their prosperity ... not the religion of property and inequality.[43]

This trend towards ever deepening economic inequality, and continuing gender and racial inequality, is becoming more extreme and more debated. American society is divided like never before. This, of course, has serious consequences for the third republican pillar holding up the West.

Failure four: The breakdown of American solidarity

The broken approach to liberty and the struggles of equality both have an impact on solidarity in the USA. The abuse of liberty has done much to individualize society, stripping out collective identities and institutions, and inequalities that are either growing or more openly debated have made every group feel a victim, with a corresponding need to circle the wagons and fight for their own stake. But a healthy West needs strong solidarity, that sense of social and moral obligations owed to others within the nation. At present, within the USA, this is grossly lacking. In fact, tribal loyalties and societal divisions are becoming more entrenched, more hostile and more toxic.

This effect can be seen in various political debates. Confidence in the police, for example, or belief in manmade global warming are now entirely partisan issues; in other words, support for them breaks down sharply along party lines. This has increased in a relatively short time. For example, from 2012 to 2015, the confidence of Republican and independent voters in the police remained entirely consistent (at 69 and 51% respectively), while Democrat confidence dipped by 13%. No other demographic group, including racial groups, saw such a sharp change.[44] The same is true on climate change. In the 1990s and early 2000s, Gallup polling found little disparity; in 2018, a staggering 91% of Democrats said they worried a great deal or a lot about global warming, versus only 33% of Republicans.[45]

The split resonates at a social level, too. In 1960 only 5% of Americans (equal in both parties) said it would "disturb" them if their child married someone from a different political party. In 2010 it was up to 33% of Democrats and 40% of Republicans.[46] *Elle* magazine featured an article in late 2018 about an entrepreneur, Emily Moreno, who has set up a dating app specifically for Trump supporters, after finding that it was too difficult to form relationships across political divides.[47] Looking for one's partner in life might be a reasonable time for serious and careful consideration of what matters, but in June 2018 there was a brief yet intense debate about a broader "civility war" in American public life, after Trump's press secretary Sarah Sanders was asked to leave a restaurant in Virginia where the staff did not wish to serve her. This has gone beyond personal values and choices in personal life to encompass social life as a whole. Despite it being a constantly disproved falsehood, a third of white conservatives still believe that Barack Obama is a Muslim and a similar proportion believe he was born abroad. A further 19% are reportedly unsure.[48] This means a majority of white conservatives are not convinced that Obama was born in the USA. There is no reason for a majority of white conservatives to be unconvinced about Obama's country of birth, except for tribalism. It has become so deep-set that people are no longer prepared to operate in good faith. The other side are not political opponents, they are liars and traitors.

In a climate of diminishing social trust and retreat into tribalism, democracy does not help unite and bring people together, but rather exacerbates these tensions. The trend of extreme partisanship and party purity is beginning to crush political processes in the USA. Yascha Mounk has suggested that this is in part a consequences of what he calls "McPolitics"—a process underway since the 1980s that has seen political parties become far more national than their previous localized model.[49] He notes, for example, that there is no good reason for Republican governors in Florida and Texas to reject additional federal Medicaid funding for the elderly in their states, except that to do so goes against Republican national opposition to Medicaid. For Amy Chua, the current political malaise is caused by a complete absence of "group-transcending ideals"—ideas that go beyond the interests of any single tribe, for the common good.[50]

The genius of Donald Trump's political rallies was, and is, to weaponize these divides. Each campaign speech identified an enemy: Hillary Clinton ("lock her up", or even the bizarre claim that she founded ISIS); Ted Cruz ("lyin Ted" whose father apparently assassinated JFK); George Soros (the funder of the migrant caravan); Mexicans ("They're bringing drugs. They're bringing crime. They're rapists. And some, I assume, are good people"); Black Lives Matter; Antifa; the media, the list goes on. What Trump has exercised so successfully is showmanship, the play on emotions, the ratcheting up of cartoon enemies and oversized personas, to create an emotional high for his supporters while entirely dismissing and delegitimizing everyone else.

Yet, as the conservative American pundit and "never-Trump-er" Jonah Goldberg has noted, "Donald Trump did not cause this corruption of the right; he exploited it. And having succeeded, he is accelerating it".[51] The heightening pace of increasing division is all that's new about the Trump era; simply a faster spin of what has always been a vicious cycle. Americans' confidence in their political institutions was sharply diminishing long before Trump became president. In 2014 only 7 per cent had confidence in Congress, down from 40 per cent in the 1970s.[52] This political crisis has been accompanied by a breakdown of civil society institutions. Back in 2000, this was explored in Robert Putnam's seminal *Bowling Alone*, which explored the loss of "social capital": the social interactions and institutions that foster an engaged citizenship.[53] Things have only got worse in the intervening two decades, particularly in the most vulnerable American communities.

Putnam went on to focus more directly on the specifics of American church-going, which serve to both connect and divide Americans.[54] In that later book, he noted that America is a nation of believers, a thoroughly religious society. Churches do continue to provide a huge number of social services—notably in education and healthcare, but also in social service provision like foodbanks and job clubs—and there is evidence that church-goers give more money to charity; the more religious they are, the truer this is.[55] But perhaps the more perceptive observation on American religion comes from J.D Vance's fascinating and tragic *Hillbilly Elegy*, his personal account of the struggles of the white working classes. Vance points out that, for all the talk of religious piety in the Bible Belt, it actually has some of the lowest church attendance in the country. Southwestern Ohio's actual church attendance (as opposed to self-reported church attendance) is barely above the rate in hyperliberal San Francisco, and well below the wealthier North East coast.[56] Looking at the USA as a whole, the non-religious now make up some 24 per cent of the population, and among the 18–29-year-olds—the future of American society—the number increases to 38 per cent.[57] The truth is that the Church is going the same way as all other forms of collective institutional belonging in the USA: it is struggling in the places where solidarity is needed most.

In a hyper-individualized society where liberty has gone toxic and the failure of equality has pitted groups against each other, and in a society marked by ever more extreme partisanship and ugly public conversation, it is a lot to ask religion—in the USA's case the Church—to correct the balance and restore solidarity. The figures above show that those looking to the Church to solve the ills of American public life are kidding themselves if they think that would be enough.

Excursus: the end of white America?

Before moving to the final problem facing the USA's Western identity, it is worth briefly pausing on the twin issues of solidarity and equality, to consider the much-discussed issue of whether white America is coming to an end. This notion of "white genocide", or, less extremely, "replacement", has been credited by a number of highly respected writers as key to the Trump phenomenon, and to broader challenges in American public life.

It is certainly true that, of all groups in American society, white working-class Americans are the most pessimistic about the chances of their children doing better than them—above even more impoverished groups such as black or Hispanic Americans.[58] Nor is this a surprise. No other group is currently seeing a drop in life expectancy, driven by increases in alcoholism, suicide and poor health cover. In Kentucky—an overwhelmingly white working-class state—life expectancy has dropped to 67, fully 15 years younger than in neighbouring Virginia.[59] And no group has been so hurt by the changing nature of global economics and industry. For all the talk of globalization and jobs being outsourced abroad, the most damaging trend to the working classes has been the robotics revolution, which allows the USA to manufacture more than it did in the 1980s with only a fraction of the workforce. Similarly, the fracking boom has significantly reduced the value of coal without replicating anything like the same number of jobs as other energy industries. The so-called Rust Belt—the Midwest and Great Lakes region of post-industrial decline, with an over-whelmingly white working-class population—has been hit particularly hard by these developments.

Without the big industries that were previously such hubs of employment, there are no jobs. Perhaps even more damagingly, there is no reason for those communities to exist. *Hillbilly Elegy* is a brilliant account of exactly that process, which saw huge numbers of people from the Appalachians migrate to the new industrial centres in Ohio, abandoning the families and support structures that their home states had had, only to see the factories close. With no work and no support networks, is it any wonder that solidarity and community have collapsed so quickly in these places? And is it any wonder that, in the pursuit of what they've lost and the dignity that has been stripped from them, they backed a populist candidate who swore to bring the jobs back, stop the migration alleged to be undercutting wages and taking the remaining jobs, and restore them to their previous status?

The economics is only one factor. As Eric Kaufmann and others have noted, a serious issue undermining community cohesion and confidence has been the speed of ethnic change in the era of globalization. A host of studies have suggested that support for Trump was driven more significantly by fears of America becoming a "majority minority" country than it was by economic factors. Twenty-two of America's largest 100 cities have already passed that point—in other words, whites are now a minority of the population—and the country as a whole is projected to become the same somewhere between 2040 and 2050.[60] A majority of white Trump supporters report feeling like "strangers in their own country".[61] A majority of Trump supporters (both white and Hispanic) believe that whites are under attack in the USA.[62] They may not be right about this reduction being a matter of design or conspiracy, but the white population of the USA is falling as a proportion of the population as a whole: from 84 per cent in 1965 to 72 per cent in 2010, and projected to have dropped significantly by the time of the next census in 2020.

This change is significant and, racist or otherwise, it cannot be denied that there is a problem with white American identity. Specifically, there isn't one, or at least not one that seems to resonate. In an age of tribalism and identity politics, white Americans seem to be the one group for whom there are not clear identity markers or a permissible set of "white" values that will not be branded as racist. Where working-class black or Hispanic people might be able to replace a splintering working class identity with an ethnic one, that option seems unavailable to white Americans in the context of rising white supremacy and white-first extremism. This point has been made by thinkers on both the left and right, including Mark Lilla, J.D. Vance, Shadi Hamid, Jonah Goldberg, Eric Kaufmann, Amy Chua and others: an identity model is needed that will be capable of embracing an increasingly disenchanted and lost American white working class, without resorting to the ethno-nationalisms that blighted so much of the twentieth century.[63] We will return to this dilemma in Chapter 5.

Failure five: No story left to tell

The moment I became convinced Trump really could win the presidency was watching the first presidential debate between him and Clinton in September 2016. More specifically, it was the moment when a seemingly flustered and shocked Clinton desperately stammered, "That's a—that's—go to the—please, fact checkers, get to work!"[64] Before rereading the transcript, I couldn't even remember which particular outrageous Trump line she was protesting about—there were so many, after all—but what has stuck with me is her call to the fact-checkers. They were never going to come to her rescue. The entire debate was one long ode to the basic fact that nobody cared. Not about the specifics, at any rate; what people were buying into was a story, and Trump's was hitting home.

The fact that Trump's story of America was full of holes, absurd exaggerations and outright lies really didn't matter so much as the fact that he had one, and a compelling one at that. The wrestling analogy has been often applied to Trump's campaigning style. Spectators know that professional matches are all scripted and pre-rehearsed, and that the absurd parodies of character on display are not real. What they are paying to see—what they are literally buying into—is the drama, the story. Trump has simply brought the world of professional entertainment to the political industry. In common with most populist political narratives, Trump's is a fairly empty and meaningless one, a hybrid of nostalgia and half-baked ideas, far more based on negative claims (things that are wrong, and who's to blame) than on positive ones (things we're going to do to improve them, together). And yet, for all that, it was a lot more compelling than Clinton's.

Three years later and it's hard to say what Clinton really stood for. The biggest point in her favour with most of her own voters was that she was not Trump: that she was not a misogynist or a racist, or an alleged sexual abuser, that she hadn't mocked disabled reporters for their disability or threatened to lock up her political opponents. Her message was a mixture of not being all those things Trump represented, and being a grown-up with sensible economic policies that passed the establishment test, well within the bounds of past political efforts. In that sense, Clinton was the technocrats' technocrat, someone saturated with decades of Washington political experience. She was also profoundly unpopular with many voters for the same reasons. When the system isn't working for so many people, persuading them to back the person on the system's side is always going to be a struggle.

Clinton wasn't alone in the failure to articulate a compelling story or moral mission that resonated with American voters. Before the Trump train started rolling, the smart money for the Republican nomination was on either Jeb Bush, brother and son of the former presidents, or Ted Cruz, the darling of the Tea Party movement. Bush failed early, despite his family connections and large campaign war-chest, suffering from a serious deficit in personality and ability to tell any story at all. Cruz was the last man standing against Trump, but in the end it wasn't even close. Jonah Goldberg has captured the Cruz dilemma perfectly: he "knew all the lyrics of populism but could not carry the tune".[65] When it came down to it, though Cruz is undoubtedly a highly skilled debater and political operator, he had nothing on Trump when it came to persuasively capturing the spirit of the moment. If he'd been facing Bush, Cruz might have won by playing Trump's game—heading to the right, and appealing to cuts, an end to globalization and Christian values. What he and Clinton were equally unable to do was articulate any meaningful vision of the future on Trump's left.

Clinton's campaign recalls others from elsewhere in the West: the Brexit referendum that had taken place earlier that year, when the Remain camp lost the narrative battle, and Matteo Renzi's attempt at the Italian presidency in 2018, which saw him finish third. All three were establishment campaigns trying to convince voters that their best interest lay in pursuing the sensible economic option while resisting the bigotry of the populists. It's a flat vision, one that offers no emotional high or sense of optimism at a time when both are essential. Business as usual is not an appealing pitch when the usual is not filling people with confidence. The safety-first approach will always appeal to many, and many more hungry for a change will just have looked at Trump and been unable to bring themselves to vote for him. That's why Clinton won the popular vote—though she lost badly in the places she really had to win—and why Remain came within a few percentage points of winning the UK referendum. It's also why Angela Merkel just about held on in Germany in 2017. But the patience for such campaigns is running thin, and it should not come as a surprise that the losses are mounting up.

As we'll see in the chapters that follow, a gap is forming between mind and soul politics. Clinton and her ilk have formulated policies that appeal to the rational actor, but they have lost the fight for the electorate's soul—the more intrinsic, meaningful depth that truly matters to the majority of people. This is the final and perhaps most critical failure of the twenty-first-century USA. Unless a new positive moral vision and goal can be proposed, one that resonates with the American people, then all these challenges are likely to continue. The only way to fight the negative anti-vision of a populist like Trump is not by appealing desperately to the fact-checkers, but by telling a better, more compelling story—one more likely to win over disaffected voters.

* * *

Just as with the EU, there's a curious irony at work among the USA's political establishment. On the one hand, they do believe in a great moral endpoint. Barack Obama in particular was fond of the idea coined by Martin Luther King that the "arc of the moral universe is long, but it bends towards justice". He often used this notion in speeches, and still argues it as a means to reassure liberal voters that the Trump programme is an aberration. Obama seems truly to believe that we are still in an overall trend towards a freer, more equal, more Western society. Many other leading American politicians of varying stripes also seem to feel that, ultimately, freedom, equality and solidarity will simply "happen", as an inevitable consequence of the West.

In fact, there is nothing inevitable in the Western project. Liberty, equality and solidarity are not values that simply occur when we leave the world to its own devices; they can only be achieved when fought for. At present the USA is failing to fight sufficiently for those key Western values. On the contrary, by the criteria laid out in Chapter 1, the USA's Western credentials are in retreat, under threat, and in danger of diminishing further. This is especially problematic in a nation so closely associated in its intellectual origins and political leadership with the fundamental idea of the West—"the last best hope on Earth", as Abraham Lincoln reportedly called it. Without a strong and profoundly Western USA, the West as a whole will be seriously, perhaps fatally, weakened.

6

THE LOST CLASS

A working-class revolution?

Since 2016 a number of writers have been at work telling a great story: of a put-upon class of left-behinds who have risen up to resist globalization and the elites who have oppressed them for too long. Seen through this romantic prism, the votes for Brexit, Trump, Salvini and a host of other populists are not examples of a worrying trend in Western politics, but a heroic tale of the impoverished David slaying the establishment Goliath, armed only with a ballot paper. It's a particularly popular narrative among populist-leaning journalists, politicians and writers who are indistinguishable in background, education and upbringing from the "elites" against which they are raging—except that they have backed the winning "anti-establishment" side.

Like most great romantic stories, this contains a critical kernel of truth. As we shall see, there really is mounting anger among a class that really has been increasingly excluded from the political process, and which has—at least to some extent—suffered from globalization and a political and economic system broadly indifferent to their plight. However, the idea that the populist upsurge can simply be explained by an international class of the left-behind is not borne out by empirical evidence. The Dutch political sociologist Matthijs Rooduijn conducted a 2018 study, looking at the voter base of fifteen different European populist parties across several countries; he concluded, in defiance of the now widespread narrative, that there is no truly significant commonality connecting populist voters, or indeed parties, whose superficial similarities can mask quite disparate ideological commitments on nationalism, economics and so on. Populists and their supporters are not simply the losers of globalization—though that is true in some countries with rising populist parties—and they are not necessarily Eurosceptic. They also do not necessarily have low levels of political trust or a desire for more direct democracy.[1]

If support for these movements can be explained as a coalition of the losers of globalization, then it is also worth noting that the core of Trump's voter base in the 2016 US election was neither particularly poor nor economically vulnerable. A March 2016 survey from NBC suggested that only a third of his supporters in the Republican primaries campaign earned less than the median US wage ($50,000), and though it's true that his supporters were unlikely to have a college education, they were only slightly more unlikely than the overall Republican or indeed national average.[2] There was also no clear correlation in the national election: the poorest Americans voted for Clinton. In fact, albeit with only a small margin, Clinton won a majority of all voters on less than the median income.[3] It is true that Trump won most of the USA's poorest counties, but he did so by winning large majorities of the better-off voters in the poorest areas.[4] Evidence shows that Trump voters were not, contrary to expectations, terribly worried about their own personal economic situation.[5] The truly desperate and left behind in the

States were disproportionately likely to back the Democrats if they voted, and disproportionately unlikely to vote at all—in many ways a far sadder indicator of the extent to which that class has been left behind.

In Germany, too, there is no correlation between unemployment (or even regions of unemployment) and populist voting. The Brexit vote in the UK, according to analysis from Antonucci, Horvath and Krouwel, again was not, in fact, particularly associated with the most poor or the working class, as such, but mostly with an intermediate lower-middle class—the "squeezed middle" with a moderate but declining income and intermediate education levels (left school at eighteen, but did not enter higher or further education).[6] Norris and Inglehart have made an important point: if the rise of far-right populists was all to do with economic factors, then it is at the very least a curiosity that right-wing populists do best in "several of the most egalitarian European societies, with cradle-to-grave welfare states, containing some of the best-educated and most secure populations in the world".[7] Of course all of these countries have ongoing issues with democratic deficits and economic inequality, but if that explains their populism, then surely populism should be far more virulent in worse-off states.

However, the story of a working-class backlash is not entirely false. Populism across the West is certainly driven by people who believe things are getting worse, and they are not necessarily, or even usually, wrong about that. Trump may not have won the votes of a majority of America's poorest, but he did win an absolute landslide among people who *felt* that they were economically worse off than they'd been four years previously: 77 per cent of them voted for Trump.[8] Economics does have a huge role in explaining why a whole segment of society has for some time been losing confidence in the West, even if in reality that segment is not the poorest, but the West's large "squeezed middle".

The cause of this loss of faith is not globalization or economics as such, but a serious breakdown in those core Western values of equality and solidarity. There is diminishing belief that society is genuinely fair, operating in the best interests of the common good and heading in the right direction. This amounts to the loss of everything that makes the West: belief in moral progress, and in the endpoint and universality of that progress—in short, the loss of a shared cohesive set of values, and with it a breakdown of common trust and belonging.

This chapter charts that loss. It begins by looking at a symptom of this shift: the dramatic decline of the West's working-class political representation, particularly through the decline of mainstream left-wing political parties. It will then look at how the breakdown in class equality and solidarity has manifested in practice, including the dramatic shifts in economic inequality, an economic system that has manifestly and negatively impacted upon solidarity, and an increasingly widening values gap between different classes. The chapter concludes by noting just how easy the mainstream is making it for the populists to win over the squeezed middle.

The decline of the mainstream political left and working-class representation

The decline of mainstream social democratic politics has been one of the most extraordinary political developments of the past decade. To be clear, there is nothing inherently Western about that kind of politics—just as there is nothing inherently Western about liberal democratic, conservative, or any other type of traditional mainstream party. The West does not depend on social democratic parties for its survival. But their precipitous decline is illustrative of the broader trends that do threaten the West. The social democratic left has traditionally been associated with the working- or squeezed-middle class that has been abandoning the West with its votes. A change of political affiliation, or ceasing to vote at all, is not necessarily a sign of diminishing confidence in the Western system, but it certainly could be an illustration of that trend. When we combine this consideration with the West's declining electoral participation and growing tendency to back parties that are at least potentially inimical to Western values, the picture that emerges is of a class that has lost confidence in the promise and direction of the Western system.

The drop-off in support for social democratic parties across much of the West has been dramatic. In the late 1990s, at their high-water mark, social democrats held power in twelve of the then fifteen EU member states. Today, in terms of national vote share, many of the traditionally biggest and most powerful social democrat parties are barely clinging on. In France, as recently as 2012, François Hollande narrowly won the presidency against the incumbent Nicolas Sarkozy, and his Socialist Party won an absolute majority in the national assembly. Five years later, Hollande was so historically unpopular that he took the highly unusual step of not standing for a second term. Instead, the party put forward Benoît Hamon, who was humiliated, scoring just 6 per cent of the vote and a fifth-place finish in the first round. The party was then embarrassed further by a disastrous showing in the legislative elections, which saw their parliamentary group lose 286 seats (from 331 down to forty-five).

In Germany in the late 1990s, the SPD had about 40% of the vote share. In the 2017 election it was half that, and the decline has been dramatic even in traditional strongholds like Bremen. The Dutch Social Democrats had their worst ever post-war election performance in 2017, falling to less than 6% of the vote share. The 2018 Italian general election saw the socialist leader Matteo Renzi lose power, and his party lose more than half its senators and almost two thirds of its deputies. The Czech

Republic Social Democrats held more than 20% of the vote share as recently as 2013, but finished sixth in 2017, and saw their vote share fall to 7%. Even Sweden, a bastion of social democracy, where the Social Democrats have been the largest party in terms of vote share and Rikstag seats since 1917, there are serious warning signs. In the 2002 election, they won just short of 40% of the vote. In 2006 it was down to 35%, and in 2010 and 2014 it was at about 31%. In 2018 it dipped to 28.3%, the party's lowest share of the vote for over 100 years.

So is there any cause for optimism among the West's traditional left-wing parties? Canada seems to stand out to some extent. In 2015 Justin Trudeau led the Canadian Liberal Party—not a social democrat party, but with a large social democrat wing—to a historic result. The Liberals received just under 40% of the popular vote, more than doubling their share from the previous election, and making the largest gain in seats in a single election of any Canadian party in history. Before this victory the party had been in the doldrums, falling into third place in the previous election. Trudeau, son of the former prime minister Pierre Trudeau, followed in his father's footsteps on a wave of positive media coverage and high personal approval ratings. Since then, however, his approval ratings have been dropping significantly. According to CBC News' "Leader Meter", seven months after taking office Trudeau had the second highest approval ratings of any Canadian prime minister since records began, 65%—just one percentage point behind the all-time record of Jean Chrétien in 1994. But by April 2019 he had dipped to a low of 28%.[9] Controversies over the Trans Mountain Pipeline expansion have played a role, as has a growing and worrying budget deficit, and a difficult foreign policy record, particularly the NAFTA negotiations. Having won the election on a surge of optimism and liberal hope, in May 2019 the polls had Trudeau in second place for re-election in October.[10]

The UK Labour Party won three successive elections in 1997 (43% of the vote), 2001 (41%) and 2005 (35%), but has lost the subsequent three elections, hovering at around 30% of the vote in both 2010 and 2015. However, it has since seen a surge in membership, making it the largest political party in Europe, and a share of the vote which rebounded to 40% in 2017—though, in the UK's two-horse electoral system, this was insufficient to oust a Conservative government that hit 42% and won ninety-eight more parliamentary seats. The picture is also mixed for the Democrats in the USA, again due to the robustness of the two-party system. However, the changing voting profile of US Democrats and UK Labour voters points to a trend much like that afflicting the European continental social democrats: they are no longer parties able to rely on working-class or squeezed-middle voters. The West's social democratic left has become a movement competing with other parties for a much smaller pool of highly educated, relatively wealthy citizens.

Some of the most comprehensive evidence on this has been gathered by the French economist Thomas Piketty. Looking at post-electoral surveys from each election since the late 1940s in France, the UK and the USA, he has been able to discern a long-term trend in the evolution of political divides in those three countries.[11] In Piketty's model, throughout the 1950s and 1960s votes for the social democratic/labour left were associated particularly with lower-income and lower-educated voters, in a largely class-based divide. That began to change in the 1970s and 1980s, as the left became increasingly associated with university-educated voters. This really took off in the 2000s and 2010s, to the extent that, for Piketty, there is now a "multiple-elite" party model in which "the 'left' has become the party of the intellectual elite (Brahmin left), while the 'right' can be viewed as the party of the business elite (Merchant right)."[12]

The strength of Piketty's model is that it is based on mountains of data, but he is hardly a lone voice. For years now plenty of other prominent economists, including Joseph Stiglitz, Paul Krugman and the late Anthony Atkinson, have been warning of the effects of wealth and income inequality. All share the same rough argument: that the left has increasingly been taken over by an elite highly educated core with a particular values culture, including high support for multi-culturalism, cosmopolitanism and internationalist political solutions, and a high sensitivity to the demands of particular minority identity claims, notably around ethnicity, gender, race and sexuality. In the UK context, the truth of this takeover can be seen in how different segments of society voted in the most recent general election (2017). The core of Labour's vote came from university graduates, 49% of whom backed Labour, versus only 32% for the Conservatives, and 11% for the Liberal Democrats.[13] In both the UK and the USA, the left has been cementing ever higher levels of support in the highly educated and relatively young populations of major cities. Clinton won the popular vote in large part due to comprehensive victories among this class in major coastal cities; she lost the Electoral College in large part because traditionally strongly Democrat-voting, working-class areas rejected her in key swing states like Pennsylvania, Ohio and Michigan.

This is not a criticism of multi-cultural, liberal political programmes, but it is to note that this relatively recent takeover of parties formerly correlated with the working and squeezed-middle classes has left that class, or at least a large portion of it, politically homeless. It also feeds a narrative, exploited highly effectively by populist and fringe parties of both left and right, that the system is stacked, with elites dominating both ends of the spectrum with little concern for a large portion of society. Beyond populist politicians, this is the critique levelled by commentators like Mark Lilla, Francis Fukuyama and David Goodhart: that the left is now defined entirely by identity politics and the exclusive concerns of a young, highly educated urban class—"Anywheres", in the designation coined by David Goodhart. For Lilla, the obsession of the metropolitan left with identity politics prevents it from ever creating a genuinely inclusive narrative for all classes of Americans, a diagnosis that Goodhart would recognize in the UK.[14]

This may have some truth to it, but there is no simple fix. For Lilla, young graduate liberals need to go out to those working-class areas that are drifting away. One wonders quite how productive this would be as a solution. As we'll see in the next chapter, young graduates who are actually engaged politically are quite rare, and if they cease campaigning on those issues that they care about, they will be more likely to drift away from politics altogether than to reinvigorate it in left-behind economic areas. Besides which, if part of the issue is that left-wing parties have become parties of graduates, it hardly seems like a winning strategy to send those people perceived as the problem to campaign to those who feel their traditional party has been taken away from them.

One gain for the social democratic left has been that it's increasingly won over minority groups. In the 2018 American midterms, 90% of black voters, 77% of Asian and 69% of Hispanics backed Democrat candidates.[15] The capture of this voting demographic has been successful partly because social democrats are clear in the vision they can provide in that space: equality and dignity for groups that have been denied it in the past. Naomi Klein is among a number of liberal thinkers who points out that appeals to minority-ethnic (i.e. non-white) groups will soon, in practice, be a pitch for the majority of American votes—probably by 2050, possibly as soon as 2030, and this is already a reality in one fifth of American cities, the state of Hawaii and the District of Columbia.[16] Other Western states are not on quite the same trajectory, but nevertheless, Klein's point is probably valid: as a forward-looking electoral strategy, appealing to minority groups makes sense.

The question is whether doing so prevents social democratic parties from making a meaningful pitch to the white section of the squeezed middle. This assumption seems to undergird much of the debate. I wonder, however, if the reality is not more that the mainstream left simply has something to offer minority groups—a clear moral end goal of genuine equality and liberation, achieved through genuine solidarity—whereas it has no answer for non-minority groups. If you have nothing to offer a particular voting demographic, then there is no reason why it should vote for you. If a party promises to be the party of your interests, but fails to deliver for you—and when it comes to economic equality, there is certainly little evidence that the system is working for the squeezed middle—then it is little wonder that this class will reject that party and its perceived broken promises.

Some of these voters have sought other parties that purport to better support their interests—by reducing migration and the flow of cheaper foreign labour, by re-opening factories—including many of the populist parties. This, for Goodhart, is a sufficiently serious trend that populism can be seen as the new socialism, insofar as its support is drawn heavily from the working classes.[17] The truth, however, is that, for all those who joined the populists, more have simply opted out entirely. In the UK's 2010 general election, there was a gap of 23 percentage points between voter turnout among the richest and poorest groups in society. The equivalent gap in 1987 was only 4%.[18] In the USA, Stephen Morgan and Jiwon Lee have demonstrated that white middle-class voters consistently have the highest voter turnout, at around 80%, while in 2016 white working-class turnout was just 57%.[19]

In the light of this perfectly rational abandonment of parties that no longer represent anything but a group of (minority) people they don't and can't belong to, the challenge for the social democratic left is not to withdraw that pledge to minorities, but to find an additional or broader offer that can also extend to white voters. As we've already established, such voters would not need to see themselves through their "whiteness" if the West hadn't seen such a breakdown in alternative forms of identity. Meaningful working-class identity has been decimated by the loss of meaningful work to go with it. As for sense of belonging to a particular nation, class, religion and so on, these types of group are increasingly dismissed as a legitimate basis of identity for any but a few particular minorities. Political affiliation, on the other hand, has in some ways become more important—though only in some ways, since party membership has declined across most Western political parties in the twenty-first century. In the last chapter we saw how political affiliation has taken on an enormous importance in people's romantic and personal lives, over and above other dividing factors. As other forms of belonging have declined, political identity has gained status and relevance. This has serious and often overlooked consequences, for the simple reason that most political programmes fail.

Eric Groenendyk, a political scientist at the University of Memphis, has explored the effect of this, with his theory of "dual motivations" in party identification.[20] Because our party identification has become an important (or more important) part of our personal identities, we have become more tribal and loyal to our parties, and experiencing a psychological high when those parties win elections and deliver on their proposals. However, if a party loses—or, worse still, wins but then fails to follow through—we suffer a blow to our identity and sense of self; we experience psychological turmoil. If Groenendyk is correct, this would explain in part the collapse of the social democratic left and the sense of betrayal felt by the squeezed-middle and working classes. The party they saw as part of their identity failed them, feeding their disappointment and loss of belief in the system. This, of course, becomes a vicious cycle: abandoned by its former core, those parties will find it harder and harder to be elected, thus repeatedly failing its ever-dwindling band of supporters.

Seen in this light, the story of the working class and squeezed middle, and the decline of the mainstream left, is part of a much broader Western trend: the loss of a moral vision that resonates with this class. Part of the evidence for this is where these voters have gone. We are not seeing a simple realignment of politics, with the squeezed middle crossing from social democracy to conservatism. It's a much more chaotic picture of a class without a clear political home, casting about for a new option: in the UK, for example, the two main parties won 97% of the vote between them in 1951; but by 2015 this was down to 67%, with three minor parties (the SNP, the Greens and UKIP) winning 21% combined, the most fragmented vote in British electoral history.[21] The problem, as we shall see, is that this class has never been more in need of a political left that can champion it: never have the worse-off in Western society been more vulnerable.

* * *

The squeezed middle is not wrong to believe that the system is not on its side, or even that the system may be stacked against it. Its rejection of the current political system and its embrace of populism can't simply be explained by economics, though many imagine that it can: it is not necessarily people's personal economic situation fuelling their disdain for the establishment and the status quo. However, economics does come into the much broader sense among the squeezed middle that the system, both political and economic, has been hijacked by a small group of elites, and does not work for the majority of the population. They are not entirely wrong there. As the market's power has grown in Western political theory, protecting it and strengthening the state's powers to support it has become the key task of Western politics.

Our Western system is complicit in a process that continues to empower corporations and market forces while stripping out the Western values of equality and solidarity. One of the particular symptoms of this process is out-of-control economic inequality, gaining considerable attention in the 2010s. Perhaps the most prominent intervention has been Thomas Piketty's *Capital in the Twenty-First Century*.[22] At almost 700 pages and offering vast reams of data, graphs and tables, *Capital* was an unlikely hit, selling more than 2 million copies and topping the *New York Times* non-fiction bestseller list. Its success was rooted in capturing the moment: inequality has become so obvious and toxic to social solidarity that an academic tome comprehensively demonstrating the scale of the issue and the culpability of our economic system struck a nerve among ordinary people. Piketty's conclusions have not gone unchallenged—plenty of critiques have been made of his data, methodology and proposed solutions. However, a consensus does seem to be emerging that the divide is serious and getting worse. Piketty argues that the ratio of capital to income is now at levels of inequality not seen since the nineteenth century. Even more serious is income inequality, as we have already seen.

Why does this matter? After all, many more optimistic thinkers have argued that economic equality is a false aim, so long as everyone is getting wealthier. The British economist Philip Booth, for example, has described himself as "entirely uninterested in the issue of inequality", seeing it as a barrier to making society as a whole richer.[23] But the reason why inequality matters is not truly economic, so much as social. For one thing, Booth's argument may have worked during the period of economic growth and rising wages, but in the decade since the world financial crash, the inescapable sense has been that the wealthy escaped relatively unaffected, while the middle and working classes have been hammered by austerity economic policies, stagnant wages, unemployment, dramatic cuts to welfare states and a general sense that the system has failed them in order to protect the banks and big corporations that caused the crash in the first place. In the UK's case, this sense was affirmed in a blistering 2018 report by Professor Philip Alston, the UN special rapporteur on extreme poverty and human rights. After two weeks of touring the UK, Alston reported that "The Government has remained determinedly in a state of denial" over the impact of its failures to resist poverty and hardship, which he linked explicitly to the austerity programme in place since 2010.[24]

In other words, it is not so much economics itself that is destructive to Western societies; the problem is the accompanying breakdown in solidarity when inequality arises. In their best-selling book *The Spirit Level*, the social epidemiologists Richard Wilkinson and Kate Pickett demonstrated inequality's effects far beyond economics and politics, including a breakdown in societal trust (further fuelling a solidarity breakdown), and a serious increase in mental health issues, stress, teenage pregnancy and crime.[25] Inequality is a moral issue in and of itself—given that equality is, or used to be, a key Western value—but it also fuels societal problems which in turn make solidarity harder to achieve. In Pickett's words, people are "dying of hopelessness".[26] Nor is the problem limited to income inequality; the way in which the labour market has evolved more generally is fuelling the sense of injustice.

One example is the evolution of the so-called "gig economy", typical of the way in which Western values have gone wrong in that it is often presented as a route to freedom and flexibility—the chance to be your own boss, pick your own hours, be free of corporate drudgery. Once again, liberty is the great justification for the way these businesses operate, while in fact they often pursue exploitative labour practices and subvert the law for profit's sake. This has been brilliantly exposed in *Gigged*, by the journalist Sarah Kessler. She points out that those working in the gig economy lack any ability to speak out about poor working conditions; consistently earn less than standard-contract workers doing the same job, but with a far higher rate of injury (for which they are not entitled to sick pay or leave); and are systematically denied basic employment rights—in the USA they are explicitly banned from unionizing, and companies are under no obligation to provide them with adequate training for their work. She also notes that the much-vaunted freedom that companies like Uber advertise to prospective workers is often a hollow promise. In practice, freedom is very limited, and at any rate 32 per cent of gig economy employees in Europe are working in that way by necessity, not choice. Unsurprisingly, they are also disproportionately poor and vulnerable employees; for example, they are twice as likely as any other type of US worker to be on a household income under $30,000.[27]

Perhaps most worrying, however, is that the gig economy is going mainstream. As more and more companies go the same route, in part to reduce regular labour costs, training costs and corporate responsibility, more and more workers are being pressed into these roles. As early as 2016, one estimate identified 40 per cent of all US employment as something less than full time with full employment rights.[28] There has been far too much public complicity in allowing these new business norms to expand. Boasting an app apparently now qualifies a company to call itself a tech firm and so dispense with any sense of social responsibility. Unfortunately, far too many commentators and politicians have failed entirely to hold gig economy employers to anything like the standards they would demand of other companies.

While employment for the poorer members of society has become less secure, and wages for workers have been largely stagnant, at the other end of the food chain sky-rocketing executive pay is now guaranteed. In the period between 1998 and 2015, pay stayed largely static for most workers in the UK. For business chief executives, however, the average wage went from £1 million to £5 million. British executives now earn 129 times the pay of the average worker in their company. In the USA, executive pay is an astonishing 347 times higher; up from just forty-two times higher in 1980.[29] This dramatic gap can be explained by several different trends, one of which is the rise in the idea of performance-related pay for chief executives. As the British Conservative politician David Davis has noted in testimony to the High Pay Commission, there is absolutely no evidence that performance-related pay in any way correlates to business performance, or that it tracks any available objective measure.[30]

This is particularly galling when companies fail, yet executive pay still seems to continue rising. The oil giant BP infamously awarded its CEO a 20 per cent increase in 2015, despite a record annual loss in the year of the Deepwater Horizon payout (his pay rise was later reduced after a shareholder revolt). We can obviously link this trend to the lack of punishment for banking and corporate executives following the financial crash, which had enormous public consequences. The economist Paul Collier has noted that the West's failure to properly regulate big companies, and its propensity to let business leaders off the hook, undermines public trust. He suggests that we need a new term for inadvertent corporate damage: "bankslaughter".[31] This would answer the fair critique that very few among the most culpable in the failure of the West's economic model have yet paid any price for their negligence.

Even when chief executives have not actively failed, the corporate pay disparity between top and bottom still has negative consequences for solidarity. More than half of all British employees now feel discouraged and demotivated by the high levels of chief executive pay, and think it has a bad effect on their company's reputation. Just under half believe that their boss is paid too much, and a majority want far more transparency about how chief executive pay is set by their company.[32] Nor is this exclusively an Anglo-American problem. Though Germany is often lauded for having employees on boards, this has proven no barrier to spiralling executive pay, which is comparable to the UK. At least some calculations give France a bigger pay gap between CEOs and average employees.[33] Germany, Sweden, Spain and Italy are not quite at that level, but have all seen the gap increase considerably since 2010. The exact rate at which this is occurring matters less than the sense of unfairness inherent in a system that seems to be failing the majority and benefiting a small moneyed elite. Solidarity and equality go hand in hand on this issue; they have been downgraded in favour of a specific conception of liberty: free market economics.

Given all of the above, it is little surprise that there have been growing calls for a radical break in the system. This has come from various right-wing populist movements—though few have a very developed answer to the crisis they are witnessing—but from other quarters too. Donald Trump and Bernie Sanders (the left-wing Democrat primary candidate who lost out to Clinton) are as different as it is possible to be in American politics, yet both their campaigns shared a claim that companies outsourcing abroad was a bad thing; that there was too much corporate money in American politics; and that trade deals like NAFTA had been bad for the American worker. Where they depart is on the wage gap. Trump has slashed taxes for the rich, while Sanders would have increased them and doubled the national minimum wage. Other populists in the West have been rather more radical. In France, the left-wing presidential candidate Jean-Luc Mélenchon called in 2017 for 100 per cent taxation on all monthly earnings over €33,000, a major increase in the minimum wage, and an end to the EU's policies of economic liberalism.

Beyond the political sphere, however, there is also a growing intellectual movement coming around to the idea that the system is sufficiently broken to require a major shock. That was the conclusion of Piketty's *Capital*, which calls for an 80 per cent tax on American incomes over $500,000—even higher than the policy of Alexandria Ocasio-Cortez, the left-wing US Democrat congresswoman and current *bête noire* of the Republican right. Even more radically, Piketty proposed a global confiscatory tax on inherited wealth. The Canadian social activist Naomi Klein is typical of a number of left-wing liberal arguments in despairing of the mainstream left's proposals to tweak, rather than radically reform, the current system.[34] More fundamental yet is the critique of the economic historian Walter Scheidel, who—building on Piketty—has argued that economic inequality has only ever been checked by one of the "four horsemen" of human history: war, revolution, state collapse or natural disaster/pandemic.[35] Needless to say, this provocative observation inspires a certain despair—if true, it would suggest that the system is weighted towards making economic inequality worse, until such time when it becomes so unbearable as to inspire revolution or violence. No wonder then that there has been a complete loss of confidence that we are moving in the right direction, or even that the system operates in any way for the collective good.

Self-defence and the immigration/welfare backlash

It seems clear that our current political and economic situation has fostered overwhelming hopelessness. In such a climate, defensiveness is an entirely rational response. Everyone wants to feel that there is a sense of justice in public life—everyone seeks to ensure that those who contribute will get something back for their efforts. It is in this context that divides are sharpening over political values like welfare and migration questions, amounting to a breakdown in collective solidarity. We can see one extreme example of this link in Greece, where a decade of European austerity politics has bitten deep, with more people in need of less available assistance. A 2018 report by the Council of Europe's own commissioner for human rights found that enforced austerity has had such a negative impact on access to healthcare—particularly to mental health services—that the programme could be judged to have violated the right to health.[36]

In a society with functioning solidarity, it is assumed that everyone will contribute to the system, and everyone will take out of the system. The old will receive pensions and assistance (such as subsidized or free healthcare), partly in return for their lifetime of contributions into the system. Children are supported by their parents and the state, not conditionally, but in expectation that they will one day support their families and contribute themselves. The European welfare state model works on the assumption that anyone, regardless of personal circumstances, may need a safety net to support them at times when they cannot support themselves. There will always be those who take out more than they put in—sometimes through no fault of their own, for instance the disabled—but Western society has functioned as one in which people's contributions, both financial and in terms of particular social and civic responsibilities, make them eligible for particular rights, protections and services from both society and the state. But this social contract can only function if cemented by social trust and togetherness: a sense of an "us", built on shared values and assumptions.

In the 2010s this has broken down, for all the reasons we have seen. There is less meaningful sense of community, and so less solidarity. In this climate, mutual trust has been replaced with an intense level of vulnerability and fears that people need to defend their own corner. In that context, two concepts become all-important: the "queue-jumper" (who takes out of the system before putting anything in), and the "freeloader" (who takes out without ever putting in). When the economy is functioning well, and everyone is seeing increases in wages and living standards, a certain level of "freeloading" can be tolerated. When everyone but a tiny class of the rich is being squeezed, and social solidarity is low, then freeloaders and queue-jumpers, however small a fraction of society, rapidly take on the status of public enemies.

It might legitimately be asked why it is not the small class of the rich bearing the brunt of public abuse. Of course, there are left-wing populist parties and movements that have made exactly this point. Few, however, have been able to win elections to deliver a political programme on that basis. Greece's Syriza did win an election, but has been hamstrung by EU-enforced economic policies. Spain's Podemos is sometimes referred to as a populist left-wing party, which has stood on manifestos of a major return to public ownership, a crackdown on corporate lobbying, punitive measures against tax avoidance, and the introduction of a universal basic income—but few of their more radical policies have been enacted, and they remain something of an outlier on the European political scene.[37] Perhaps because of the struggles of socialism after the end of the Cold War, it has been significantly more difficult for Europe's left-wing populists to win places in government than it has been for their right-wing counterparts.

One of the easiest rallying cries for populist politicians of both political wings, as well as for mainstream political parties in search of an easy PR boost, is the call to cut down on welfare spent on those public enemies. This includes both domestic citizens who are the new "undeserving poor" and migrants perceived to be taking jobs and welfare provision that they have not earned, denying those who feel they have earned it from getting their fair share. That this is a live concern can readily be seen in polling. According to the British Social Attitudes Survey, "Support [in the UK] for increasing taxes and spending more on health, education and social benefits fell from 63% in 2002 to 32% by 2010—and had only increased slightly to 37% by 2014. The level of agreement with spending more on welfare benefits for the poor fell from 61% in 1989 to 27% in 2009, and remained low, at 30% in 2014." Benefits for the unemployed have become particularly unpopular.[38]

However, there seems to be growing support for increased government spending in general,[39] though particular areas of government welfare spending remain unpopular—the British who want to see further cuts to support for the unemployed significantly outnumber those who want the cuts reduced, for example.[40] Ipsos MORI polling has shown that almost a third of the British believe government welfare costs to be higher for Jobseeker's Allowance than for pensions—in reality the UK government spends fifteen times more on pensions, which form the bulk of the welfare budget—and that, overall, the British "estimate that 34 times more benefit money is claimed fraudulently than [the reality of] official estimates: the public think that £24 out of every £100 spent on benefits is claimed fraudulently, compared with official estimates of £0.70 per £100".[41] The narrative of welfare abuse and unfairness has been driven relentlessly by the tabloid press across the West, but it is impossible to say which came first—the media narrative, or audience enthusiasm for the message. This public support for reduction of benefits for the poor reflects a sense of systemic injustice (reward for the undeserving), both driving and driven by the great fears among an increasingly large share of the population that the elites just don't care about them, and would rather help anyone else. This idea is perhaps explored most starkly in J.D. Vance's *Hillbilly Elegy*; among rural small-town workers, Vance finds real disgust and distrust of those seen to be abusing the system, and the sense that it is too difficult to get by and raise a family as a hardworking citizen, yet too easy for others to attain the same lifestyle by living off other people's taxes.

Of course, these feelings of resentment and losing out apply doubly to migrants. Immigration is almost always unpopular— the overall majority in Europe is for a reduction in migration— but it is noticeably less unpopular among the wealthiest class. For example, in 2014, the European Social Survey of twenty-one European countries found that the richest 20 per cent were significantly more pro-immigration than the bottom 20 per cent.[42] Regardless of income, polling has shown that the average person overestimates the number of migrants living in their country in all but two of the EU's member states; in nineteen EU countries, the average person's estimate is more than double the size of the actual migrant population.[43] Even leaving aside raw numbers, proponents of migration can point to plenty of data showing that migration is a net economic positive for every country in the West, with migrants paying more in taxes than they take in social costs, and helping to fill jobs necessary for economic growth. But this simply doesn't matter when solidarity has already broken down.

The squeezed middle and the working class does not see the macro-economic picture when opposing migration; what they experience is a perceived mass arrival of queue-jumpers, who will gain priority for state provision already under significant strain due to austerity economics. Despite the many valid economic defences of migrants, there is evidence that they do keep wages lower in many industries.[44] As for the perception that migrants take housing or social services, this impression too can have some truth to it. In 2015 the Dutch minister responsible for resettlement of refugees, Klaas Dijkhoff, was attacked in the small Dutch village of Oranje. The reason was not difficult to understand: Dijkhoff was there to announce that the town was to receive yet more refugees, with 700 settled there against local residents' wishes. Before the refugees arrived, the town's entire population had been 130.[45]

* * *

As with inequality, the economics of migration is not its most important aspect. The critical issue—the one that threatens the very foundations of the West—is that a whole class of people now believe that they are losing out and that the system is not on their side. This destroys solidarity between that class and everybody else, migrants included; and it fuels the sense that the West's great economic promises have turned out to be nothing but air. It is not simply the losers of globalization and the poorest in society fuelling the new politics—rather, it is those people who really ought to have benefited from the West, the lower middle classes, who are now losing confidence in it. This is not one class casting around for new answers and a sense of identity, but more like eighty to ninety per cent of the population (depending on the country in question). The West risks losing everybody outside the very small category of highly educated, economically secure, urban and broadly cosmopolitan "Anywheres"; everyone who feels increasingly insecure, abandoned, and betrayed by failed Western promises.

This is both a social and an economic mega-class. The philosopher Matthew Stewart has pointed in *The Atlantic* to the rise of a "new aristocracy".[46] The super-rich (0.1% of the population) enjoy an increasingly large slice of the economic pie, but critically their slice has not come equally from everyone else's. Ten per cent of the population is no better off, but hasn't lost out either. Whereas, in past ages, the upper class was defined by an evidently extreme level of privilege—landed nobility—today, the socioeconomic elite is now anybody in that 9.9% that at least hasn't become worse off. The big loser, or the underclass, is everybody else: the entire bottom 90%. As Stewart notes, "At their peak, in the mid-1980s, people in this group held 35 percent of the nation's wealth. Three decades later that had fallen 12 points—exactly as much as the wealth of the 0.1 percent rose." This grossly unfair context is what's empowering the populist waves of both left and right. It fuels the anger of a growing minority, and the apathy and disengagement of an even larger group. In this atmosphere of betrayal of the many by the few, it is not difficult for populists to claim that they alone are on your side. Leaders like Donald Trump don't want to tell you to get behind migration and globalization because it's beneficial to the economy overall. On the contrary, they give voice to the idea that the system needs to get back behind the people it has left abandoned. The mainstream left doesn't seem to be rising to the challenge.

There has been too little honesty in grappling with the grievances and worries of the squeezed middle. It is easy to dismiss concerns about migration as inherently racist or xenophobic. To be sure, there is plenty of prejudice around, and if you look at reported hate crime figures in the USA, the UK, France, Germany and elsewhere, there is reason to think that it could be getting worse at the end of the 2010s. But we are unlikely to make progress there unless we can accept and respond to the fact that migration is unpopular, and that this is due to a sense of misplaced justice and an uncaring political class. We also need greater honesty about the Western economic model more generally. The economist Paul Collier has written that one of the great *mea culpas* of Western economics ought to be the confession that trade is not, in fact, a win-win for all.[47] International trade can benefit everyone, but only if aligned with policies of economic distribution. He gives the example of steel: if the UK trades with China, that can mean that the UK's overall consumption goes up—but not in Sheffield, where steel is no longer made. That is, not unless the government purposely distributes the gains from

Chinese imports to the parts of the UK that have lost out from the deal. Such policies have been all too rare, and the result has been the avoidable creation of losers of globalization. This isn't news, of course, to anyone living in those cities or regions—the American Rust Belt, the Welsh coal mining communities, the French towns dealing with "*désindustrialisation*" and so on.

By failing to acknowledge where such concerns are legitimate, all the Western elite does is feed the narrative that the West, in its current form, is not working or designed for the squeezed-middle and working classes. The mainstream of liberal democratic politics has made life far too easy for the populists, their near-complete lack of any overarching sense of purpose and mission feeding the hopelessness that is infecting society. In its place we are seeing symptoms of what the political theorist Chantal Mouffe calls a "post-democratic" society, in which the people as a whole (the *demos*) is no more than a zombie category, and the political realm is dominated by technocrats without an ideological vision beyond sustaining our current economic system.[48]

The Slovenian Marxist philosopher Slavoj Žižek has described populism as "simply a new way to imagine capitalism without its harder edges; a capitalism without its socially disruptive effects."[49] This is exactly the challenge facing the West more broadly. The economic model that was once the West's great success story is becoming self-destructive, undermining the equality and solidarity that are needed to balance commitment to liberty. Winning back a class that feels abandoned and betrayed will take a new model, one able to prove that—in contrast to the story of the twenty-first century so far—we are all in this together, and share some sort of common political goal.

7

THE LOST GENERATION

Yascha Mounk's *The People vs. Democracy* has a chapter entitled "The Young Won't Save Us". In a broader thesis that liberal democracy is in dire trouble, the German political scientist notes that the younger generation are no more liberal or democratic than their parents and grandparents. In fact, worryingly, they seem to be among the most illiberal and anti-democratic, and growing more so.[1] This should not really surprise anyone. A whole generation—"millennials", those born approximately between the early 1980s and the mid-to-late 1990s, and the post-millennials who are only now coming to adulthood—has no memory of the Cold War. The only political and economic reality they have known is that of the West, characterized by liberal democracy and, increasingly, by its period of decline.

As we saw in Chapter 2, these younger generations are less religious than their predecessors were. They are also less likely to be Marxists, or to adhere to any ideological movement. In fact, they are less likely than any previous generation to belong to movements of any sort, or to believe in any ultimate goal.[2] In Chapter 1, I argued that the West is an intellectual space defined by a commitment to moral progress towards an endpoint, namely the trinity of republican values (liberty, equality, solidarity), and by a belief in the universalism of this project. The millennial and post-millennial drop-off in believing and belonging, therefore, matters enormously. The West's young do not believe in existential goals or "big ideas", and do not belong to collective groups or institutions. Different countries have contributed in different ways to the overall trend, but the threat to Western progress and Western solidarity is obvious.

The challenge is not just that the West's lost generation has no solidarity between its own members; also becoming clear is that the younger generation is alienated from its elders, feeling betrayed by the perception that the West has not lived up to its promises as it did for older generations. This chapter charts how this happened—how the West lost its young. It starts by looking at the signs of youth rejection of the West, including a growing scepticism of liberal democracy. It will then argue that this trend is something distinctive and new, significant beyond timeless young rebellion. Crucially, the symptoms of the lost generation reveal an ever-greater rejection of a sense of Western moral purpose, while the causes of this ailment reveal an endemic breakdown in intergenerational solidarity. The two trends reinforce one another, and they are poisonous for the future of the West.

* * *

It does not seem as if the young have much confidence in liberal democracy as a system of government. In fact, it is the young who are at the forefront of many of the trends doing the greatest damage to liberal democracy, including fuelling the fires of some of the West's most authoritarian and anti-Western forces. These include not only populist parties with authoritarian streaks, but also more sinister para-political and extremist groups ranging from far left to far right, and extremism of various stripes, including religious. The second great symptom of the loss of a generation is perhaps the sadder one: an increasingly large share of the young are simply opting out of their experience of the West. As we saw when looking at the challenges facing the EU, in many Western nations the young are voting with their feet. The Bulgarian political scientist Ivan Krastev has described migration as the great revolution of the twenty-first century.[3] Instead of fighting for revolution and change within, now people emigrate away in search of something better—away from the nations and politics they associate with betrayal, broken promises and hopelessness.

In those Western states where the young do not leave—either because they've reached the top of the Western economic ladder and have nowhere to go for a better life, or because they lack the finances, skills or right to emigrate—the young simply disengage from Western politics. Youth turnout has always tended to be lower than for other sectors of the electorate, but has dipped to historic lows since the turn of the millennium. Using the UK as an example, British Election Survey data reveals that youth turnout was similar to that of all other age brackets in the 1964 election, but then declined consistently, and dramatically from the 2000s. In 1992, 63 per cent of 18–24-year-olds voted; by 2015 that was down to 43 per cent. The 2017 election did see a bounce-back to the levels of 1992, but this was in a context of higher turnout across the board.[4] So some nations are left with a generation defined by those lacking the education or ambition to leave and a dwindling population, while others, perhaps the better off, are left with a generation characterized by either anger or a far more destructive kind of hopeless apathy.

It is worth noting that there are some positive signs amid the malaise, particularly in terms of alternative forms of democratic participation among young people, and we will explore this in more detail below. For example, the political scientists Daniela

Melo and Daniel Stockemer have demonstrated that young people in the UK, France and Germany are less likely to vote, but are significantly more likely than other generations to sign petitions and get involved in protests and demonstrations.[5] Recently this has been emphasized by high-profile, youth-led campaigns, particularly the Fridays For Future protests, an international movement of schoolchildren protesting against climate change. However, these signs of life aside, the overall trajectory seems to be more like an abandonment of the governmental political scene, and this reveals a damaging loss of faith in the direction of the West. As with the squeezed middle, the expectation that we are on the road to somewhere better has come to an end among the West's youth.

* * *

As we saw in Chapter 1, liberal democracy is in trouble, and has been for some time. It remains, however, the best surviving effort at creating a political expression of Western values, particularly the trinity of republican values. As such, the fact that the younger generations appear to be losing confidence in liberal democracy is cause for concern. In the USA, a nation whose political identity is synonymous with democracy, only 29% of those born in the 1980s consider it "essential" to live in a democracy.[6] There has been diminishing support across the generations, but the younger you are, the more drastic the drop-off has been. As we explored in Chapter 1, Mounk's data suggest that 71% of Americans born in the 1970s think living in a democracy is essential, while only 51% of those born in the 1980s agree.

Mounk has used World Values Survey data to chart these trends across the West. In almost every long-standing democracy, grandchildren are significantly less likely than their grandparents to believe that democracy is essential. The trend is particularly acute in the Anglosphere and in France and Switzerland.[7]

The specific economic situation of the country does not seem to affect this trend—Australia is the most successful economy in the West, as the only developed economy not to have a recession since 1990, yet its young are falling out of love with democracy faster than the Greeks, Italians and Spanish, who have witnessed the worst of the crisis begun in 2009.[8] Nor does strong traditional attachment to democracy and Western values seem to put a brake on this disenchantment: it is apparent even in supposed bastions of liberalism like Sweden.

It is not merely that the young are unconcerned about the value of democracy; they seem increasingly prepared to witness its overthrow. In 1995, 34% of American 18–24-year-olds felt that a political system with a strong leader who does not have to bother with Congress or elections was either "good" or "very good". By 2011, that number had climbed to 44%, and is projected to rise further; already it is significantly above the overall national average of 32% across age brackets.[9] Interestingly, the American youth did not back Donald Trump, the closest the USA has had to a strongman candidate in some decades: 55% of millennials backed Hillary Clinton, versus only a third for Trump.[10] However, the sands are shifting, and while Trump's particular strategy and election pitch may not have appealed, millennials do appear to be abandoning the Democrats; one source shows a 9% drop over just two years.[11] This generation of Americans is either seeking something outside the two traditionally available options, or opting out entirely. That said, a new wave of Democrat figures—including the millennial congresswoman for New York's 14th District, Alexandria Ocasio-Cortez—do seem to be attracting a new generation of young voters. Whether or not mainstream US politics loses its young may depend on how this trend develops in future years.

Some have identified age as the basis for a new class warfare, with a significant values gap between millennials and older generations. Among those making this argument in the UK has been the centre-right Resolution Foundation, which has been running an intergenerational commission fronted by the former Conservative minister of state for universities and sciences David Willetts. Torsten Bell, a researcher at the think tank, points out:

> in 1974, 40 per cent of voters supported Labour in almost every age group. Age was a political irrelevance. But by 2017 it had become a key driver of whether someone votes Labour—a 30 year old was almost twice as likely to vote Labour as a 70 year old. 70 year olds were also twice as likely to vote Tory in 2017 as 30 year olds.[12]

The political scientists Pippa Norris and Ronald Inglehart also identify this values gap beyond party lines, in terms of social questions. Since the 1970s, they argue, there has been a gradual intergenerational shift towards post-materialist values, including cosmopolitanism and multiculturalism, and a clear shift on attitudes towards LGBT rights, among others. Seen in this light, the rise of populism is at least in part a cultural cleavage between younger cosmopolitan liberals and older populists.[13] Of course, this might suggest that the young are a good news story for the West: more universalist, more liberal, more resistant to the backlash against Western politics that so many populist parties represent. But the younger generations are not only falling out with liberal democracy; they are the key driving forces behind some of the West's populist movements.

Much depends, inevitably, on the definition of populism. The polling we've seen shows that young Americans are losing confidence in liberal democracy, but they didn't, on the whole, go for Trump's "America first" rhetoric. British youth are also falling out of love with liberal democracy, but similarly seem to retain robust support for a more cosmopolitan, pro-migration attitude: they overwhelmingly voted to remain in the European Union, with estimates of over a 70 per cent youth vote for Remain.[14] Likewise, younger German voters have been the most consistently supportive of Chancellor Merkel's asylum seeker policies. Those are the positives, and if we see populism as illiberalism, then this generation might not be lost to the West after all.

But populism can also be seen as the deconsolidation of politics, and here come the negatives. The young may remain generally cosmopolitan, but they are also exhibiting remarkable electoral volatility, and the capacity to drive fringe movements. France is a good example. In the first round of the 2017 presidential election, more than half of all voters under the age of 24 voted for either the extreme-left Jean-Luc Mélenchon (30%) or the far-right nationalist Marine Le Pen (21%). The centre candidates from left and right achieved only 19% of the vote combined. Among 25–34-year-olds, Mélenchon and Le Pen each received 24% of the vote. Despite the stereotype of the Front National as a party of elderly Catholic voters, only 10% of the over-70s voted for Le Pen; of the 60–69-year-olds, 19% backed her.[15] In other words, younger voters were significantly more likely to back the FN than older voters (the true core of Le Pen's support is robustly middle-aged).

A similar story unfolded in Italy in 2018. The most popular choice among young people was the Five Star Movement (M5S), a curious populist party originally co-founded by the comedian Beppe Grillo with an eclectic political programme that might be best summarized as left-wing anti-establishment. Around one in three under-28s are thought to have backed the M5S.[16] The movement has half as many supporters over 65 as it does among the under-35s.[17] La Lega, the populist right-wing party that swept the Italian north, claimed 10 per cent of first-time voters. However, perhaps the bigger story was that a reported 35 per cent of eligible first-time voters didn't vote at all, significantly below the national turnout (around three quarters), in a nation which usually has one of the highest turnouts in the Western world.[18] Even in Sweden, a nation widely regarded as having one of the world's most stable liberal democratic settlements, the younger generations seem to be turning away from the established left. Traditionally, the centre-left Social Democrats have been able to rely on a high share of the youth vote as a key pillar of their electoral strategy. In 2018, the young scattered across the political spectrum, leaving the Social Democrats with just 20% of their vote. Thirteen per cent of 18–21-year-olds backed the right-wing populist Swedish Democrats, 12% the liberal Centre Party, 12% the feminist Left Party and 6% the Greens.[19]

The lesson from these and a string of other Western elections in the 2010s—Spain, Portugal, Greece, the Netherlands—is twofold. One, as has long been recognized, we are seeing a new electoral division focused more on age than on class, with significant value gaps forming that can, to some extent, be mapped in results at the ballot box. Two, the young generation is not simply going left; rather, it is going everywhere but where it was before. Young people in the West may not be sure what they want, but they are seemingly convinced that the current system is not it.

One significant counter-example worth considering is Germany. In the most recent election, polling suggested that 57% of first-time voters would back the incumbent Angela Merkel and her centre-right CDU/CSU, with a further 21% backing the traditional centre-left Social Democrats.[20] This is the so-called "Merkel Generation"—a whole cohort of young voters who have come to maturity only really knowing her chancellorship, which began in 2005. Germany has a strong economy, with the lowest youth unemployment in Europe and one of the best-educated young demographics. Moreover, in a world of remarkable instability and chaos, there is evidence that Merkel is regarded by many young Germans as "the adult in the room". This perception of strength, security and a saviour figure had made it hard for populism to appeal from elsewhere on the political spectrum. The great question, now that Merkel has announced her retirement, is what Germany's youth will do without such an option on the table.

The trend is a little different among the new Westerners of Central and Eastern Europe. Here, as we saw in Chapter 4, the young have fallen more decisively behind right-wing populism, amidst remarkable electoral success for a string of nationalist populist parties. In Hungary the most popular party among students is the far-right Jobbik, and young people are far more likely than older generations to back the party. The nationalist right-wing Law and Justice Party in Poland was the most popular among first-time voters in every Polish election, national and local, of 2016–18, and in the European Parliament election of 2019. In Slovakia the trend is not quite as pronounced, but even so almost a quarter of first-time voters backed the extreme-right People's Party in 2016, a significantly higher percentage than the party's total vote share of 8 per cent.[21] Perhaps paradoxically, however, young Central and Eastern Europeans are still much more likely to believe that it is necessary to live in a democracy than their Western European contemporaries—no doubt the legacy of communism has a huge bearing on that fact. Seemingly, the votes for populist movements don't reflect an abandonment of the democratic principle—otherwise we'd perhaps be seeing far lower turnout, rather than disproportionate support for populists.

* * *

To vote for the extremes is one thing; at least casting around for new political identities is in the spirit of the West, which continually searches for a moral vision. The greater danger is that the young become so disillusioned with the prospects of reaching that endpoint, with the political options available to them, that they simply forget or abandon the West. As we already touched upon in the introduction to this chapter, this has gone beyond psychological or emotional abandonment in much of the West. Young Westerners are abandoning their countries.

Europeans leaving for a better life is not a new historical phenomenon. The USA, Canada, Australia, New Zealand, South Africa, Brazil, Argentina and a number of other former colonies owe their current ethnic make-up in large part to waves of European emigration, which was generally economic in nature. However, at least from the 1960s until the mid-to-late 2000s, the Western economy was a phenomenal success story, and large-scale emigration from Western nations simply did not happen. Instead, Western nations became the places to which people migrated for a better life, as we can see in the changed ethnic composition of virtually every Western nation since the 1960s.[22] In the 2010s, however, the picture has changed again.

For the new Westerners—the EU "class of 2004"—the impulse to leave has been largely driven by economic ambition. It is possible to earn a lot more money in the UK or Germany than the average wages at home, and with the right to move freely and work across the Eurozone, who can blame those who take the opportunity? But, as we saw in Chapter 4, the effects can be stark. Population losses are devastating to the economies of Central, Eastern and Southern Europe: according to the IMF, by 2030 emigration could have lowered GDP per capita in Bulgaria, Romania and some Baltic states by as much as 4 per cent.[23] Particularly devastating has been the loss of the young generation, benefiting from post-communist freedom and higher education, which is essential to economic growth.[24] More catastrophic than the economic loss, as Krastev notes, is the cultural loss. So many of these countries have only recently reclaimed their national identities, traditions and cultures; now they are seeing an existential threat posed not by foreign masters, but by the young simply moving away and forgetting. This trend is not confined to the former Communist Bloc. Italy is a founder member of the European project and currently witnessing a stark emigration trend, particularly among the younger generation. The number of Italians registered as living abroad rose 60 per cent from 2006 to 2017, to almost 5 million.[25] Similar stories can be told in Spain, in Portugal and across the European south.

Hidden in those figures are the consequences of internal migration. The twenty-first century is marked by mobility, and, as argued in Chapter 1, by a breakdown in any sense of community belonging. The two trends have combined to make it easier, both practically and emotionally, for people coming of age in this century to leave where they've grown up and move elsewhere, not just abroad but within their own country. The job market plays a major role in this, as does the higher education market. The conservative American political scientist Patrick Deneen has pointed out that universities are not only becoming increasingly vast businesses, but that they are sucking in all the talented youth and concentrating them in a relatively small number of institutional settings, where they are placed on a conveyor belt of education and employment ideals that will never see them return to where they grew up.[26] The US education machine—and similar models are true of Canada, the UK, Australia and several others—harvests the most promising young people from across the nation, but gives nothing back to the places that raised them. The American system is particularly devastating because the costs of higher education are so obscene, and the pricing to some extent incentivizes people to leave their own states.

Cities are the great beneficiaries of this trend. Places like New York, London and Berlin, to name but a few, are increasingly "young" cities: places people move to for study and work, and which they only leave once they have families of their own to raise. This is a great economic and cultural resource for those locations; for everywhere else, the effect is draining. These regional inequalities result in resentments that harm solidarity, with the flight of the educated young a direct hit to two of the West's three republican values.

* * *

It is easy enough to conclude from all of the above that the West's young are disillusioned and unhappy with the West as it stands. To which the cynic might counter, so what? The young are famous for being disillusioned with the system. In this line of argument, the youth of the 2010s is no different from all the previous generations of teenagers and young people who have given rise to counter-cultural movements and political radicalism, and there has always been conflict between the young and their parents. Every revolution in history has drawn on a pool of angry young men. The former extremist turned liberal Muslim writer Ed Husain has described Islamist radicalism as one of a number of means (also including Marxism) by which young men have struggled to find political expression.[27] In this sense, the disillusionment of the young is not particularly new.

Compared to the French student riots of 1968, or the primarily youth-driven resistance to the Vietnam War in the USA, or young support for the Black Panthers, the current intergenerational divide seems at the very least less explosive than previous conflicts drawn on age lines. The political scientist David Runciman has compared today's democratic struggles in the West to the most recent serious attempts at armed coups in established Western democracies: France, where the last such attempt was in 1961, and Greece, where the colonels successfully overthrew the democratic government in 1967. He concluded that the chance of an armed overthrow driven by the younger generation is far less likely today than it was then. However, he thinks this is because of an ageing society with a lack of political energy—which could bode equally ill for the future of the West.[28]

What's more, in some ways, this disillusionment is not like anything that has been before. For one thing, it is more widespread. The radical left, particularly in the West, has always drawn primarily on the young, but overall remained a fringe movement even among that demographic. In the 1970s, the young were more likely than the old to back the far left in the UK, but only a very small proportion of the young ever actually did so.[29] Otherwise, youth voting patterns were set by class, and did not differ greatly by age group.[30] The same was true of most Western countries, although those with more proportional parliamentary systems do exhibit a greater range of party choices, and so throw up larger radical groupings from time to time. In the late 2010s, however, there are significant generational gaps in support for particular parties. Dissatisfaction is no longer limited to finding political expression in fringe movements—instead the fringe is taking over the political landscape across the West, on both left and right.

Furthermore, there is a major difference in context. The astonishing revolution in communications technology and social media has had far-reaching consequences, not least what the British journalist and think-tanker Robert Colvile has dubbed "the great acceleration". All aspects of public life, including politics and the media but also personal relationships, are now defined by an extraordinary increase in both speed and scale.[31] This makes political movements faster to develop, but also harder to sustain. The dissatisfaction spreads faster, but the solutions are more fragile. The same explosion of social media and online life has also meant that fringe groups can be much more effective than in the past. Given that they were by definition a minority interest, before the internet age there was always a limit to their agency. Now, such groups never have to gather in person, and can communicate and co-ordinate remotely: far more people can be involved, and messages spread far more quickly. Right-wing and Islamist extremist movements each account for only a percentage of a percentage of the Western population, but their ability to connect online has enhanced their ability to organize and proselytize, and made them harder to police.

This change applies to anyone with a smartphone, but of course that means it applies far more to younger people. In fact, research in the US has found that 95 per cent of American teenagers have access to a smartphone, and 45 per cent are online "almost constantly".[32] One of the more bizarre expressions of this rapid online radicalization among young men is the so-called Incel movement. Incels are an almost entirely online subculture of primarily angry young white men who describe themselves as "involuntarily celibate"—a condition they blame primarily on women and feminism. The subculture has long been linked to a growing family of online white and male supremacist groups. Using internet forums and message boards, this group—despite being geographically dispersed and accounting for only a tiny number of people—has been able to gain huge public prominence, in large part due to a series of terrorist attacks carried out by Incels. One of the most notable of these was carried out in 2014 by Elliot Rodger, who murdered six people in a shooting spree in California and left a 137-page Incel manifesto that had been widely shared online and inspired a series of other attacks. Several of these have focused on high schools and university campuses, including the most deadly, when Nikolas Cruz killed seventeen students at a high school in Parkland, Florida in 2018, with the message that Elliot Rodger "would not be forgotten".

The power of social media in political and radical organization is just one example of the key point: that even if the cynics have it right, and young people are always radical outsiders critical of the system, this doesn't mean that the present young generation will necessarily follow tradition in coming around to the West with age. For one thing, as Mounk has demonstrated, each successive generation has been less pro-liberal democracy than the one that went before; so to some extent this is a cumulative build-up of resentments across a number of generations. For another, as we will see below, the trends driving this dissatisfaction look set to get worse, not to improve. Over successive postwar decades, the West has got wealthier, and intergenerational justice was a widely understood part of the social contract. Neither of those points can be taken for granted any more.

Perhaps most crucially, though, the young's diminishing belief in the West matters because of demographic reality. If it is true that generations are the new classes in terms of political cleavages, then the young are set to be thoroughly disenfranchised over the coming years. Europe is an ageing continent, and one which is going to be increasingly politically dominated by the elderly. Some estimates believe that by 2020 a quarter of the EU population will be aged 65 or over. By 2050 it could be as high as one third.[33] In Eastern and Southern Europe, the young are leaving their countries behind, exacerbating the natural trends in living and dying. In Germany the ageing population has raised serious political questions over the sustainability of the economic model. In the UK and France, the ageing of the population would look far worse were it not for newly arrived immigrant populations keeping the birth rate up.

It is not really birth rates that are the issue; it is that people are simply living longer. In the UK it is estimated that by 2040 there will be 10 million over-75s, and that the "super-old" (those aged over 95) will have increased by 390%.[34] Meanwhile, the number of young adults and children is expected to remain fairly stable—there were 12.4 million children in 2016, and the ONS predicts only 12.7 million in 2041.[35] You have got it all wrong if you would argue, in the wake of Brexit or Trump, that things will turn out fine once the old die and are replaced by the more liberal generation following behind. The political agenda of the next few decades is going to be ever more dominated by the priorities of elderly voters. If their values and political beliefs really are very different from those of their younger counterparts, as the data seems to suggest, then the young are only going to become more disenfranchised. To try and draw attention to this oft-overlooked trend, David Runciman has gone so far as to provocatively suggest lowering the eligible voting age to six, in order to try and rebalance intergenerational bias in the voting patterns of the UK.[36]

All these symptoms of malaise among the Western youth point in one direction only. An entire generation has lost confidence that the West can deliver for it. The young no longer believe in the West's sense of progress, nor can they envisage its promised utopian endpoint. Their lack of conviction in those principles is such that they haven't, overall, rallied behind any particular alternatives. There is only a lingering and growing sense that what we have now is not working for them.

Solidarity breakdown

Why are the young abandoning the idea of the West? Inevitably there is not one single factor, but several do jump out. Particularly, overarching almost everything is the loss of intergenerational solidarity and resulting sense of betrayal.

Solidarity, as discussed in Chapter 1, is the sense of duty and obligation owed to others. The term has deep roots within both religious and secular political philosophical traditions. When it comes to generations, this is most commonly thought about in terms of families. Parents are held to be responsible for raising their children, supporting them and helping them to raise families of their own. The children in turn are thought to have responsibilities to care for their parents in old age and to raise children of their own. In the political context, intergenerational solidarity works—or, perhaps, worked—in a similar way. It was expected that the political process would take into account the impact of decisions on future generations, including those not yet born, and also that overlapping generations would ultimately benefit collectively from avoidance of short-term decisions only in their own immediate best interests.[37]

In a host of ways, this intergenerational model appears to have broken down—in economics, environmental politics, and family relations. In each case the generations have grown apart from each other, and it is the young who have lost out as a result. It is no surprise that they feel betrayed and that they voice this feeling, further damaging intergenerational solidarity. Western economic and social policy has changed markedly in the past forty years. Until at least the 1970s, European governments in particular prioritized full employment as a key policy commitment. In the UK, for example, pre-1976 unemployment was rarely above 3 per cent—but since 1976, it has barely ever dipped below that level.[38] The change came about due to deliberate policy decisions to rethink the way economics worked, embracing what some refer to as neoliberal economics (a legion of alternative terms are available). Welfare states had been a staple of the European economic and social model since the Second World War for both the left and the right, declining only recently and largely due to policy choices. For decades in the postwar period, both Europe and the broader West (particularly the USA) saw a remarkable growth in living standards. This too is no longer true, in large part as a consequence of a decade-long economic crisis.

Of course, even at the height of the *trente glorieuses* (1945–75), when welfare states, near-full employment and increasing living standards were becoming standard across the West, there were problems. The commitment to full employment arguably held back several European economies for many years, and there were plenty of economic dips. The overall trajectory, however, was upwards. And, crucially for the stability of the West, intergenerational solidarity was a reality. Welfare states and economic growth meant that it became standard for each generation to be wealthier than the last, an inheritance of progress and strength. As we know, this is no longer the case, and we can chart the change in various ways.

For one thing, wealth is now accumulating among older generations, and not being passed on. The economy of the West is showing significant favouritism towards a few, older generations. For example, in the UK, those born in the 1970s had an average personal wealth (including property and pensions) of £53,480 by the age of 31. For those born in the early 1980s—that is, those in their 30s in 2019—average personal wealth is just £27,350.[39] British household income has stalled after generations of growth. The reality is even starker in other countries. A 2018 International Monetary Fund study in Italy found that since 1995, the average real net-worth wealth of over-65s had increased by 59 per cent. This is the only age group where people are better off today than people of the same age were a quarter century ago. The bracket 55–64 broke even, and all younger brackets were worth less than their mid-90s counterparts. The most dramatic loss was for the under-35 category, down 60 per cent on the same age group's wealth in 1995.[40]

Across the West, the same story can be shown again and again: the 2008 crash notwithstanding, the past twenty-odd years has been a good period for the older generations, and a disaster for younger people. The impact of the economic crisis has fallen particularly heavily on the West's youth, especially in terms of employment and austerity cuts, which—with some exceptions, notably Greece—have tended to hit hard provisions that primarily benefit younger people (education, housing), while leaving the priorities of older people (healthcare, pensions) relatively well protected. Adding insult to injury, the debt deficit of most Western nations has continued to spiral, meaning that not only are younger people paying the price for the crash now, but they will be doing so for their whole lives in servicing the national debt. That this has been allowed to happen is, in itself, one sign of the breakdown in intergenerational solidarity.

Employment and housing are two areas where this economic pain has been notably acute. Unemployment in the UK post-crash has been particularly hard on the under-25s: other generations have actually seen unemployment dip during the austerity years. In Italy, unemployment among young people in 2017 hit 35%, and would have been even higher had so many young people not already left to go abroad. Spain was even higher (39%); in France it had been at around one in four for some time. Portugal, Cyprus, Croatia and Finland were all over 20%, despite 2017 being a significant improvement on 2016 in almost all these countries and across the EU.[41] In each case, the youth unemployment rate was well above the national average. Even where unemployment seems relatively low, there is mounting evidence that younger people account for a disproportionate share of precarious and temporary jobs, with lower rights and securities.[42] The UK is one of a number of Western states with a lower minimum wage for younger workers, and which has withdrawn housing benefit for under-25s as part of cost-saving measures during the austerity regime.

This brings us to one particular flashpoint in the youth sense of betrayal: reforms to the labour market sold as being in the interests of young people, but rejected by them en masse. The clearest example—most of them are in Southern Europe—was the 2014 "Jobs Act" introduced in Italy. The Act was the flagship policy of Matteo Renzi's premiership, designed to get young people in particular into the labour market. It did so by making

it easier for companies to fire people, and incentivizing permanent contracts, but with fewer employment rights. Though
widely applauded by economists at the time—notably by the
European Commission and the OECD[43]—evidence of the legislation's success has been mixed.[44] More to the point, despite
being designed to get young people into jobs, it was hugely
unpopular with young people, culminating in a protest in Rome
of up to 1 million Italians in October 2014. This in part explains
why so many young voters rejected Renzi in favour of populist
alternatives in the 2018 general election.

The reason for this is not hard to fathom. Young Italians
didn't simply want jobs; they wanted the same social contract
that their parents and grandparents had had: jobs with enormously high levels of security and protection, effectively a "job
for life". The state had supported this for several previous generations by borrowing, and making cuts and reforms elsewhere.
Young Italians simply didn't see why they should be the ones to
miss their turn, in a system that has effectively operated since the
Second World War. They saw Renzi's reforms as a betrayal of the
social contract, with older generations benefiting from years of
prosperity and safe jobs and then denying the same to their own
generation. Whether or not such a feeling is good economics, it
breeds intergenerational distrust all the same.

A similar story can be told of housing, the cost of which—
partly as a consequence of growing and ageing populations[45]—
has long been wildly rising across the West. The UK has managed to grossly accentuate this crisis by selling off a high
proportion of its social housing stock without reinvesting the
proceeds in younger generations, flogging a collective asset for
the benefit of a single generation in a fire sale. As breakdowns in
intergenerational solidarity go, the British approach to housing
makes for an extraordinary case study. Not content with privatiz-
ing a great deal of its social housing, successive British govern-

ments of both left and right have also failed miserably to incentivize the building of new homes, or to do anything significant about the rental market, which has seen prices increase dramatically faster than for any other consumer commodity—save actual property prices. The beneficiaries of this changing situation have been the baby boomer population. Back in 2007, fully 17 per cent of the over-50s owned a second home in the UK, and made up a hugely disproportionate share of landlords; home ownership for the under-30s has been in steep decline for years.[46] Young people in the UK live in ever smaller, worse-standard, privately rented and expensive properties, with all the profits going to their parents' generation, which owns the buildings.

The UK has been an ignominious leader in this field, but plenty of other Western countries have done their best to emulate the model. The USA has also presided over a supply crisis in affordable homes and correspondingly steep house price values, while seeing only small growth in the value of wages. Absurd housing bubbles in the USA, the Republic of Ireland and Spain helped drive their respective economic crashes in the late 2000s.

A final issue of intergenerational solidarity and economics lies in higher education. Here there are major variations across the West. In Austria and Denmark, for example, undergraduate study is free. The same is true for Scottish students at Scottish universities (though not in other parts of the UK). Other Western states, including France and Germany, maintain very low tuition fees at undergraduate level. By contrast, a *Business Insider* report found that the USA was joined by several EU members—including the UK, Hungary, Estonia and Lithuania—among the world's ten most expensive countries for a university education. This was calculated not only by the size of tuition fees (the USA in particular charges eye-watering amounts), but also by the proportion of household income spent paying for university education. By the latter calculation, Hungary is actually the most expensive country for higher education in the world, with up to 92 per cent of an average salary being spent each year on university education.[47] In the USA the equivalent is 53 per cent.

On this issue, it is American and British millennials who feel betrayal most strongly. Data collected by *U.S. News* show that in 1998–2018 average tuition fees at private national universities rose by 168%. Out-of-state tuition and related fees at public national universities had jumped even more, by 200%; in-state tuition and related fees at public national universities had increased an astonishing 243%.[48] Even adjusting for inflation over this period, the cost of a college education has gone up sharply, by about 3% above inflation since 2007. Student debt is now the second highest consumer debt category in the USA, behind only mortgages and ahead of credit cards. Total student loan debt in the USA is now worth over $1.5 trillion, and the loan–debt balance is growing.[49] The UK's sense of betrayal is focused on the introduction of tuition fees, which were first brought in at a low level under Tony Blair's New Labour government in 1998. In England—Scotland and Wales have separate education systems under devolution—fees were then almost tripled as a result of the 2004 Higher Education Act, to £3,000 a year (not including living costs). The maximum tripled again in 2010 to £9,000, set to rise with inflation. Both the 2004 and 2010 increases saw student protests, without any success.

Millennials' sense of injustice in the UK is twofold. For one thing, previous generations were funded entirely by government grants to attend university, which was deemed an important asset to the country's economy. If anything, higher education has become more important to the national economy in recent years, as the tech revolution and globalization has transformed economic trends, but the bill is increasingly footed by the young themselves. Prices have gone up, but there is now increasing doubt that many degrees are worth the cost incurred. A report by the Institute for Fiscal Studies found that graduates continue to earn a lot more than non-graduates overall, but that this effect was significantly reduced after controlling for pre-university characteristics such as family wealth. Further, they found that several degree courses—including those in English literature, creative arts and philosophy—actually lead to certain men who study those courses earning less than their equivalents who did not. (This is not true of women with undergraduate degrees, who do much better than their male counterparts at outstripping non-graduate competitors in the job market.) There are also a number of universities, particularly among the newer universities founded after 1992—usually former polytechnics—whose graduates can, depending on various factors, earn less than non-graduates.[50]

One sign of how millennials and post-millennials have felt and acted upon this betrayal of the social contract has been the fate of the Liberal Democrats. The Lib Dems (as they are popularly known) won 23% of the vote in the 2010 general election, and entered into coalition government, an exceedingly rare circumstance in UK political history. Key to their success was winning 30% of the 18–24 age bracket, and 44% of university students, in large part thanks to a very public campaign pledge to fight not only against increasing university tuition fees, but for scrapping them altogether. In government this commitment did not last, and the announcement that fees were to be tripled was confirmed within months of the election. Student support for the party plummeted from 44% to an estimated 13% by the following election in 2015, when the Lib Dems were left with just eight seats in Parliament.[51]

The recent economic climate has hit hard for young people bearing college debts in both the UK and USA. Among Eastern European nations with tuition fees that are high relative to salaries, the effect has been the brutal emigration pattern we have already discussed, with young people forced abroad to make enough money to justify their education, leaving the country with little actual benefit from its own graduates. As with the Italian and other European millennials resenting labour market reforms, these are not simple issues. There are fair questions to be asked about where the burden of education funding should lie, and why people personally benefiting shouldn't be expected to pay for the privilege. But education is an area where the costs have been handed over consistently to young people, while public services used particularly by older people have been relatively protected in the UK and USA. In other words, this debate has accentuated millennials' perception of the baby boomers as asset strippers who enjoyed rising prosperity, guaranteed jobs, affordable housing, generous welfare states and heavy state subsidies when they were young people, all of which they now seem unwilling to fund for their descendants, instead leaving them with the bill for the state's past generosity.

* * *

Attitudes towards the environment are another interesting example of the struggles of intergenerational solidarity. Of course climate change is a global, and not a specifically Western, issue— but (as we will explore in Chapter 9) it is obvious that a great deal of the action needed is going to have to, and should, come from the West. Young Westerners are clearly aware of this. The first thing to note is that environmental and ecological concerns rank far higher as a worry for millennials than for older voters. This difference is more generational than partisan. For example, a Pew survey in the USA found than millennial members of the Republican Party are far more likely than older Republicans to believe that human activity is the key cause of climate change (36% vs 18%) and that the government should do more both to protect animals and habitats (60% vs 34%) and to reduce the effects of climate change (47% vs 27%). Among Democrat millennials, the equivalents are all over 90%, slightly higher than for older Democrats.[52]

Similar trends are apparent across the West. Environmental concerns are youth concerns. Studies in Europe have shown that, the younger you are, the greater the likelihood of you accepting higher fuel prices to protect the environment, for example.[53] This is not hard to explain. The 2018 IPCC report warned that we have only twelve years left to limit global warming to 1.5C, otherwise we will face catastrophic consequences in floods, droughts, extreme heat, poverty, and the complete eradication of coral reefs.[54] The longer major reforms are delayed, the greater the cost of resolving the problem, and the more likely that people alive today will see drastic damage to our shared world. Indeed, this is already happening—extreme weather is already taking a heavy toll on many parts of the world, a process which is only likely to get worse. What we are witnessing is sheer ecological vandalism; the betrayal of future generations by a Western political class that has seen all the evidence, yet can't seem to bring itself to take the necessary steps.

Action by Western governments has been sporadic, and has rarely met the standards that younger voters in particular have demanded. Earlier international agreements such as Kyoto or the EU's carbon trading market were not sufficiently ambitious to meet the scale of the crisis, and at any rate Western nations have largely fallen short of the little that was agreed. Of the thirty-eight signatories to the Kyoto agreement, two—the USA and Canada—withdrew; the remaining thirty-six, though they did meet their overall target, did so mostly as a natural result of the financial crash and industrial outsourcing to the developing world, rather than through proactive efforts and policies to change behaviour at home.[55]

The most recent and theoretically far-reaching treaty was the 2016 Paris Agreement, which has been ratified or acceded to by

183 states plus the EU, together representing more than 87 per cent of global greenhouse gas emissions. However, a series of studies have criticized that agreement as not going nearly far enough, and the respected scientific journal *Nature* found almost two years into the agreement that no major industrial nation had yet met its pledged emissions reduction target or implemented most of its proposed policies to do so.[56] Donald Trump has already withdrawn the USA from the agreement, and Republicans continue to campaign for abolition of the Environmental Protection Agency, despite it having been founded by Richard Nixon. With no binding mechanism on governments to meet their climate commitments, there is plenty of reason for scepticism that the West will make the progress needed.

As an issue of intergenerational solidarity, the West's abnegation of responsibility over the impact of climate change is indicative of a broader political context in which the future itself is a low priority. For young Westerners, the frustration is not only that an issue they care about is being ignored, but that existential threats are being ignored to sate more immediate policy concerns. Some of the anger at that situation can be seen in the mounting number of campaigns and protests run by young people and even children on this issue. The global Fridays For Future protests by school students began in November 2018, inspired by fifteen-year-old Greta Thunberg's three-week school strike outside the Swedish parliament. The Fridays for Future website now lists national contacts for twenty-five countries that have started campaigns.

* * *

It is economic and policy decisions that have fed the collapse of Western intergenerational solidarity, and their consequences are not only political. They have wrought real societal changes that will have implications for decades to come. For example, the economic changes around housing and employment have dramatically changed the dynamics of family life in the West. Young people are starting families later, in large part due to economic circumstance, perpetuating the demographic crisis of an ageing West. They are leaving home later—the average young person in the EU doesn't move out of their parents' home until the age of 26.[57] This is significantly later than the average even a decade previously, and this set-up has been shown to have negative consequences for family life, wellbeing and the extent to which young people feel wholly a part of wider society.[58] It is a product of Western economics, but with consequences for solidarity and social cohesion that far exceed most analyses.

Other changes are no less destructive. The increasing political value divides between generations are having consequences on family and social life. The UK's 2016 Brexit referendum was typical of many recent votes that have divided sharply along generational lines and led to accusations of older generations betraying their children's futures. In the aftermath of the vote there were widespread articles in that vein, some of which called for older people to be denied the vote, or even looked forward to the day when a whole generation would have died off and left a more liberal mainstream. The same happened later that year, after Trump's victory in the US presidential race. To be sure, many of these perspectives were humorous or facetious, but several were simply angry. The tone of those online pieces translated to social media, but worse, to the dinner table. Intergenerational political conflict is fuelling the breakdown of solidarity. The young feel betrayed, the old that their values are being publicly dismissed and despised. The cycle of negativity and accusations of bad faith continues.

8

MIGRANTS, ISLAM AND WESTERN VALUES

Several chapters in this book have referred to issues around migration and the West. It is not a question that can be ignored, since it dominates so much of political and media discourse. The stakes are high not only because the debate is so entrenched in those settings, but also because how Western governments choose to address concerns about integration of migrants is a critical test of the depth of Western values. This chapter argues that the response of the 2010s risks seriously undermining those same values, and so the West itself. If this isn't addressed in the right way, then migrants and their descendants—and particularly Muslims—may well become another group lost to the West.

For all that migration has been a critical policy issue for decades, there has rarely been much consistency in how Western governments have come to evaluate or assess the purpose and ethics of their migration policy.[1] Two criteria largely dominate that discussion. One is the extent to which migration is economically beneficial, and the other is to what extent migrants have integrated into their new state—in other words, how effectively newcomers have become British, American, Swedish and so on. Most Western governments' approach has oscillated between these two questions, seeking either to maximize the potential economic gains, or to encourage assimilation. The Australian points-based immigration system is a good example of the former. Potential migrants are assessed according to the level of economic benefit they will bring to the state (by filling a labour shortage in a key industry). The assimilation tactic, meanwhile, is perhaps best captured by the German state of Baden-Württemberg, which introduced what was widely criticized as a "Muslim test"[2] in the mid-2000s, demanding that prospective new citizens prove their liberal commitments and ability to fully assimilate.

It is important to note that these two criteria—the economic value of immigrants and their capacity for assimilation—are certainly not the same thing, and not even necessarily compatible. It is entirely possible to be an enormous net economic contributor and yet never assimilate at all, or equally to fully embody a new cultural identity while representing an economic black hole. Both these approaches also raise moral challenges for how the West conceives of itself. For one thing, the economic model can perpetuate a dehumanized vision of migrants, in which people are just grist for the mill, unworthy of any meaningful social value beyond their labour. In the words of Pope Francis, "The prevailing mentality puts the flow of people at the service of the flow of capital, resulting in many cases in the exploitation of employees as if they were objects to be used, discarded and thrown out."[3] Our ability to restore the Western commitment to solidarity will require us to see people as people, with an innate human dignity, and to move beyond seeing them solely as economic units. A failure to do so has made forming communities and collective purpose more difficult, and undermined the sense of importance attached to the West's values.

MIGRANTS, ISLAM AND WESTERN VALUES

Western fears over Islam and the Great Replacement

However, it is the use of tactics aimed at fostering assimilation that has arguably created the bigger challenges for living out the West's values in practice. The fear that immigrants—both first-generation newcomers and their descendants—will undermine the West by not integrating is particularly directed in the post-9/11 world against Muslims. In reality, it is the Western response to the challenge of integrating migrants—and particularly Muslims—that risks undermining each of the key pillars of Western identity: moral progress and vision, the trio of republican values, and universalism.

In terms of actual presence, the Muslim population of the West remains very small. In the USA it amounted to only 1.1% of the total US population in 2017.[4] In the UK it was between 4 and 5% at the time of the 2011 census, though public perception has it at closer to 15%.[5] In Poland, Hungary and Slovakia, it is less than 1%, and yet forms the subject of a great proportion of political speeches and media hysteria. In New Zealand, which witnessed one of the West's deadliest anti-Muslim terrorist attacks in March 2019, Muslims make up just 1% of the population, despite a significant rise in numbers in the 2010s. The Muslim population of Australia, from where the Christchurch attacker hailed, is just 2.6%. But whatever the reality, in the minds of many Westerners Islam presents an issue of immense importance for the future sense of a Western identity. The spectre of jihadi terrorism has played a huge part in this. 9/11 provoked a radical shift in American self-confidence and led ultimately to a major shift in both American foreign policy (particularly military intervention) and domestic surveillance. Islamist terrorist attacks in various Western nations have fed media narratives of a West under siege, and have marked Muslims as a domestic threat in the eyes of some non-Muslim citizens.

In parts of the West, this narrative of Islam as a potential enemy is more deeply rooted than the recent struggles with jihadi extremism. Driving the Moors out of Iberia was critical to the formation of Spain as a state, and southern Spanish cities like Córdoba and Seville clearly display the long and enduring influence of Moorish culture, despite the takeover of buildings and cultural ideas for Christian Spanish purposes. Things are more recent and more visceral in the Balkans, among those peoples who were once under the Ottoman Empire. Hungary's status as defender of the West against Turkish aggression was a key part of its formation as a national culture. For all that, the polling evidence does suggest that fears about Islam increased dramatically across the West after 9/11 and the beginning of the War on Terror. Historical trends may play some part, but the great spur has been the wave of radical Islamist terrorism from the 2000s. Fears have been stoked further by the 2010s phenomenon of Western-born Muslims leaving home to join the war in Syria. Just under 6,000 Western Europeans went to fight for ISIS, including about 1,900 from France, just under 1,000 from Germany, and around 850 from the UK.[6] Both the shock that Western Muslims could actually want to go and fight to protect an evil regime, and the fear of what to do with any of those fighters who choose to come home, has contributed to an atmosphere of hostility and panic.

Terrorism may have provided the initial or most dramatic catalyst, but Western fears over Islam have also spread to issues of integration—the ability to become Western. In France, which has a higher Muslim population than most of the West (probably around 7.5 per cent), about half of those surveyed by Ifop in 2016 and 2018 felt Islam to be incompatible with French republican values.[7] This doubt that Muslims can become fully Western has been fed by any number of books and articles arguing that Islam is a specific problem too broad for the West to overcome.

Douglas Murray's *The Strange Death of Europe* is one such work that includes a litany of notes on the problem of integrating Muslims ranging from the mundane (pubs closing on British high streets) to the more fundamental. At the latter end of the spectrum, he discusses the "open secret" of sex attacks on women by gangs of immigrants, concluding that "the more refugees a country took in, the greater that problem became."[8] Others address issues as varied as FGM, anti-LGBT attitudes, child grooming gangs, the need for halal food and the observance of modest dress as examples of a values gap too wide to bridge.

Media treatment of these issues has repeatedly strayed into dishonesty or sensationalism. A number of reports on grooming gangs have been revealed to be deeply flawed, as have claims about increased incidences of sexual assault. Media bias has been shown to dramatically inflate the coverage of crimes committed by migrants—particularly Muslim migrants—versus column space or air time given to crimes committed by other criminals or terrorists.[9] In other cases, the reporting has simply been farci-cally exaggerated, as with the regularly debunked trope of right-wing news outlets that various European cities are full of Muslim-controlled "no-go zones". Even the usually staid *Wall Street Journal* fed into this narrative with an astonishingly poorly researched piece by Andy Ngo entitled "A Visit to Islamic England"; in which almost every claim and statement could be shown to be factually incorrect by anyone with even a passing knowledge of London.[10]

More broadly, underpinning arguments about the values gap between Muslims and Westerners is the sense that Muslims all believe and act in the same way, and so that having a Muslim minority means having to accept—or even, in extreme accounts, conform to—these supposedly anti-Western beliefs and prac-tices. This is false on both counts. For one thing, the spectrum of beliefs, practices and importance of faith among self-identifying Muslims is extremely broad, as it is among followers of every religion: 64 per cent of American Muslims said in 2014 that religion was "very important" in their lives, almost exactly the same percentage as among the total American population.[11] It should go without saying that the vast majority of Muslims are as horrified as anyone else over grooming gangs, and readily condemn FGM and rape. For another thing, it is quite possible for the West to continue to legislate and condemn practices that it deems to be unacceptable—FGM, rape and grooming are already illegal, and there are no Muslim opt-outs. The theologian Miroslav Volf reminds us that to understand is not necessarily to agree, and certainly not necessarily to excuse:

> Empathetic understanding of the Moroccan Muslim who killed Theo Van Gogh, the director of *Submission*, will not make me believe that his behaviour was somehow excusable. But understanding will prevent me from concluding "Issuing death threats and killing people for advocating views deemed unacceptable proves that violence is at the heart of Islam".[12]

In parts of the West, legislation has gone far beyond defending the law and Western values to what can only really be deemed as a targeting of Muslims. The "burkini ban", for example, as implemented by at least twenty local governments in France, seems unnecessarily dictatorial. Having the police force women to wear skimpier bathing costumes than they are comfortable with is not a victory for liberalism, feminism or for secularism— it is an entirely unwarranted assault on individual freedoms conceived in order to target a specific minority group. Another example of attempts to police perceived Muslim intolerance is Baden-Württemberg's "Muslim test" for prospective new citizens, who are quizzed on their allegiance to the German constitution—their views on homosexuality, whether they believed that a wife should obey her husband, and whether they thought there was any truth to the accusation that Jews run the world.[13]

Obviously, there are several problems with this approach. For one thing, the questions asked clearly indicated that the test was particularly targeted at Muslims—meaning that the test came from a prior assumption that Muslims cannot, in fact, be good liberal Westerners: they must be one or the other. Similar tests have never been suggested for integrating other communities. Marking out Muslims in this way feeds public fears. The second problem is that it asks Muslims to clear a far higher hurdle than is applied to anyone else, including born and raised Germans. If it is anti-Western to be opposed to gay marriage, then it is certainly curious that the state of Baden-Württemberg maintains a church tax on behalf of local faith groups, including the Catholic Church, which is institutionally opposed to gay marriage. Had he been forced to take this test, it would presumably have revealed that the German Pope Benedict XVI was not capable of being German. Of course, it is not unreasonable to test whether prospective citizens understand the constitution and that they are prepared to consent to it. However, there is a serious gap between understanding and consenting to the law, and being expected to prove specific political or social views beyond that.

Moves like this reflect a fear that, unless protections are in place, Western values—or even Westerners themselves as a people—could be overtaken or replaced. This says far more about the West's insecurities over the depth and commonality of its own values than it does about a real threat posed by Western Muslims. It is not a lack of certainty over who Muslims are, but rather a lack of confidence in who Westerners are. In 2012 the French writer Renaud Camus published *Le Grand Remplacement*, a book warning of a great replacement in his country, with the "ethnic French" replaced by migrants from North Africa and the Middle East. Camus has made a career out of provocation, but this particular idea seems to tap into a growing vein of thought, and is widely cited by thinkers in other Western countries.

Parallels can be seen particularly in the USA. Chapter 5 explored the fear of "white genocide" or "white replacement" among some white Americans. The rallying cry of a large portion of the American alt-right is "You will not replace us!"

The theme of replacement also underpins the conservative British journalist Melanie Phillips' *Londonistan*, a polemical but widely discussed book about how London is now minority white British: although white British people are still the largest single group in London, they no longer represent over 50 per cent of the population.[14] In Australia, the journalist Andrew Bolt was castigated in 2019 for an article written after the white-supremacist Christchurch attack on Muslim worshippers, in which he claimed, "There is no 'us' any more, as a tidal wave of immigrants sweeps away what's left of our national identity."[15] In truth, however, before the obvious tragedy of the New Zealand shooting, Bolt and plenty of others had been writing this and more on a regular basis, without seemingly breaking any taboos.

Fears of a non-Western takeover are not particularly rational. For one thing, much of the West now desperately needs migration in order to survive. It is a matter of diversify or die for much of Southern and Eastern Europe. Italy, for example, is now the second oldest country in the world (behind only Japan), with a diminishing birth rate. In 2017 there were 458,000 registered births in Italy, down by 120,000 from 2008.[16] Germany now has more citizens over the age of 60 than under 30. Without migration, population decline would be chronic, with the welfare state struggling to support an ever larger elderly population with a smaller pool of workers. In addition to the ageing population, we know that emigration has been a serious strain on much of Central and Eastern Europe, to the point where the Polish government—despite its vociferous public condemnation of new arrivals in Europe—has been quietly encouraging immigration to address its mounting demographic crisis. This has seen some 2 million Ukrainians come to Poland in 2015–18, and more than 13,000 work permits granted to economic migrants from the Indian subcontinent in 2017. Despite its official opposition to migration and rhetoric on the great replacement of European values, in 2017 the Polish government issued the second highest number of work visas to non-EU migrants of any EU state, behind only the UK.[17]

So much for the economic arguments for opposing immigration—what about the concern that the West's defining values might be lost after the arrival of so many newcomers? There is probably less to worry about here than we might assume. For one thing, these new arrivals provide the only like source of renewal for national cultures. It is surely better that a culture—with all its music, literature and language—should survive with a broader ethnic make-up than that it should die entirely. The latter scenario is not implausible in Bulgaria and Romania, for example. Also, as Eric Kaufmann has explored in *Whiteshift*, what is deemed to be the majority culture is more elastic than people might think. The category of what counts as "white" is most likely to simply expand as the majority of the population inter-mixes and inter-marries.[18] Throughout Western history, new arrivals have been shaped by their new environment far more than the other way round. The US journalist Colin Woodard's work on American nationhood(s) explores the foundation of eleven rival American cultures that have shaped the contemporary USA. He has noted that American communities' values structures have proven incredibly durable since their foundation.[19] The waves of migration to the USA in the nineteenth and twentieth centuries brought some additional cultural accumulations such as new foods or dress, but made almost no impact on central political, economic or moral systems.

Europe too can provide plenty of lessons for shaping an apparently diverse population into a cohesive mass. It is worth remembering that the ethnic identity of most European states is a largely mythical construction. German, British and Italian identities, to name just three, are not natural, but were forged between several previously distinct national and ethnic peoples. "We have made Italy, now we must make Italians" is an oft-quoted aphorism from the nineteenth-century Italian-Piedmontese statesman Massimo d'Azeglio, perfectly capturing the task of nation-building undertaken by many European nation states that only truly emerged in the nineteenth century. Besides, one of the central underpinning beliefs of the West has been that its values are not particular, but universal. Adopting a universalist and evangelical mindset from Christianity, the West has spent its history wholly committed to the idea that the West can, and should, expand to other places. The only real difference is one of context. For most of its history the West has been exporting its ideas, in the expectation that people will become Western in their own countries. Now, more than ever, the West is trying to make Westerners of new arrivals within its own borders.

In principle, then, there is good reason to think that the West is sufficiently capable of absorbing newcomers. There are also reasons for optimism that we can overcome fears about replacement. Despite the fact that there are still very clear and worrying racist trends across the West (see Chapter 5 in particular), there are also hopeful signs that racist attitudes are declining among the majority of the population. Recent studies, for example, have shown that young white Americans are much less likely than older generations to express prejudice towards minority groups, and that such prejudices are in decline among all age groups; support for segregated schools among white Americans is in significant and rapid decline.[20] Other research has shown that implicit bias against minorities (with the exception of the obese) seems to have been reducing across the board in the 2010s.[21]

Nevertheless, we are still faced with the risk of complacency. Just because huge numbers of people with disparate identities and values have previously been integrated into the West's identity and vision of itself does not mean that this will happen again without some effort on our part. At the core of current fears may reside a kernel of dangerous truth. Previously the West has been able to absorb people because it had a very clear sense of what its values were, and was convinced of their power. In other words, there was something to absorb people into. If the West's values are now muted, and do not have the deep-rooted support of most of the West's citizenry, then that integrative process proves more difficult. It will require a conscious effort on the part of Western societies to consider how they want to go about the process of integration.

In short, the task facing the West as it relates to newcomers and Islam is essentially the challenge of this book: to find a story and moral vision through which a diverse people can come together, and to find a way to create this collective ideal without betraying what the West fundamentally is. There are a number of potential options which lie before us, several of which ought to inspire serious fears for the future of the West.

Option one: Become the "other"

By far the least likely route forward is to do exactly what the French writer Renaud Camus and others are warning against: to actually abandon Western values entirely and embrace an alternative vision; in other words, to be complicit in the supposed takeover and surrender any claim to Western identity. This scenario has been satirized by the French novelist Michel Houellebecq in *Submission* (2015), a bestselling but controversial book whose prominence was greatly increased by its feature on the cover of satirical French magazine *Charlie Hebdo* the day of the terrorist attack on the *Hebdo* offices. Houellebecq imagines France adopting sharia law after an electoral alliance between a conservative Islamist party and the Socialists, who decided that a coalition was necessary in order to stave off Marine Le Pen and the far right.

It's a clever satire, but despite Houellebecq's contention that it depicts "an evolution that is, in my opinion, realistic",[22] there is little sign that anywhere in the West is on any such trajectory. The closest thing the West has to an Islamist party—at least in the eyes of its critics—is the Dutch party Denk, a spinoff from the Dutch Labour Party founded by two Turkish-origin politicians; it won a grand total of three parliamentary seats in 2017, on a manifesto of tolerance and solidarity toward migrants. If there is any expectation of the West becoming shaped by the Other, it will be a subtler process. The only plausible version of the West replacing itself with another vision of the world is one where, in trying to outcompete rivals that seem to be gaining ground, the West ends up embodying policies that lead to the same place. This is infinitely more likely to be anti-Muslim than Islamist. We have already seen attempts by some mainstream Western governments to draw the sting of ethno-nationalist populist parties, adopting a more radical approach to migration or assimilation. In Denmark's most recent general election in 2015, the centre-right Venstre party remained the senior partner in its parliamentary coalition, but only held off its surging bloc-mate—the far-right Danish People's Party—by echoing most of its anti-migrant rhetoric and policies on the campaign trail.

Option two: Crackdown and repression

Policies of hard assimilation demanding the repression of Muslim identity are already evident in the West. For example, in addition to the burkini bans mentioned above, some schools in the south of France insist on pupils eating pork, in a transparent effort to force Muslims either to exclude themselves from public life, or else to abandon their religion. As of summer 2018, nine out of twenty-eight EU member states had either national or local restrictions on the wearing of headscarves or veils.[23] Efforts at restricting migration specifically from predominantly Muslim countries, or refusal to take Muslim refugees, are also policies designed to prevent Islamic migrants from having any status in Western countries. A growing number of elected politicians in the West are making such policies a key plank of their platform. Some are highly explicit about it. During the 2016 Dutch election campaign, the far-right politician Geert Wilders and his Freedom Party stood on policies including the "de-Islamification" of the Netherlands, the banning of the Qur'an and the closing of all mosques.[24] They won 13 per cent of the vote and twenty seats, good for second place on both counts.

These are political approaches, but there are also societal pressures that can, in practice, amount to the same thing: the exclusion or repression of Muslims. The Pew Research Center, for example, produces a regular index of both religious restrictions (policies enacted by governments that prevent religious freedom) and social hostilities (acts of pressure by fellow residents or citizens that can also impinge on religious freedom, such as vandalism, violent assaults and desecration of religious texts). On the 2016 social hostilities index, no Western country appeared in the "Very High" bracket, but quite a few were in the "High" bracket: Germany, the UK, France, Italy, Switzerland, Romania, Denmark, Australia, Spain, Austria and the USA. Worryingly, several of these were showing increasing hostilities, particularly against Jewish and Muslim groups, and Europe had seen the largest annual increase in social hostility of any region.[25] Examples could be drawn from almost anywhere, but in Canada police-reported hate crimes increased by an astonishing 47 per cent in 2017, with

2,073 crimes reported, mostly driven by antisemitism or Islamophobia.[26] Among these was the Quebec City mosque shooting in February that year, which killed six worshippers. There have been many kinds of vandalism directed against mosques across the West, including broken windows, graffiti, or even pig heads being thrown into them.

More insidious are efforts to exclude Muslims from political or public life through innuendo. In the UK this was perhaps best illustrated by the London mayoral elections in 2016. The contest was fought between Zac Goldsmith—a Conservative MP from the smart suburb of Richmond and the Etonian-educated son of a famous financier—and Sadiq Khan, the son of a Pakistani bus driver and the Labour MP for the highly diverse working-class district of Tooting. Most observers predicted a close race. The incumbent mayor, Boris Johnson, had proven that the Conservatives could win in London if they got a high turnout among the middle-class suburbs, and Goldsmith's liberal and environmentalist credentials were expected to play well in that context.

What was unexpected was that Goldsmith's campaign instead decided to focus on Khan's Muslim identity. In a series of articles and attacks, Goldsmith's official campaign accused Khan, known as a soft left-centrist, of being a terrorist sympathizer, who could not be trusted with the capital's security. This reached its nadir with an article penned by Goldsmith in the right-wing *Mail on Sunday*, entitled "On Thursday, are we really going to hand the world's greatest city to a Labour party that thinks terrorists is [sic] its friends?", accompanied by a large image of the London bus blown up in the deadly 7/7 attacks.[27] Goldsmith insisted throughout the campaign on referring to Khan as a "radical", while denying that this was a racist dog whistle. What was astonishing about this onslaught was that Khan is no radical Islamist, but the epitome of a liberal Londoner. He is pro-abortion and pro-transgender rights, voted for gay marriage as an MP—receiving a number of death threats from actual extremists for doing so—and has campaigned as mayor to keep local pubs open. As the conservative political commentator Peter Oborne noted in a scathing attack on the Tory campaign, "If Zac Goldsmith's campaign succeeds, it tells every single British Muslim that there is no role for them anywhere in the British democratic system".[28]

Whether through legislation or social hostility, reacting defensively to the West's fading sense of self by lashing out against Muslims is deeply problematic. It is a rejection of the Western commitment to liberty and equality. To "protect" the West by repressing Islam in this way is to end up rejecting the whole canon of Western liberalism, and also to exhibit a weakness in Western confidence. If you need laws or restrictions to protect your values, then they are not deeply held by your people. If the West participated in a "cultural takeover", then it would simply cease to be itself; but the same is equally true of the crackdown option. In attempting to save itself, the West would abandon the very principles that make it what it is—liberty, equality and solidarity. Neither can be acceptable, or successful, paths to restoring the West.

Option three: Multiculturalism

The term "multiculturalism" is often used as a normative description of the West's increasingly diverse societies. I am using it here in the stricter sense of the policy adopted by the Canadian government of Pierre Trudeau in the 1970s and 1980s, the UK government of Tony Blair in the late 1990s and early 2000s, and various other Western administrations to greater or lesser degrees. It is the idea of affirming and supporting different cultural groups to continue to live out their own identity in full—an idea in direct opposition to the French model of *laïcité*, you might say. In the Canadian case, which is where the policy was followed most explicitly, this was understood to imply explicit promotion of cultural diversity and support for the rights of minority cultures to preserve and develop their specific identity. Unlike the last option we explored for regaining Western identity, this principle comes from a well-meaning liberal agenda: promoting the freedom to define one's own identity and to claim multiple different identities. The appeal of multiculturalism is obvious. It encourages people to tap into deeply held aspects of their identity, rather than suppressing them, and avoids the repressive tactics that can simply "other" or exclude minorities.

However, the most meaningful critique of multiculturalism has been that, although it seeks to promote inclusion, it still serves to exclude minorities. As the UK's former chief rabbi Jonathan Sacks argued in *The Home We Build Together*, this was a policy designed to promote tolerance—but one that had run its course by the late 2000s.[29] For Sacks, and many others in different contexts, the desire to support minority groups often ends up losing sight of the need also to promote the whole, and create meaningful solidarity across groups—not just freedom for each of them and equality between them. In the Netherlands, Paul Sniderman and Louk Hagendoorn have argued that multiculturalism has actually led to greater levels of social exclusion between groups, rather than inclusion.[30]

It can also mean that people are unhelpfully reduced to a single aspect of their identity. This is a point explored by Lori Beaman, Jennifer Selby and Amélie Barras, who have analysed the experience of Syrian refugees in Canada. They found that, in an eagerness to make these refugees feel at home, many areas of resettlement have ended up over-emphasizing the Muslim element to integration, insisting for example on the need to provide mosques and Muslim-specific services.[31] This was undoubtedly of benefit to many, but just as many other refugees were not in fact particularly religious; basing their identity and support networks entirely on faith was not necessarily helpful or desirable for them. Multiculturalism can fetishize and limit identity to a single category, forcing people to inhabit a public label that they would not otherwise take on and operate in a silo, apart from others. As we have seen throughout this second part of the book, that is a dangerous and un-Western situation for our societies to be in.

Option four: Creating an engaged middle ground

The three first tactics explored here have each come with serious reservations. Becoming the other is an existential self-destruction. Crackdown and repression is anathema to Western values of freedom and equality, and does much to drive minorities further to the extremes. Multiculturalism fails to build any meaningful sense of solidarity. So what is left that is authentically Western?

The task is to engage across differences, but with the goal of forging a common society around the values that define and cement the West. Given the fact of diversity in the West today, whether people like it or not, this shared identity must be built out of disparate groups—which will require both engagement with people's deeply held identities, but also directing them towards a common moral purpose and commitment to the West's fundamental values. The fears raised by Islam and migration more broadly should not spell the death of the West, but serve as an impetus for the West to finally wake up, and see the necessity of a real discussion about its values, how they are experienced (or not) in the lives of its citizens, and what it should demand of citizens in their name. These debates could—in fact, must—raise difficult challenges about the expectations of citizenship, but this is a good thing. Complacency and an empty approach to values has been the single most damaging feature of the West's malaise in the twenty-first century.

Given that Islam has become, however unjustly, the pinnacle of Western identity anxieties, it stands to reason that one of the starting points will need to be a role for strong interfaith projects that both take the faith aspect seriously and also seek to build mutual understanding and commitment to a common mission. There are plenty of projects of this sort already underway, at a low level. Following the controversy over Pope Benedict XVI's Regensburg lecture in 2006, popularly—if not necessarily entirely fairly—understood as an attack on Islam, a group of Christian theologians and leaders published "A Common Word Between Us and You", which in turn spawned a major interfaith initiative bringing together some of the most senior leaders and intellectuals in Islam, Judaism and Christianity. It has led to the development of programmes, courses and conferences at many leading universities.[32] Since 2000 there has been a remarkable mushrooming of similar networks and projects across the West. In the UK alone, there are more than 200 interfaith organizations, ranging from small local projects to national initiatives like the Inter-Faith Network (IFN) and the Faith and Belief Forum (previously known as the 3 Faiths Forum).

There are often challenges to these interfaith projects. One is that many have tended towards the elitist. Bringing together community leaders, heads of churches, leading scholars and the like is a noble endeavour, and there are plenty of examples of such approaches having successes. However, there is limited evidence of any trickle-down effect from these relationships. Despite its 240 interfaith groups, the UK seems to be overseeing an atmosphere of declining religious literacy and growing mistrust towards Muslims. One 2016 survey from ComRes captures an indicative picture of the situation, with findings including that only 28% of British adults believe Islam is compatible with

British values; 43% believe it to be a negative force in the UK; and 72% believe that most people in the UK have a negative view of Islam.[33] The connection between representative leaders and ordinary individuals of the same faith is often less clear than one might imagine. The majority of the religious probably have little direct regular engagement with their religious leaders; the vast majority do not regularly attend religious services, never mind interfaith initiatives.

A second issue is that interfaith projects reduce the task of integration to something done by and between religious actors. As we saw in Chapter 2, large parts of the West are majority non-religious. Even where the faithful still dominate, organized religion's political and social importance has been declining for some time. The challenge in terms of integration is not primarily between faith groups in today's West; on the contrary, the gap to be bridged is between a generally disunited and apathetic majority and a minority group of active believers. This problem is also exacerbated by the tendency among Western politicians to focus their efforts in this space on the people who are easiest to meet. Western politicians love being seen meeting with liberal Muslims, and hate being seen with those who have more conservative or "problematic" views. This is not hard to explain, given the significant media attention and public castigation for appearing to condone politically incorrect views on issues like sharia law, abortion, LGBT rights and so on—nor, as Tim Farron's case has shown, is this limited to believers of the Muslim faith. Unless we can get meaningful engagement working with conservatives as well as liberals, any reconciliation process will be of limited value.

Inevitably, the true answer lies beyond what the state can accomplish on its own. As we will see in Chapter 10, the way to build genuine solidarity is through engaged local groups, working towards a common endpoint. This is perhaps especially important when it comes to identity and Islam. Building trust for an "alien" community (as it is often perceived) cannot be done in the abstract, but must be done in the particular, and face to face. This is most easily accomplished when combined with a clear, deliverable goal of shared interest.[34] That said, this does not let the state off the hook. Much more could be done to better support the structures that can help. Keeping such community programmes going is not easy, particularly if local government is not prepared to play an active role, both in terms of funding and facilitation. Community initiatives are also easily undermined by national state action. Engagement is much more difficult when government policy seems to actively prevent Muslims from being just one group among many. Police and local authority trust in the Muslim community across much of the West is far lower than trust in the white population. This is not a coincidence but the result of a history of confrontation and policy choices.

* * *

Virtually every state in the West is wrestling to some degree with the question of how to think about immigration. The confusion in their thinking is in many ways symptomatic of the West's broader crisis. Policies that reduce migrants to nothing but economic units are a sign of the general trend of treating the West's values and ideas as a secondary concern, behind the needs of the market. Our policies for integration and assimilation, meanwhile, often end up compromising our own Western identity—whether it's freedom and equality being undermined by repression of Muslims, or solidarity being undermined by an uncritical multiculturalism.

Fears of a takeover, particularly from Islam, also expose the West's contemporary existential crisis. If so many people believe that a specific small portion of the population could radically change the overall culture, this amounts to a tacit admission that Western values are not felt to be widely shared or understood, making them vulnerable to any alternative that emerges. Fears over Islam expose the West's lack of self-belief, not any genuine "clash of civilizations". Part Three of this book picks up these challenges, in all the forms we have seen them in throughout Part Two, and looks towards the future. Given the extent of the damage charted here, is there a way to win the West back?

PART THREE

HOW TO WIN IT BACK

9

RESTORING THE MYTH

If there is one idea that could finally bury the West, it is that there is no need for a vision—no need for us to aim for a particular end to our story. But the West at its best is defined by a myth of progress towards a great moral utopia. This sense of necessary progression—from barbarism and backwardness to civilization and a republican future—is inherited above all from the West's Christian past, and any number of Western secular visions have endlessly reinvented that same idea. It is our founding myth, serving as a point of unity that allows people to set aside differences and tolerate misfortunes or even temporary crises, in order to achieve something profoundly important in the future. Ideals that transcend group identities are the glue binding together otherwise disparate tribes. This sense of dynamism and progress has underpinned Western expansionism and evangelicalism—the belief that we are headed somewhere of such universal benefit that others ought to join us on our journey.

Whether or not you view that past expansionism and evangelism as positive, there is no denying that the contemporary West has lost confidence in its own myth; and it is equally apparent that there is currently a disastrous block on the West uniting its people or making any further progress. The triumphalism of the end-of-history era now seems horribly misplaced, leaving us with the existential challenge of whether the late '90s and the '00s really were the apex of what it is possible for the West to accomplish. Was that it? Or can we yet see some hope for a West that aspires to be much more?

The current signs are not good. Too much of the political sphere seems to have given up on ambitious plans for the future. Idealists have been largely replaced either by demagogues and autocrats, or by technocratic managers determined to maintain the status quo system, regardless of its desirability. The story of the European Union in the 2010s has been typical of this trend. For far too long it found itself presiding over a successful economic model and devoted all its efforts to maintaining that system and fostering the passive consent of its citizenry. Quietly, even without anyone ever really noticing, it morphed from one of the most ambitious and morally driven political projects in world history, to a project that, in the words of Jürgen Habermas, has followed "the lure of technocracy".[1] This disease has been spreading throughout the West, a sort of post-politics in which management—particularly economic management—trumps idealism and Western values. The issue was first identified as early as the 1970s, particularly by Habermas and the German sociologist Claus Offe, but the warnings of a mounting bureaucratization and oligarchy in politics were not much heeded.[2]

Instead, things have got much worse. Politicians have started making an asset out of the emptiness of their ideas. In early 2019, a minor political earthquake in the UK saw eleven MPs—eight from Labour and three from the Conservatives—leave their parties to found a new group initially christened The Independent Group (subsequently known as Change UK). Its founding statement declared: "Our aim is to pursue policies that are evidence-based, not led by ideology, taking a long-term perspective to the challenges of the 21st century in the national interest, rather than locked in the old politics of the 20th century in the party's interests."[3]

The plausibility of evidence-based policy, free from the supposed shackles of ideology, is one of the most insidious fallacies of contemporary politics. There is no such thing. An evidence base relies on some sort of criteria for success, and those criteria are a matter of intellectual and imaginative construction. To reduce politics to picking the most effective pragmatic solution is to strangle the importance of values and beliefs. We do not need less ideology; if anything, we need more. If we start from a position of trying to find the best managerial responses to short-term issues, we will never see radical change to anything. Why does this matter? Because ongoing progress and reform is the bedrock of the West's identity as an intellectual idea—if we settle for how things are now, the West has no dream on which to thrive; the West loses its Westerners.

There are any number of reasons why the Remain camp lost the UK's EU referendum battle in 2016, but one that stands out above all others was its abject failure to tell any positive, visionary story about EU membership. Instead, campaign videos trotted out an endless parade of lacklustre business leaders and politicians to patronize voters with a message that voting Remain—in other words, protecting the status quo—was the responsible, adult thing to do. The message wasn't necessarily wrong, but was pitifully lacking in any appeal to the heart or to identity. Hillary Clinton played the same game, pointing to her opponent's many foibles and presenting herself as the sensible choice, but without ever really clarifying just what she wanted America to become under her presidency. What was missing from these campaigns was a story compelling enough to counteract the reactionary, but highly effective, stories of anti-Westerners, from both within and without. Crucially, as Naomi Klein has identified, that story needs to be values-based, not policy-based.[4] If we could start with a set of shared values that define where we want to go, the West would be less vulnerable to cold technocracy on the one hand, and to personality cults on the other. As things stand, progressive Westerners as well as ethno-nationalists have begun to put too much onus on a hero. There is a constant temptation to latch onto a single populist progressive figure, as an alternative to the hard work of confronting the deep-seated problems in Western politics.

Emmanuel Macron is the classic example. His 2017 presidential election victory came at a time when much of the West's political establishment was reeling. The previous year, Donald Trump had won in the US and Brexit had been victorious in the UK, despite the predictions of almost all the polls. The sense of relief across the West when Macron won was palpable. However, his defeat of Marine Le Pen in the presidential run-off was interpreted uncritically by too many, seen as evidence that progressive liberal democracy was in better health than advertised, and all that the West needed to staunch the bleeding was a socially liberal centrist with a bit more optimism about them. The Italian daily *La Repubblica* declared that Macron's election marked the "turning point" for populism—a particularly poor prediction given the subsequent collapse of the centrist vote in Italy's 2018 elections. The subsequent plummeting of Macron's popularity and his presiding over weeks of *"gilets jaunes"* social protests on Paris' streets suggests that these hopes of a centrist miracle, absent a genuine set of values and underpinning ideas, were misplaced.[5] We are going to need more than superficial re-brandings of the Macron variety. Fortunately, significant change is perhaps easier than we often imagine.

RESTORING THE MYTH

Eggs, Omelettes and the potential for major change

As the old saying goes, you can't make an omelette without breaking some eggs. Changing the political and economic system can be painful and difficult, and for that reason is often avoided, in favour of tinkering and optimising the system that we have already. What is curious, however, is that the current system was built on an awful lot of broken eggs, without any sign of an omelette being prepared. Since the 1980s, but particularly since the 2008 economic crash, the assumptions in Western political life have been torn apart. The welfare state, organized labour, taxation and inequality are all radically different today from what they were before, with serious and far-reaching consequences. It is difficult to find much evidence that all this change has been of significant benefit to most Westerners, or that it was at least systematically aimed at some better endpoint. Inequality has widened, living conditions for the vast majority of the Western population have plateaued, and only the wealth of a small minority has mushroomed. All this might have been forgivable, even happily consented to, if there had been any evidence that the West was enduring this pain in search of something better—if there were any evidence of a masterplan, or an identified utopia to which we are headed. There hasn't been, and so it is little wonder that the populist upsurge and disenchantment with mainstream politicians has been so pronounced—particularly against those on the progressive left who are meant to be on the side of the majority.

The greatest divide in Western politics is between mind and soul. The former concerns political visions which are based on a rationalist understanding of belonging and purpose. They are designed to appeal to the rational actor who operates according to their own best interest. The latter are those based on the idea of belonging as existential, for whom such identity transcends

215

rational policy making. Historically, most visions sat at neither extreme, but operated as a sort of trade-off between the two. Today, however, we have replaced the traditional divide along left-right lines with one between technocratic rationalists with nothing to offer the soul, and emotive populists prepared to abandon the rational. In such a contest, the soul will win out more often than the mind.

What previously helped bridge the gap was that sense of vision for the future. This will be harder to recreate than it was to establish before. As we saw in Chapter 2, there has been a collective loss of belief in the plausibility—let alone the positivity—of the West's moral endpoint, the universal application of the three republican values. People still speak of the arc of history, and it underpins assumptions about liberalism, but it is not felt as it once was. The decline of religion in the West has left a hole, as has the decline of Marxism and other secular ideologies. People are not so inclined to believe in myths any more.

The one exception is in the sphere of science and technology, the last great bastion of Western confidence in Western progress. Tech barons like Elon Musk still talk of a utopian future, albeit one based on endless technological, rather than societal, evolutions. It is no coincidence that the West's sunniest optimists, like the British scientist Matt Ridley and the Canadian-American psychologist Steven Pinker, base their confidence on progress achieved through science, medicine and technology. Ridley, for example, is positively blasé about climate change, believing that—given economic growth and scientific innovation—there is essentially nothing to worry about.[6] The advance of science and technology has indeed been extraordinary, and continues to develop apace, but it would be a mistake to place too much confidence in it as a solution to our existential difficulties. Already the businessmen (and they are all men) who run the tech giants are afforded a huge amount of power, with too

216

little oversight or public intervention. The scandal over Facebook's data mining and selling of personal information in conjunction with Cambridge Analytica has exposed definitively what had already been apparent to many for some time: tech companies are companies first, and they do not necessarily have the best interests of society at heart. Technological progress, particularly when driven by the private sector, is no substitute for a moral model of politics and society.

But all is not lost for the West in terms of recovering its myth of progress. Belief in science and technology alone is not enough, but it is symptomatic of a continued underlying confidence that some things, at least, can get better, driven by Western innovation. Recent decades are illustrative of the fact that the West is perfectly capable of overseeing hugely significant social and political change, even if that change hasn't been positive—witness the nigh-on elimination of the Greek welfare state—and even if Western leaders haven't worked out what they are trying to do in rehauling society. The hope is that we can still direct that energy into a great moral mission for the future. Specific policies are less important than the symbolic recommitment to concrete proposals for restoring the West's myth.

But what is that myth to be? In 2003 Pope John Paul II lambasted Europe—though it could have been the West more broadly—for its "loss of Christian memory" and heritage, characterizing Europeans as "heirs who have squandered a patrimony entrusted to them by history".[7] His vision of a restored Christian Europe, founded on Catholic political theology, is of course no longer plausible in an increasingly diverse and secularized West. However, his challenge did serve a reminder that the values discussed in this book have a heritage and foundation. We do not need everyone today to agree to an exclusively Christian sense of moral progress, but we do need a common understanding of the transcendent power of shared values. Our values, in other words, have to be proven to matter in practice. The less abstractly and the more concretely the West can demonstrate its moral commitments, the more powerful the myth will become. Progress becomes momentum, and the narrative of the West gathers steam as it lives out its own values.

Presented below are just three major areas in the values system of the West to which we could make concrete commitments in the 2020s and beyond. Many other values could have been suggested, but it won't surprise the reader to learn that the ones chosen here are the same three pillars of the West explored throughout this book: the sense of a moral endpoint; liberty, equality and solidarity; and universalism.

The future we want to see

Environmental politics provides a huge opportunity for the West to restore a myth of progress shared by all its citizens. At its heart, it is a story of potential redemption. The West has been disproportionately responsible for ecological and climate damage, which leaves it with a particular obligation to fix the mess it has created. It also has the best means to do so, enjoying the highest level of technological advancement in the world. Not only is there a redemptive case for resolving a situation of our own making, but it gives us the opportunity to use the technological revolutions that do still command a shared sense of optimism and progress. Furthermore, since this is an issue that will disproportionately affect future generations, this is a shared story—of a cleaner, safer world—that could revive the intergenerational solidarity currently vanishing in the West.

As we saw in Chapter 7, concern about climate change is one of the few areas that cuts across party lines for younger Westerners. In both the USA and Europe, younger voters are more supportive of national or international action to protect the environment. The lack of progress by Western governments has been grossly disappointing, but there is still hope for a more radical future. Already Paraguay, Albania and Iceland obtain all their electricity from renewable sources, and Norway is almost at the same level. California has legislated to achieve the same, and the Australian states of South Australia, Tasmania and ACT look set to reach 100 per cent renewable energy in the next few years.[8] Making this switch is obviously easier for some nations than others—hydro and geothermal electricity generation requires geographical features which are not present everywhere—but the aim to switch to renewable electricity sources across the West within the next twenty years is not implausible if governments make firm commitments to that end.

This state action needs to be combined with tougher sanctions for dirty and irresponsible industries. The destruction of so many habitats and public spaces by chemical and oil companies in Louisiana and elsewhere is an absolute disgrace, made worse by the paltry penalties (if any) exacted upon the culprits.[9] There can be no excuse for such companies: concerns that important industries—particularly the automotive industry—were incapable of adapting to legislation and ethical requirements have proven to be unfounded, at least among companies prepared to innovate and change their modes. The Chinese car market already boasts more than 400 different models of electric vehicle,[10] and in Norway almost 60 per cent of new cars sold in March 2019 were electric.[11] There is nothing to fear from pressing these industries harder to adapt and innovate.

The more positive aspect of this agenda is the burgeoning enthusiasm in Canada, the USA and elsewhere for a Green New Deal, which proposes investment and an economic stimulus package to simultaneously deliver more sustainable industries and challenge economic inequality. It does not yet have sufficient support in the US Congress to be deliverable, but it is an idea of growing popularity. Nine senators and more than sixty House representatives have officially backed it, and there is even polling evidence suggesting that as many as 80 per cent of Americans could back some version of the idea.[12] The appeal of a Green New Deal to Westerners should be obvious: it combines a moral vision and solidarity for future generations with an attempt at challenging contemporary economic inequality and the breakdown in solidarity. If it could be made to work economically—or even if it could be shown to operate at only a moderate loss in the current system—then it could be exactly the ambitious policy that the West needs to gain back its *raison d'être*.

Failing that, as an absolute minimum, the West's governments could commit more strongly to actually meeting the IPCC report target, with significant policy reforms; this would be a serious symbolic and practical statement of the West's solidarity with future generations and the wider world, and a clear step on the path to re-establishing an overall moral purpose and aim. Of course, the challenge goes far beyond the actions of states. The environment is a matter of personal and collective societal responsibility. There are already any number of campaigns in this space designed to make homes, businesses, places of worship, schools, universities and virtually every private organization play their part, alongside a long history of environmental campaigning leading to major changes without government intervention.

One interesting initiative making a difference without the need for state action has been the huge growth in social impact investing—not limited by any means to environmental projects, but they do make up a sizable portion of the practice. Social impact investing is an approach to financial investment, made with the expectation of making profit, but also intended to deliver a measurable and significant positive impact on society or the environment. The Global Impact Investing Network found that at least $228.1 billion was invested this way in 2018, around double the previous year's total, in a sign of mounting interest in the field.[13] The *Financial Times* praised the idea, profiling some of the most successful environmental projects in a special report.[14] This demonstrates that Western action on the climate crisis need not all be sacrifice and legislation—there are positive market- and civil society-based responses that could show the critical importance and collective responsibility of this issue. The more successes there are in this field, the greater the renewal of the West's idea of progress.

* * *

The environment poses an existential threat caused by human (and particularly Western) ecological negligence. The changing nature of technology and the workplace is more a cultural shift, but one which will also have major consequences for the future.

Historically, there is nothing new about emerging technology making vast numbers of jobs effectively obsolete, or radically changing the nature of normal patterns of human labour and behaviour. Most notably in Western history, the Industrial Revolution changed large parts of the West from a predominantly rural society based on agriculture to an urbanized society based on industry. Vast internal migrations completely transformed Western societies and previous modes of belonging. We may now be reaching that point again, but it is more dangerous than before. The Industrial Revolution gave rise to new industries that eliminated or reduced the need for many previous jobs, but it also created new, very intensive industries that required huge workforces. The new revolution in artificial intelligence and robotics is completely different: instead of replacing one role with new roles, it is eliminating the need for human employees altogether.

To put this in perspective, in 1955 seven of the top ten American employers were sustained by the demand for vehicles.

All required large workforces to deliver industrial products. In 2017, only two of those companies were still in the top ten, and only sixty of the Fortune 500 of 1955 remained on that list in 2010.[15] Today, most of the largest employers are retail chains or tech giants, and the majority of money and market share is dominated by firms with comparatively small workforces. Google, for example, has fewer than 100,000 employees in 2019. Compare this with General Motors, which had over five times as many employees when it topped the Fortune 500 in 1955—at a time when the US workforce was more than 50 per cent smaller.[16] To be an entrepreneur now means running industries that require nothing like the workforces of the past. It is often said that huge parts of the US Rust Belt and its equivalents in many other Western nations are angry with politicians for sending their jobs abroad.[17] There is some truth in that, but far more have been lost to robotics—to the simple fact that many jobs can be done more cheaply, consistently and safely by machines. As technology advances, this is only likely to become more common, and to affect more than the blue-collar jobs with which it is often currently associated as a threat. Various countries are already experimenting with automating minor, routine matters of justice like traffic offences, removing lawyers and judges from the equation in all but the most contentious cases.

As with every previous economic revolution, this is causing and will continue to cause major disruption and pain. People are losing jobs; whole towns built around particular industries are losing their purpose, and are being forced to reinvent themselves or die out. In much of the West, these transitions, which have been underway for decades, and are possibly now accelerating, have seen rather too little care from the state. The seeds of discontent in areas that have started voting for anti-establishment parties were largely sown by Western governments failing to demonstrate that they had any intention of redistributing the economic gains of technological advance and globalization to those areas that had lost out. There was no meaningful sign of collective solidarity, or of much forward planning for progress to a better future.

There are things that can be done here. The new knowledge economy will require a highly educated workforce. For one thing we need a recommitment to the value of solidarity, a theme that is the focus of the next chapter. For another, the way for the West to survive and thrive through this momentous upheaval will be for it to commit to the future it wants to see. Rather than bending over backwards and allowing any company with an app to abnegate all social responsibility, there needs to be more of a focus on shaping the economy and political order around the new employment and tech realities. Trade union membership is in decline, and much collective bargaining has been systematically broken in parts of the West—though not everywhere: the French unions, for example, remain powerful. In a gig economy where people's jobs are linked to irregular hours, new labour laws and collective organizations are needed. New, more responsive unions for gig workers would be a start. Pushing back against new-age firms and their dubious employment practices would be better still. Best of all would be a comprehensive plan and policy to better establish codes of conduct on how the revolution touches ordinary people. This policy should be underpinned by an international body—since the internet makes the tech revolution a fundamentally international endeavour. The Cambridge Analytica scandal revealed the tip of an iceberg in how ill-equipped most Western states are to deal with cyber issues. Models of public scrutiny and law enforcement are scrambling to keep up and are too rarely fit for purpose. If we can change this in a decisive way, we can re-establish our shared understanding of the society we wish to see.

Moral internationalism

It may seem odd to look at ways of renewing the West outside its borders, but in truth that is one of the most Western possible responses. The West has always, for good or ill, looked to spread beyond itself and transmit its values to others. That is hardly surprising given that universalism is a distinctively Western characteristic. It is not just that the West is committed to a moral endpoint for itself, based on liberty, equality and solidarity, but that it believes those values to be universally applicable, and that others should be on the same journey. For the West, the case study for the depth of its values is how it treats the wider world, but recent years have seen it turn inward. The EU has come to suffer from "enlargement fatigue": the progress in helping to develop new members—with robust democracies, strong economies and a flourishing civil society—has slowed, if not stalled. Beyond Europe, there has been an increased reluctance to intervene abroad or to meet international aid commitments. There is plenty that could be done to change this, and to restore a level of moral internationalism.

One is close to home. Western commitment to supporting democracy and state building in the Balkans is essential. Bosnia and Herzegovina, Serbia, Macedonia, Albania, Montenegro and Kosovo are all facing serious challenges, not least a crisis of legitimate leadership and a struggle to establish a civil society strong enough to build a functioning democracy. A worrying 78 per cent of Bosnians are currently in favour of violent protest as a means of securing urgent political reform.[18] In the 1990s and 2000s, the EU and USA played a major role in peacekeeping and rebuilding after the Yugoslav wars—albeit after a disappointing lack of effort to prevent genocides in the first place. This work has continued, particularly via charities and other NGOs working on peace and reconciliation.

However, we are some way short of the USA's stated commitment in the 1990s to a "Europe: whole and free", which is no longer a key foreign policy objective in Washington. The EU's efforts to foster democracy and liberalism seem to have slowed to a crawl. This is immensely dangerous; the Balkans remains a powder keg region that could explode at any moment, with devastating consequences. Step one for the West in rediscovering its moral purpose must be to re-engage in the hard process of reconciliation and democracy building. The encouragement of civil society, particularly a functioning independent media, is essential. The EU has a critical role to play here, and could make a strong case for itself as an agent of European peace and prosperity by redoubling efforts to bring the remainder of the West Balkans up to the same standards it has already helped to emerge in the former Yugoslav states of Slovenia and Croatia—hardly perfect states, but they have shown real signs of economic development and green shoots have come up of a growing, authentic local democratic and civil society culture. The populist anti-capitalist left in Slovenia, for example, has shown signs of being able to translate street level activism into legitimate political platform, with a functioning party (Združena levica).

The task of furthering democracy and economic development on the West's borders also extends south and east from Europe into Africa and the Middle East. The Schuman Declaration, the founding document of the European project, talks explicitly of Europe's (admittedly paternalistic) obligation to develop Africa. There are models to build on here, particularly the formation of the Union for the Mediterranean, a process driven with great enthusiasm by the French president Nicolas Sarkozy in the 2000s. This has resulted in around fifty co-operative regional projects between EU, Middle Eastern and North African states, mostly focused on economic development, sustainability and civil projects, particularly around the role of women. In contrast to the

EU, this institution has a less ambitious remit and a far smaller budget, and is purely inter-governmental, with decisions made by consensus among the forty-six members. Imagine, then, how much more the EU could accomplish along the same lines.

The model could be expanded relatively easily. To do so would not only be a sign of the West's commitment to global development, but would also be of mutual value. National and continental populations in the developing world are growing dramatically, without the healthcare or subsistence infrastructure to sustain that level of growth. The result will be a greater strain on resources and, likely, an increasing stream of forced migration to the West. This makes supporting developing states both a good moral thing in and of itself today, and an imperative for the future; a failure to act now is to store up more crises to come. As with the environment, this is a matter of justice in terms of intergenerational solidarity as much as it is an immediate necessity.

Foreign aid has come in for serious criticism in recent years. The economist Dambisa Moyo hit headlines for her book *Dead Aid*, which she argued that government-to-government foreign aid, while good for resolving immediate natural disasters, otherwise foster corruption, conflict, a culture of dependence, and a diminishing middle class.[19] Much of her analysis is less than convincing, and the call to phase out all such aid within five years is both entirely implausible and globally dangerous, given how much of the aid is tied into crucial disease prevention programmes. The book does, however, add fuel to the fire for critics arguing that foreign aid lines the pockets of dictators with Western citizens' hard-earned taxes. The truth is that the mission of aid has often been done badly, but it is clear to see how essential it is to the broader identity of the West—and there has been ample evidence in this book of the breakdown in Westernness when crises of equality or solidarity arise.

Paul Collier's *The Bottom Billion* offers some concrete examples of how we can move away from official aid to other forms of development.[20] The poorest billion people on earth, according to Collier, are kept in four poverty traps that can only be resolved by intensive effort on the part of richer countries. He shows that this is not only a moral issue, but also an imperative to stave off hard-headed economic disaster, given the cost to other countries when states fail. In Collier's model, breaking the poverty traps requires aid, but also several non-financial kinds of development: military intervention on occasion—as in Sierra Leone in 2000—as well as preferential market access for the poorest states, and in particular the sending of skilled administrators and governance experts to help build the necessary political leadership.

It has to be recognized that these arguments are open to accusations of neo-colonialism and a modern reimagining of the "white man's burden". My response to this is that, given the past culpability of Western states in the economic, environmental and military damage done to much of the developing world, there is a moral obligation to repair and restore. Even were that not the case, the gap between the richest and poorest nations is now so enormous, not least in technological terms, that it is not plausible for it to narrow without a conscious commitment by the West to the development of the rest of the world. The United Nations, for example, has warned that unless we close the gap in science, technology and innovation, it will prevent many of the Least Developed Countries from attaining the 2030 Agenda and its Sustainable Development Goals, which is likely to significantly hinder any efforts at building a future green economy.[21] Fortunately, that same issue also provides a possible hopeful model for the future, in the form of the Technology Bank for Least Developed Countries, established in 2017. This should avoid some of the worst risks of neo-colonialism precisely because it is a real partnership between developing and developed countries, in which the former have real input into what they want and need to set their own goals.

One issue that is likely to hinder efforts at change in the developing world is the crisis of international debt. For the majority of African nations, for example, the cost of borrowing exceeds the rate of domestic growth, which is slowing across most of the continent as the 2010s close, while interest rates are rising. This has happened before: in the mid-1990s, much of Africa was largely excluded from the global financial system due to a mountain of unpayable public debts. The solution reached in 2005–6 was a forgiving of debt on so-called "Heavily Indebted Poor Countries". The results for much of the following decade were very positive: the debt burden was significantly reduced, good policy was introduced and many of the thirty African countries that received debt relief saw significant positive growth and development.

The 1953 London Debt Agreement provides another model of significant debt restructuring, in order to rebuild West Germany after the war. That accord wrote off roughly half of all Germany's pre- and postwar debts, making other portions interest-free or seeing interest significantly reduced. This move, alongside Marshall Plan loans from the USA, was critical in kick-starting a desperately struggling West German economy, which in turn helped to ease the process of European reconciliation through the emerging European project. Public debt is a barrier to economic development, but also contributes to richer countries locking poorer ones in poverty traps. Finding ways to refinance or forgive these debts would be a strong stance for international solidarity, and may at any rate have long-term and security and economic gains for the West.

* * *

Beyond purely economic and financial intervention abroad, promotion and protection of human rights is probably the most prominent symbol of the West's commitment both to international morality and to the universalism of republican values. In many ways, human rights are the secular legal embodiment of the West's values, although those values themselves have a Christian heritage; the human rights movement was originally largely driven by Christian intellectuals seeking a legal embodiment of Christian notions of human dignity.[22] This combination of symbolic power and legal enshrinement is a potentially powerful one for protecting and renewing the spirit of the West.

In the decades since the Universal Declaration was first published, there have been many different advances in the Western approach to human rights, including the EU's Charter of Fundamental Rights. However, it is troubling that these advances now seem to be coming into question. A number of Western states, including the USA, have undertaken policies on asylum seekers and border controls that Amnesty International believes breaches the 1967 Protocol to the Refugee Convention, which has been part of US law since 1980.[23] The European Court of Human Rights, meanwhile, has been held up as a *bête noire* of much of Europe's political right, not least among the Brexit-supporting right in the UK. This weakening commitment to human rights is worrying precisely because it suggests that the values represented by that notion are unimportant. When Western politicians put human rights on the backburner for the sake of neoliberal economics, or because refugees are deemed to be a security threat greater than the powerful West can endure, the message sent is that neoliberal economics and security are the cardinal values of the West—not liberty, equality and solidarity. Yet this will not do as a new narrative for the West, because—as we saw in the chapters on the EU and USA in particular—the utopia of neoliberal growth and perfect security is a fair-weather mythology. It has nothing to do with dignity or identity (only a negative identity of "othering"), which leaves

Westerners with nothing to believe in or to sustain them when economic performance or security takes a plunge.

Resisting that abandonment of Western values will require a fundamental recommitment to human rights, both at home and abroad. The deal struck between the EU and Turkey on refugees is one example of a pragmatic arrangement betraying Western ideals. Turkey's recent record on human rights is appalling, including significant restrictions on the press and political opponents, up to and including credible allegations of government complicity in unlawful killing,[24] as well as ongoing reports of human rights abuses in Kurdistan. Turkey is no safe place to divert refugees, let alone to pay billions of Euros for the privilege. A tougher and more robust defence of human rights in the international sphere—even if, as in the case of Syrian refugees, it inconveniences the West—is essential. There should be firm blocking of efforts to undermine or reduce the authority of international human rights courts that can reign in the worst temptations of nation states.

Often, the measure of values' power or insignificance is how they are applied when there is nothing to gain. Assisting development and democratization abroad has long-term potential benefits for the West in economic and strategic terms, as could a new approach to international debt. Taking in refugees, on the other hand, presents no immediate benefits to a host nation at all. Indeed, unlike most other forms of migration, it involves accepting migrants purely on the basis of their circumstances. Refugees tend, by definition, to come with complex needs, including poor mental and physical health. In addition, while it would be unfair to lay the blame for all of the world's 20 million refugees at the feet of the West,[25] it cannot be denied that the West has been especially culpable in both the environmental and the war-related damage that has led to many of the world's most significant refugee crises, particularly today in the Middle East.

With that in mind, what does the West's record look like as a moral leader on migration? The answer is decidedly mixed. The UK is among several Western states that has used the "systematic deployment of destitution and indefinite detention as forms of border management", in the words of the theologian Anna Rowlands.[26] This has included detaining asylum seekers in camps prior to assessing their claims and banning them from working to support themselves. These tactics have become worryingly mainstream. The most egregious example comes from Australia, where the state does everything in its power to detain asylum seekers, going beyond anything the Europeans have yet accomplished by intercepting them at sea and putting them (including children) in detention camps on Nauru, a different sovereign country. Reports from the camps drew international condemnation after regular reporting of a crisis from healthcare professionals, including reports of children making repeated suicide attempts.[27]

That is just the treatment of refugees who do get taken— many do not. In 2017, the twenty-eight member states of the EU gave asylum (or some equivalent protected status) to 538,000 people. This is an assuredly large number, but the burden has by no means been shared equally. Astonishingly, over 60 per cent of those refugees were taken by Germany alone—325,400 people were granted protected status in Germany that year. Among the other larger EU member states, the UK took 15,700, Italy 35,100, and France 40,600. Taken as a proportion of their own population, Germany, Austria and Sweden took by far the most, each settling more than 3,000 refugees per million of their own population. At the other end of the generosity scale, Slovakia took just ten refugees per million of its population; Poland and the Czech Republic each took fifteen per million. The UK took 240 per million, as did Bulgaria.[28]

There are positive stories in the West of generous leadership on refugees, particularly in Merkel's Germany, but the overall picture has been one of taking every possible move to dehumanize and deter asylum seekers, regardless of the merits of their case. This cannot be acceptable for the West as a moral leader committed to liberty, equality and solidarity. It stands in stark and unfortunate contrast to the pride that some Western nations once took in their commitment to refugees. Lord Alf Dubs was a child refugee from a Czech Jewish family taken in by the UK thanks to Nicholas Winton's *Kindertransport* to escape the Nazis. In 2016, as a Labour peer, he proposed an amendment to the new Immigration Act to offer safe passage to unaccompanied refugee children. The amendment eventually passed in Parliament, but was controversially abandoned by the Home Office in 2017 after resettling only 350 of the original target of 3,000. This stance against refugees, or even, apparently, against more humane processing procedures, undermines the whole sense of the West as having a moral purpose. The use of detention facilities for the most vulnerable makes a mockery of any commitment to liberty or solidarity.

There is a challenge, of course, in reconciling delivery of this Western solidarity with the equally Western notion of liberal democracy—which entails opposition. Germany, Canada and Sweden have all demonstrated that with proper planning it is possible, though not easy, to take in large numbers of refugees, but not without provoking a certain degree of serious popular dissent. Solidarity with asylum seekers requires political bravery, but to be really sustainable it also needs a sea-change in public opinion. This is easier said than done, but it is worth noting that, despite some political costs, the vast majority of Westerners continue to support taking in refugees fleeing warzones. The Pew Research Center found in 2018 that 77% of people in the EU countries surveyed back this stance, versus 21% who did not; there was majority support for granting asylum in every polled EU member state except for Hungary. In the USA, the same survey found 66% in favour versus 29% against.[29] So there is hope to build on for a new, healthier public narrative towards migrants. Part of the process must be changing the tone of the debate on refugees—from a reluctance to help, to renewed pride in the West's moral purpose.

* * *

Leadership from the EU in all these arenas of foreign intervention will be crucial for the health of the West, because the EU is the institution most ambitiously and explicitly founded on the three key Western pillars. As explored in Chapter 3, it was not so long ago that a series of triumphalist books claimed the EU represented the future superpower to rival the USA, with an economic model that could compete with the biggest national economies while retaining a social model that valued health, family and society. Those days now seem to be past, and while the EU has a critical role to play in the future of the West by reining in backsliders like Hungary and helping to develop further-flung parts of the world, it may be that the EU is past its apex, and will need to settle for a less ambitious endpoint than its great advocates had hoped for. After all, the genius of the European project has been an ability to reinvent itself to meet the needs of the time. In the 1950s, the reconciliation of France and Germany was a key goal; in the 1980s, the rehabilitation of Spain and Portugal was critical; and in the 2000s, it was bringing the new Westerners back into the fold. It may be that in the 2020s the EU can rediscover a purpose beyond itself once more. Alternatively, it may be time for new models.

Many of the challenges that the West is facing are transnational and imposingly enormous. Climate change, threats from extremist Islamism and Russia, and the shifts in global economics—including global economic fraud, theft and tax dodging—are all bigger than the capacity of any one Western state, even a super-state like the USA, to deal with alone. Whether through the EU, NATO, the UN, the Council of Europe, the Union for the Mediterranean, or another body that does not yet exist, something supranational will be required to meet these future existential challenges. If the European project of the 1950s provides any model, it is that determined efforts to build a moral project with a clear mission can work—so long as its member states are prepared to make the necessary sacrifices, and brave enough to commit to something. The courage to take up moral internationalism is currently lacking, and until that changes, the West is going to struggle to confront the global issues before it.

Restored liberty and equality at home

The need for a new moral internationalism is about demonstrating the depth of the West's values in its dealings with the rest of the world—essential for continued belief in universalism. The nature of an introspective crisis, however, is that it also requires domestic changes. In particular, to prove its commitment to a moral endpoint, the West needs to restore, front and centre, the trio of republican values. As we've seen throughout Part Two of this book, solidarity is in the most difficulty of the three, which is why the final chapter deals in depth with how to restore it. There is much, however, that can be done to support the other two values.

The West's commitment to freedom has never been entirely clear cut. Isaiah Berlin's famous differentiation of positive and negative freedoms has been a critical fault line in Western political discourse. One model is particularly prevalent in the North American context, and to some extent in Australia, where frontiersman ideas of independence loom large in the public imagination: the idea that maximum freedom means simply being left alone, truly independent and self-sufficient. This has also become, at least in principle, a defining feature of the neoliberal economic models governing the West, which have looked to strip back any regulation or public interest of corporations to a minimum, in a competitive free market. There has always, however, been another vision of freedom, and not only on the political left. In this model, liberty is about achieving one's own potential and making one's choices to the best of one's talents, with the recognition that it is not always possible to do so without outside assistance. Two people, one of whom has a fortune spent on their housing, health and education, the other growing up in abject poverty, might both be able to enjoy negative freedom from interference, but—through no fault of either individual—one is far more likely than the other to be able to fulfil their own potential, and enjoy positive freedom to "do".

A critical insight of Catholic Social Thought, which has spread to Western ideas more generally, is the notion of the common good: not a utilitarian idea of what is best for the majority, but rather a recognition that humans cannot achieve the fullness of their potential as atomized individuals, no matter what the libertarians might dream. In other words, it is the idea that we operate in essential networks of relationships and structures that can either empower us to enjoy the freedom of self-actualization, or can enslave us in traps that we cannot escape. The West at present has all too many such traps. But that does not absolve individuals of the obligation to work hard and to struggle to get where they want to be—the concept of self-actualization in the common good does not mean that everything is simply given to you. However, it does recognize that the West cannot truly stand as a bastion of liberty without breaking down some of the structures that prevent people from fulfilling their potential.

This includes a hard look at the West's entrenched educational inequality. A report from UNICEF entitled *An Unfair Start* looked at this issue across the West and returned some stark findings in 2018. Its very first line notes: "In the world's richest countries, some children do worse at school than others because of circumstances beyond their control, such as where they were born, the language they speak or their parents' occupations."[30] One of the report's main findings is that many Western countries have huge gaps in education equality at the point when children start school, and that these gulfs of opportunity are never bridged. One of its key recommendations is the provision of high-quality preschool education, regardless of social status. It also reiterates one of the 2015 Goals for Sustainable Development: "By 2030 [countries should] ensure that all girls and boys complete free, equitable and quality primary and secondary education leading to relevant and effective learning outcomes".[31]

Meeting this goal would be a clear sign of commitment by Western states to encouraging freedom through the best available opportunities, regardless of parental circumstances. A broader goal to eliminate child poverty in the West would be even more ambitious and difficult to deliver, but would be an even more impressive effort. It should be deeply concerning that, according to Eurostat, "in 2017, an estimated 24.9% of children in the EU-28 were AROPE [at risk of poverty or exclusion] compared with 23.0% of adults (18–64) and 18.2% of the elderly (65 or over)".[32] The fact that there is already a sustainable development goal to address this inequality shows that this is not an international failure to identify a moral purpose for the West—what we are seeing is a failure on the part of national governments to commit to that moral purpose by applying the West's values in practice.

There are plenty of other examples on which we could draw to reinforce commitment to positive freedom by breaking structures preventing it, notably economic inequality (see Chapter 10) and the extraordinary levels of personal debt on which so much of the Western economy is based. In the UK, for example, a TUC report found that the average UK household had more than £15,000 worth of debt (not including mortgages), the servicing of which accounted for more than 30 per cent of household income.[33] It is going to be difficult for people to take up training, or take risks with new businesses, or even to raise families, with that sort of burden round their necks. And there has already been some recognition of the need for a more humanized, responsive model of economics and politics that will allow people to fulfil their own potential—in fact, this viewpoint appears in a great many political programmes. Theresa May attempted to make it the focal point of her government before she and her administration became too bogged down in the impossible morass of Brexit negotiations. In a September 2016 speech, she announced a plan to "set Britain on the path to being the great meritocracy of the world", a place "where advantage is based on merit not privilege; where it's your talent and hard work that matter, not where you were born, who your parents are or what your accent sounds like." She wanted positive freedom for all in Britain—for it to be somewhere "where everyone has a fair chance to go as far as their talent and their hard work will allow."[34]

Unfortunately, putting such rhetoric into practice has proven difficult, and not only for May's government. Nevertheless, the hope is there, and the idea is understood; now we just need someone brave enough to make the tough choices needed to realize it.

* * *

Just as liberty is not an uncontested Western value, so too equality can be understood differently in different Western political visions. The rise of identity politics in the Western context has been one response to the demand for equality, and one that applies not so much to individuals as to communities. When the statistics show that black Americans are, as a group, likely to be significantly poorer (in terms of both mean and median income), more likely to be incarcerated, more likely to be in a violent confrontation with the police, and more likely to be unemployed, it is not surprising that this provokes a reaction. Campaigns to assert minority identities cannot easily be split from the recognition that while the West stands for equality, some Western groups are systematically disadvantaged.

We could look at almost any minority group across the West and propose policies and measures committing the West, both concretely and symbolically, to its values. The one that stands out as the most hopeful at present is the struggle for gender equality. As explored in Chapter 5, there has been a huge surge of public attention in recent years around this issue. The #MeToo campaign helped to spark a major public conversation about sexual harassment. In 2018 one of the consequences of this was the Time's Up Movement, which has gathered hundreds of volunteer lawyers and a defence fund of more than $20 million. What long-term impact this might have is too early to know, but it has served to highlight that there is much left to be done if the West wants to be known for its valuing of equality. So too has wider discussion of gender equality issues at the end of the 2010s, including the gender pay gap and analysis of the make-up of corporate boards and senior management.

Beyond the general conversation re-energizing the fight for gender equality, there have been some promising examples of concrete reforms that could be easily rolled out more broadly. For example, the UK and Germany have both introduced legislation designed to name and shame businesses with a gender pay gap. Since 2018 in the UK, all companies with more than 250 employees have had to report their pay gap each year; since 2017 in Germany, every company of over 200 employees is obliged to provide workers with data on the average pay of comparable staff, if they request it. To improve the balance at governance level, as of 2018 Austria demands that the board of any company with 1,000 employees must have at least 30 per cent women members (and at least some men). To help overcome barriers presented by parental leave and gender-unequal family demands, Sweden, Germany and Denmark have all introduced major parental leave reforms designed to encourage men to take a greater share of the statutory leave and the burden of early-years child support, helping to reintroduce mothers to the workforce.

In the political sphere, France, Slovenia and Belgium have all introduced legislation designed to ensure more equal representation between men and women among parliamentarians and local councillors. In Slovenia this has been accomplished via a quota system and a training programme for women candidates. In Belgium men and women must be equally represented on electoral lists. France has introduced a local-level system whereby teams of men and women are elected as binominal candidates, to guarantee gender balance in municipal authorities.

None of these policies alone can overcome all of the struggles for equality, and you cannot simply legislate a problem out of existence. However, you can raise the prominence of the issue, and show your commitment to tackling it. Policies can help within a broader campaign to change culture. The West needs a fundamental recommitment to the idea of equality. These policies are not enough to do that on their own, but they would all be a good start if they could be replicated across the West—both in and of themselves, and in providing a burst of energy and public attention for broader movements and campaigns that can sustain broader social change.

* * *

This is a critically dangerous moment for the West. It is slowly emerging from the economic crash, but if history tells us anything, it is that it is that revolution, state breakdown and explosion happen not at the nadir, but when societies are beginning to recover, and reforms are beginning to loosen the reins. That is the moment when people get out of survival mode and, with a little more time and freedom to consider their surroundings, begin to question why the system is like it is. That is the point where people begin to question why all the eggs have been broken, and yet there is little sign of the omelette we were trying to produce.

In other words, it is more important now than ever that the West recalls and lives out its fundamental values, and provides a strong answer to the question of where we are going. A fair criticism would be that much of what is presented above is a matter of legislation and state policy. But this is not a scattering of good ideas for their own sake—it is part of a broader reaffirmation of the moral purpose of the West. In one sense, the specific policies are far less important than the principle: making a case for and a sincere show of recommitting to the West's fundamental values, which are all that it has. Those values are unlikely to be taken seriously if they remain abstract, as we have clearly seen in the spiritual abandonment of the West by so many groups in Western society. To keep the myth alive and propel it forward, we need concrete achievements, like the policies above. Together they could form a powerful narrative on which to build the future.

10

RESTORING SOLIDARITY

The previous chapter discussed the need to restore a shared myth for the future. Yet such a myth cannot come from nowhere. To have any purchase and claim on the imagination of Westerners, it needs to build on what the West already has: those values that define what it is to be Western. To progress, we need a shared idea of what connects us. The full triplet of republican values is critical to a strong sense of Western self and purpose, but the key one is solidarity. So it is particularly problematic that, while all three values have gone wrong to some extent in the twenty-first-century West, solidarity has been particularly overlooked.

Without the ability to restore solidarity on a par with liberty and equality—if there is no belief that we are in it together—then there is little incentive to build a common future of liberty and equality. Solidarity is an idea of obligations: of what is owed to people within society. As we saw throughout Part Two, that sense of mutual obligation has broken down between generations, between economic classes, and between certain countries of the West and others—and it was never particularly strong between various majorities and certain minority groups. For the

West to rebuild the mission that defines and drives it, we will need to win back those who have ceased to believe that the West has their interests at heart.

There are three particular areas that need invigorating for this process to be successful. First, the West has become bad at talking about and embracing identity. Efforts to rebuild a meaningful solidarity are serially undermined by the poverty of our conversations around identities. Fixing our conversations about identity in Western public life is essential. Second, our ability to do that is limited by the disastrous collapse in civil society, which makes forming relationships of trust, or building a representative political system almost impossible. Finally, our Western economy needs a rebooting, to put it back into its rightful place as a tool in the service of the people, rather than their master.

Fixing the identity debate

Of course, for resurrecting solidarity, identity matters enormously. Robert Putnam has found that societies with less diversity have higher levels of social trust—in other words, people find it easier to harbour a sense of common interest and mutual obligation the more they can see of themselves in their neighbour.[1] Such group identities need not be rational; in fact, they very rarely are, as explored by Kwame Anthony Appiah's *The Lies That Bind*.[2] Nevertheless, they are fundamental to people's sense of self. Francis Fukuyama has called this the "soul aspect" of a person—that part of you essential to your sense of dignity.[3]

As such, efforts to suppress or ignore identity are neither sensible, nor desirable. The meaningful binding together of societies in the West will have to build on the positive energy that can be generated by the dignity and pride of identity belonging. Done badly, of course, identities can compete explosively and tear a society apart—Yascha Mounk describes national identity as a "half wild animal".[4] Yet the full suppression of such identities does not defuse conflict; it just prevents any positives from identity being used to empower society. This is an obvious lesson from history. Those regimes that have suppressed particular ethnic or religious identities have very rarely succeeded in eliminating those identities, and have often felt the disastrous consequences of that failure later on (Yugoslavia is a common example, but plenty of others are available). The French model of secularism is famed for its attempt to create a republican identity entirely detached from all religious identities. Yet France faces some of the most severe challenges with Islamist extremism, with an increasing ghettoization and sense of exclusion among French Muslims. As we saw earlier, almost half the French believe that Islam and French republican values are incompatible.[5] What hope is there for bonding together a notion of French solidarity under such circumstances? France is hardly alone in suppressing particular identities. The USA has never had the French difficulty in embracing religious identities—at least, domestically; it has frequently underestimated their relevance in foreign policy—but it has become worse over time at recognizing the importance of other identities, particularly racial.[6]

In some cases, there have, of course, been good reasons for supressing particular identities. Germany has very good reason to be wary of encouraging nationalist visions of identity in the wake of Nazism, as does Spain post-Franco. Many European states have to wrestle with a historic national identity associated with imperialism, colonialism and all its consequences. This has prompted various efforts at building solidarity without any underpinning identities. Communist Europe tried to eliminate national and religious identities in favour of an internationalist communist identity. The failure of that model was exposed by the West's recovery of Eastern and Central Europe in the 1990s, and the fact that some of the world's most virulently nationalist regimes are now found in former communist states. The philosopher Jürgen Habermas has tried to build a model of "constitutional patriotism" (*Verfassungspatriotismus*) that eliminates messy nationalist identity in favour of an attachment to liberal values and norms, over and above any specific identity claim. This notion has been influential in the attempts to establish a constitutional basis and a *demos* for the European Union, but the absence of any identity claim that fundamentally matters to anyone probably explains why such efforts have failed so comprehensively, and why national identity has returned even to Habermas' native Germany, including among a new generation of far-right nationalist parties.

In a mark of the West's confusion over how to treat the issue of identity, certain identities, particularly those associated with minority groups, are now viewed—at least on the political left—as holding a sacred legitimacy, their need for specific protection and promotion putting them in a separate category from majority identities. At the same time, other identities have been condemned as anathema—as too tarnished by some historic sin ever to be redeemed. Those associated with historic oppression are particularly likely to be condemned—for example, any notion of a white identity is open to the accusation of association with racism, colonialism and—particularly in the USA—slavery. This has also been applied, more contentiously, to national identities. This differential treatment of particular identities, whether positively or negatively, sits uneasily with the overall demand for equality.

Between celebrating some identities, and denying the validity of others, the West has created a scenario in which it is finding it difficult to have real conversations about identity. In fact, this confusion—about why some people are allowed to have identities and others are not—is now so hard-wired into public discourse that a meaningful encounter has become far more difficult than it should be. James Walters, an Anglican priest and senior lecturer at the LSE, has noted the difficulty of getting today's students to have real discussions about their differences: "We have taught young people to respect one another's beliefs in a way that has now paralysed the conversation".[7] All perceived efforts to privilege or criticize any one belief structure have been ruled out of court. We are not going to get a proper debate about the place of identity in Western cohesion until we can begin to accept that it is natural for people to privilege those things which are sacred to them, and also that this will create differences of viewpoint between them.

As we saw in Chapter 2, the changing place of religion further complicates the picture. The shared moral and religious assumptions that underpinned much of public life in previous eras made it relatively easy to establish shared values that cut across ethnic and national markers of blood and soil. The US Declaration of Independence could state baldly and without much fear of contradiction that it was "self-evident" that all men were created equal, because when it was declared almost everyone was either Christian or at least saturated within a Judaeo-Christian worldview supporting the same. (One claim by the famous clergyman and educator Ezra Stiles in 1760 was that there were 445,000 Congregationalists in New England in 1760, out of a population of only 450,000—even allowing for some academic scepticism as to their precise accuracy, these figures speak to Christianity's dominance in society at that time).[8] The fact is that many of today's "self-evident" values—secularism, humanism, human rights, democracy—are no such thing, but evolved logically from within a Judaeo-Christian intellectual tradition of human dignity in the image of God. Detached from that cultural base, their principle—and the fact that we should all, naturally, believe in it—is not nearly as clear-cut as many would like to insist.[9]

Politics and much of Western intellectualism has been slow and often ineffective in responding to these shifting identities.

Too often, identities have been sidelined and ignored, despite the fact that they remain the only known reliable basis for building political solidarity. An apocryphal story from the world of International Relations holds that in the early 1970s the CIA rejected a research proposal from an analyst in Tehran, who wanted to conduct a study of Iran's emerging religious leaders. The CIA's grounds were that this amounted to useless sociology; as a result, US intelligence was left scrambling to understand the new political dynamics after the Islamic revolution of 1979. While the West—burned by experience—is starting to recognize identity as an important feature of foreign policy, it is often bizarrely overlooked domestically, as if identity only mattered or applied to non-Westerners. The first step towards re-establishing a truly strong solidarity across the West is to acknowledge that the most durable historic model for doing so rests on empowering identities, not suppressing or ignoring them. Foundational to any attempt to build a sense of an "us" will need to be a conscious effort to encourage public debate on the nature of that "us-ness". This must move beyond merely sharing differences, or bland efforts at presenting empty lowest-common-denominator values; identities must start actively critiquing and challenging one another.

Ignoring identity is not simply missing an opportunity for building solidarity, it is playing with fire. The American historian Carl Degler saw the danger back in the mid-1980s. Witnessing an academic elite that thought it could dispense with any study of identity in history, he warned his colleagues, "We can write history that implicitly denies or ignores the nation-state, but it would be a history that flew in the face of what people who live in a nation-state require and demand ... If we historians fail to provide a nationally defined history, others less critical and less informed will take over the job for us".[10] The same charge could be laid against today's historians, but also against social theorists, politicians, civil society leaders and religious leaders. By failing to engage in proper public discussion of identity, we leave all the dangerous potential of such identities to others, to use and abuse as they see fit.

Rebuilding civil society

Crucially, the ability to have these conversations relies on there being spaces, both institutional and intellectual, where such debates can take place. To fix the identity question, we need not only to acknowledge its importance, but also to have a healthy civil society. The lack of this in the 2010s has been problematic both for identity discussions and more broadly for the West. So if we wish to rescue the West by resuscitating solidarity, we will also need to rebuild civil society.

To understand what's gone wrong with civil society, we need only look at one stereotype, which does seem broadly to hold true: the contemporary left believes the solution to every problem is more state intervention, and the contemporary right believes the solution to every problem lies in more freedom for the market. What both approaches have in common is that they tend to undermine solidarity. Centralized state policies, while necessary for addressing many issues, have also helped to feed the tendency in Western politics towards excessive technocracy, operating at too great a distance from the citizen and abandoning the importance of those crucial identity markers. As for market-based solutions, we have seen the result throughout this book: in the name of economic expediency, we have created a society of gross and damaging inequalities, a labour market that prizes the power of corporations over any societal costs they might inflict, and people reduced to no more than economic units in a machine. The big state deprives communities and groups of the dignity that comes from participation; the state rolled back to make way for the market undermines any sense of collective societal responsibility for our neighbours.

There is nothing new in identifying such a split, and the traditional solution has lain in the power of a third force—civil society—to hold the other two accountable and keep them in balance. In the 2010s, however, civil society is as weak as it has been in decades. As several previous chapters have explored, there has been a complete erosion in institutional belonging, particularly among the young and outside the middle classes. Robert Putnam's seminal *Bowling Alone* explored this in depth, and is widely quoted, but in the almost-twenty years since it was published there is now significant data to suggest that the trends Putnam identified (the breakdown in social capital, the struggles of clubs and unions) have only got worse. In fact, the conservative American writer Timothy P. Carney found in *Alienated America*, a conscious effort to revisit Putnam's thesis, that there is now an extraordinary class breakdown in belonging. According to Carney, every other college-educated American is a member of a team, club or society, versus just 31 per cent of those who have no more than a high school education.[11] Both statistics represent a serious drop from the 1960s, but it is the less educated group that has seen the biggest reduction in civil society belonging.

The trend is by no means limited to the USA. Wealthier Westerners in general are much more likely than poorer Westerners to be part of societies and other forms of institutional belonging—and this is a problem for solidarity because the wealthier only make up a small minority of society as a whole. Membership of civil society organizations is down across the board, but particularly among poorer and younger Westerners. It is perhaps no surprise, then, that a sense of local community and social solidarity is also much lower among poorer and younger Westerners. In the USA, among self-identifying lower-class respondents to the 2010–14 World Values Survey, only 4% said that they "completely trusted" their neighbourhood, while three times as many of the "upper-middle-class" respondents said the same. A full 39% of the lower class trusted their neighbourhood "not very much" or not at all; the figure was just 18% for the upper middle class.[12] In the Netherlands, only 52% of the working class believe that most people can be trusted, versus 79% among the upper middle class; in New Zealand, the equivalent is 43% versus 64%; and so on.[13] Overall levels of trust vary—and the World Values Survey has more than one question on trust, each capturing different aspects in different countries—but the overall trend is clear: wealthier people have far higher levels of trust (a key part of solidarity) than those who are less well off.

Without societal trust, there can be no sense of mutual obligation, and no solidarity. We need a robust civil society to help build those relationships and that sense of belonging, between both groups and individuals. Some countries have tried harder to encourage this than others. Germany, for example, has a flourishing scene of *Vereines*—registered voluntary societies ranging from football clubs and shooting clubs to self-help groups. This is a positive, but the changes in Germany's patterns of employment and, in particular, the undermining of organized labour has led the sociologist Oliver Nachtwey to suggest that Germany is witnessing a significant social decline. Political parties and trade unions are falling apart, partially concealed by relative economic success.[14] It is not as simple as encouraging people to join a football team: civil society necessarily also requires a rejuvenation of political and economic intermediary bodies to increase social trust and work towards meaningful solidarity.

It is also important not to spare charities and civil society from basic critique. An independent enquiry for the UK's Civil Society Futures project noted in its final report that "We know that civil society is not yet fit for this purpose [deepening democracy and social participation], it lacks confidence, skills and credibility and there are too many examples of charities and institutions being part of the problem".[15] Sadly, many of the most significant bodies in civil society have been discredited in part through their own failings. The Catholic Church is one of the biggest providers of social belonging (not to mention practical charity and aid) in the Western world, but has seen much of its public credibility hammered by sex abuse scandals, and a seeming inability to provide the transparency and responsiveness necessary to restore public trust. Abuse scandals have also rocked institutions including the international development charity Oxfam, the BBC, and sports teams in various countries. The media, a key pillar of a functioning civil society, is also suffering a trust crisis. Some of that has been driven by politicians attacking the media for perceived (or often real) bias, but much has been self-inflicted too. "Most U.S. adults, including more than nine in 10 Republicans, say they personally have lost trust in the news media in recent years", according to a report from the Knight Foundation. Most put this lack of trust down to a perceived lack of accuracy and excessive bias in the media.[16] Efforts to reform civil society need these organizations to get their own house in order. A culture of trust requires hard evidence of transparency and capacity to deliver.

Assuming that those commitments are in place, the next great need for restoring civil society is support for efforts to revive local community. The Indian economist Raghuram Rajan calls this a need for "inclusive localism."[17] During a previous period of Western existential crisis—the late 1920s and early 1930s—the same observation was made of the need for strong local organizations that could return dignity and agency to communities denied them by the competing poles of market and state. Back then, this realization led to the development of the idea of subsidiarity in Catholic Social Thought, which—as we saw in Chapter 3—was explicitly built into the European project at its founding. Following the 1931 papal encyclical defining subsidiarity (the duty to devolve what can be devolved), Christian Democrat parties, Catholic guilds and trade unions developed, which—alongside a revival of Church-based civil society organizations—would be instrumental in the rebuilding of much of Western Europe after the Second World War. We may now have moved away from organized religion leading the way, but we ought to be seeking new means of following this long-established Western principle: that subsidiarity is essential to the thriving of local communities, and that the alternative can be destructive to the point of "grave evil".[18]

There are models on which to build here. The time has seemingly come for community organizing: alliances of local organizations and individuals—including faith groups, businesses and community groups—engaged in door-knocking and deep listening exercises to establish issues of local importance, and then to act upon them. The movement in the UK has developed training models and resources, with thousands of people engaged directly in addressing local issues, and significant projects in education, employment, housing and mental health now under way. Supported by government funding, the intention is to have 10,000 trained community organizers by 2020. A linked movement is now underway in Australia. A different but also influential model of community organizing is already well known in the USA. Not only does community organizing deliver campaigns of local importance, but there is evidence that people who participate in such programmes become significantly more civically engaged and committed to local volunteering in their area and beyond.[19] Furthermore, these relationships are long-term, enduring long after the initial campaign has ended.[20] Higher levels of participation also lead to greater sense of community and of "psychological empowerment", the sense of being capable of accomplishing meaningful change.[21] In other words, we can be confident that these sorts of programme are not only nice in principle, but actually effective in building solidarity and the confidence to deliver change.

As argued in Chapter 1, many Westerners feel powerless, excluded, and hopeless when faced with the system as it stands. The psychological empowerment needed to believe that you can change the system—and therefore to participate in civic and political engagement aimed at creating that change—is difficult to forge at a national level, but is far easier to create at the local level.[22] It is easier to care about and act upon particular concerns in our own immediate area and among people we know. But by building the confidence to work towards local improvement, it is possible to give people faith in their capacity to confront the bigger issues, too. Having local communities empowered to find radical solutions to problems is the most effective means of building the confidence and expectation of solidarity among citizens that they will need in order to re-engage at a national or Western level.

There are other models besides community organizing. One related but more faith-based enterprise, also in the UK, is the Near Neighbours programme run by the Church Urban Fund, a charitable agency of the Church of England. This scheme provides small grants for local community projects, with a particular focus on bringing together disparate segments of society (particularly across faith lines) for interaction and joint action. Research from the University of Cambridge's Woolf Institute has studied the programme favourably, suggesting that it had successfully created a greater sense of community in target areas, and built the capacity of those involved to do further work, in the "snowballing effect" described above.[23] Innovative new civil society approaches are also being pioneered around social care and housing in particular. Various countries across the West are experimenting with the Dutch *Buurtzorg* (community care) model of nursing, which sees trained teams of nurses deliver care in the community, primarily through health coaching; this allows older people to live independently and in their communities for longer.

Some of the most interesting initiatives have been efforts to confront the need for housing while also seeking specifically to provide richer social cohesion. La Borda, a co-operative housing scheme in Barcelona, provides low-cost housing with an emphasis on coexistence and social collaboration. Vrijburcht ("Free Castle") in Amsterdam was founded in 2007 and features not only fifty-two homes but also a café, workspaces, a theatre, a nursery and a small harbour. Again community living has been emphasized. The Empty Homes Doctor scheme in Leeds is a not-for-profit business working closely with the city council to help local people turn disused properties back into homes— empty homes often blight communities, particularly those recovering from economic difficulties. There are other examples from across the West. However, these tend to be fairly small-scale, and—as ever with civil society—to be impactful they will need help from both state and market. All of the successful housing schemes mentioned have been reliant to some extent on local government support, whether financial, in terms of expertise, or simply moral support through backing a risky enterprise that might have failed. Most also required the sponsorship or support of banks and businesses. Part of the challenge facing us in the rebuilding of civil society is the difficulty in engaging people who have got used to the idea that local community is an irrelevance in their lives.

David Cameron, on becoming the UK's prime minister in 2010, promised a new approach to "Big Society", and indeed a government paper was produced on how to build it. There were interesting outcomes, including the establishment of Big Society Capital, which works with investors to provide social investment to charities and local groups. But the notion was only ever partially implemented. The promises to empower local government, charities and mutuals were severely undermined by the severity of the imposed austerity cuts, which have devastated local councils' ability to deliver services, and significantly increased the burden on charities—particularly those that previously received substantial support from central and local government, such as adult care services.[24] For many of Cameron's critics, the "Big Society" amounted to nothing more than an ideological cover for cutting funding from key services. Had the scheme been properly funded and delivered, it might have served as a valuable means of kickstarting civil society.

* * *

A final critical note on the collapse of civil society is the plight of local politics and political parties. Chapter 6 looked in some depth at the plight of the social democratic left, but the malaise has spread across the political spectrum. A constant refrain across the West is that politicians have become too remote from the people they serve, and that parties seem ill-equipped to deal with a changing political landscape. This in part explains the sheer volatility of party structures across the West. New parties are arising all the time, and often with sudden political success and decline. In 2017 Emmanuel Macron briefly sparked hope among socially liberal centrists when he first won the French presidency and then achieved major parliamentary success with his new En Marche! party—but this was fool's gold. There is little evidence that that party has any cohesive deep ties into local communities. On the contrary, in common with a number of recent European success stories, it is a party built around the personality of the leader, with limited genuine interaction between members and leadership.

Even well-established parties have been reduced to vehicles for individual cults of personality, in which leaders talk a good game of reaching out to the base, but with limited evidence of any meaningful control of the party, or even a functioning check and balance, by members or constituents. We are kidding ourselves if we think that the US Republican Party leadership sees its rank-and-file membership as anything more than a funding opportunity and a base of hard-pressed volunteers for electioneering. The fate of the Italian Christian Democrats should perhaps have served as a warning. The dominant party in Italian politics from 1944 until 1994, the DC then collapsed utterly under the weight of the enormous Tangentopoli corruption scandal, simply ceasing to exist. Since then, the centre right of Italian politics has been a procession of schismatic personality cults, most prominently that of Silvio Berlusconi; today that political space only survives as a less successful version of the populist right.

Part of the challenge may lie in the very idea of party politics as the most effective means of connecting collective will to national policy. In *Post-Democracy* (2004), the political scientist Colin Crouch put forward the idea that there are still free elections in the West, but little meaningful power held by citizens—and, as we saw in Chapter 4, even the presence of free elections is coming into question in parts of the West. Citizens have lost influence on political decisions, lobbyists, economic elites and a small core of professional political managers hold all the power.[25] It is a frequently observed cliché among political scientists that there is no Latin word for democracy, and no Greek word for representation. Our model of representative democracy, based on political parties, made a great deal of sense before the advent of mass communication, and when political representatives really were local people expressing the views of their neighbours. It arguably makes little sense today.

In this new technocratic politics, the electorate is reduced to something like the viewers of reality TV. They can vote and have some limited swaying power, but the rules, events and design of

the programme remains resolutely under the control of the production company. It is little wonder that politics has taken on
the appearance of entertainment, with larger-than-life characters
savouring the drama of it all. In too many cases, we—the electorate—participate in the sense of voting and following the twists
and turns of those personalities, but do not truly contribute to
the running of our Western democracies. No surprise, then, that
so many elections are now being won by perceived outsiders—
those with larger-still personalities who claim to present a break
with our unrepresentative system. The Brexit referendum in the
UK—a democracy with a non-proportional system of representation—was significant precisely because it represented a genuinely rare vote giving people a real opportunity to determine the
future course of the nation.

Breaking the cycle may require something more radical than
just the building of the voluntary sector. Again, there are emerging models we can use as inspiration. The Leap Manifesto in
Canada is one effort at gathering together a range of community
activists across different segments of society to produce a cohesive political programme: a set of demands that better reflects
the interests of grassroots organizations. At the time of writing
it has gathered more than 50,000 signatories, including from a
wide range of disparate community groups—faith and belief
groups, trade unions, citizens' initiatives, smaller political parties,
student unions, environmental campaigns, and indigenous peoples. Individual signatories include some of Canada's leading
intellectuals and activists, such as Charles Taylor and Naomi
Klein, as well as some of Canada's best-known celebrities. The
ultimate success of this scheme remains to be seen, but it represents an interesting new approach for sourcing policy decisions:
across coalitions of actors working on the ground.

A more radical approach comes from the G1000 experiments.
These began in Belgium in 2011, randomly selecting 1,000 ordi-

nary citizens—in proportions reflecting the national demographics—to meet and discuss the future they want for national politics. In the original Belgian model, the process began with a public consultation of 6,000 citizens, using an online questionnaire; the second phase saw their ideas presented to the summit of 1,000, before a third phase in which a subset of thirty-two participants formed a panel, developing specific policy proposals reflecting the conclusions of the summit. Experiments at local and regional levels in the Netherlands, Canada, Poland, the UK, Ireland, Spain and elsewhere have proven that the model works, insofar as it is capable of producing consensual policies that reflect local concerns, and it has had a long-term positive impact on citizens' political participation.[26] Unlike referendums—which offer a vote but little participation in the selection of its options—these proposals allow the public to be involved at every step in the creation, selection and delivery of policy. This might provide a more radical and responsive means of invigorating local (if perhaps not national) politics, even if there is little evidence thus far of governments acting upon the locally responsive policies it produces.[27]

On a less radical but more deliverable scale, there is the option of participatory budgets—local people voting on the allocation of a portion of the local or municipal budget. The system has been gaining in popularity since first being introduced in Brazil in the late 1980s. In Iceland, this has seen more than €2 million euros devoted to projects chosen by local people. Scotland is proposing to go much further, with at least 1 per cent of local budgets reserved for participatory budgeting by 2021. Various models have been tried in parts of the USA, Canada, and elsewhere. So far, the amount designated for participatory budgets has been relatively small, and the approach has been marginal to the wider political process. A relatively small shift could see major gains in terms of community engagement with local government and involvement in identifying how taxes should be spent in the best interests of the community.

Social trust is certainly aided by a better engagement with identity, but it also requires institutional frameworks to allow relationships to form, and for local communities to find a sense of dignity and means of participation in their own renewal. This rebirth of civil society at the local level can in turn fuel empowerment and participation at a national and even international level. As such the West will need to commit greater investment in and support for civil society initiatives, while also requiring charities and third-sector bodies to up their game in terms of transparency and efficiency. To re-engage people in their own communities will also require a new approach to politics, one that takes people out of the game show audience and more into a genuinely participatory space. There are plenty of available models to explore, and we have looked at just some of them— but certainly the system as it stands is unfit for purpose. It must change if we are to restore solidarity in the West.

"In it together" economics

So far this chapter has explored the need for a new approach to identity and belonging through the reinvigoration of civil society, including local politics, to help provide people with dignity and empowerment within institutional frameworks where relationships of political and social trust can develop. We cannot ignore, however, the destructive role that our current economic model has played in undermining solidarity. It is impossible to persuade people that we are a collective group if our economic policies appear to wage constant war on particular segments of society. Unsurprisingly, then, the final element necessary for renewing solidarity will be addressing certain aspects of that economic system.

First and foremost, we need to relegate the science of economics back to its proper place. Economics is a tool, a means of achieving society's ultimate ends. It should never be an end in and of itself, yet too often that is what it has become. Chapter 3 on the struggles of the EU shows the full consequences of failing to recognize that truth. How did we ever end up in a situation where economists were deciding to force more than half of Greece's pensioners below the poverty line, over the wishes of a democratically elected Greek government? Far too often, policymakers begin with the economic question and then work backwards to the social consequences. This attitude has been utterly destructive to creating genuine solidarity, since people rapidly come to perceive (correctly) that their interests are not being served—sometimes leading them to turn away from politics, and sometimes leading them to turn on each other. To that end, there are at least two areas we could look to in bringing economics more in line with the social goal of solidarity: addressing inequality, and fostering social responsibility.

* * *

It is long past time that Western governments take fundamental action to confront economic inequality. Its consequences are undermining any ability for society to pull together. The links between inequality and poor health, crime and anti-social behaviour, teenage pregnancy and low levels of social trust have been demonstrated at length by a number of writers, perhaps most prominently by Wilkinson and Pickett in *The Spirit Level*.[28] Aside from moral debates over the fairness of the distribution of wealth, this creates a basic pragmatic need to resolve the issue: unless inequality is addressed, communities will continued to be damaged, and it will become increasing difficult to form any meaningful level of social trust in the West. The stakes for politics and public life are as high as it is possible to imagine, as we saw with Walter Scheidel's provocative suggestion that inequality can only be reversed once the social strain is so unbearable that it has provoked state collapse or war.[29]

Even taking a more positive view than Scheidel, and allowing that policies can address inequality, we have now reached a point where decades of worsening economic inequality have probably taken us beyond the point where minor tweaks to the system will be adequate. The challenge here is something of a chicken and egg situation. Inequality fuels a social breakdown in solidarity, yet to really address inequality will require a significant political and economic programme that—in Western democracy—will only likely be possible if a significant proportion of the population can be persuaded to fundamentally alter the system. It is hard to achieve such shifts without strong social solidarity, yet inequality is itself one of the factors undermining social solidarity. Here we see the complex interaction of identity, civil society and economics. The most powerful tool for breaking inequality lies in cultivating a powerful Western identity that unites people to the point where inequality becomes intolerable to the conscience of the group. It is, accordingly, little surprise to see that those states with the highest levels of social trust also tend to have the highest commitment to challenging economic inequality.[30] As my colleague at Theos Nick Spencer has put it:

> Inequality becomes harder to justify, harder to sustain, if you find yourself breaking the same bread and drinking the same wine with others you would otherwise never meet ... At the final count, it is only here, not in the cataclysmic circumstances of war, not in the chirpily optimistic calls for democracy or debate or leadership, but in the deep, pre-political understanding that we are called to be with one another, that we will find a political answer to the problem of inequality.[31]

This is absolutely right, but nevertheless it would be naive to leave the whole process to a resuscitation of civil society. There is a role for the Western state in showing a symbolic commitment towards rectifying the situation it has been instrumental in creating. This book may demand more than lip-service on human rights, but at least Western governments have sent the right message in signing up to international treaties, establishing courts and appointing special envoys. There have been virtually no similar signs of commitment to resolving economic inequality or rethinking Western economics in the 2010s.

At the very least, as a matter of basic justice, there needs to be a much more honest approach to taxation and regulation, one based on international reciprocity, that prevents money earned in one country from being favourably taxed in another. Disappointingly, at the end of the 2010s relatively few bold solutions have been put forward even on the political left—and almost none on the political right. That could change if the US Democrats elect one of their left-wingers to fight the next presidential election, or if the various social democratic parties across Europe could stage a revival—but at present there is lack of leadership and imagination in politics to challenge this. This is disappointing, but perhaps unsurprising given the reliance of Western economies on the neoliberal free market economics that structures them.

One of the most destructive trends in contemporary Western economics has been the belief, popularized by the Chicago school of economics in the 1970s, that the only true responsibility of businesses is to maximize profits. As the economist Paul Collier notes, this was quite a departure from how corporations had been seen previously, and also flew in the face of basic common sense.[32] Corporations do not exist in a vacuum—they are part of society, not separate from it. They rely on society as much as they provide to it, in terms of infrastructure, housing, education and healthcare. The consequences of their decisions are also deeply felt in society. If a company closes, the effect is not only on the immediate employees but also on the wider community. If a company is responsible for pollution, or puts a strain on local infrastructure (for example, seriously increasing traffic), the consequences will be felt by the local community, too often short on options for holding that company to account.

If we are to restore solidarity through tackling inequality, we need a reformed sense of stakeholder capitalism: a form of capitalism recognizing that all those with an interest in the results of a business ought to have a say in its governance—not only shareholders but also employees and the local community. Some parts of the West have been better than others at instilling this philosophy. Germany, for example, has led the way in worker representation on boards, as we saw in Chapter 9. The casting vote stays with the shareholders, but the practice has still been shown to have an impact on wage inequality and to help counter many corporations' short-termism, instead forcing them to take a longer view in light of the needs of their employees.[33] There is reason for optimism, therefore, that such equality-driven measures can build solidarity. A number of other nations, including Austria, the Netherlands, Hungary, Sweden and Norway, insist that a third of supervisory board members be drawn from the workforce—a positive step, although insufficient to force significant change if a majority of shareholders are opposed. We might expect such policies from the Northern European states, but the Hungarian example is notable. Elsewhere in this book, Hungary has been criticized for a breakdown in solidarity, yet on this specific issue there is some hope. This is a helpful reminder that solidarity is a complex issue, and that making gains in one area will not prevent other policy areas from undermining the process. None of these measures will be enough on their own, but must be delivered as part of a culture of renewed commitment to solidarity.

While certain Western nations have taken promising steps towards stakeholder capitalism, there has been a disappointing lack of progress elsewhere. While campaigning to become leader of the UK's Conservative Party (and so prime minister) in 2016, Theresa May called for employee representatives on company boards and for legally binding votes from shareholders on executive remuneration.[34] Alas, beset by her own party's infighting and the struggles to deliver on Brexit, nothing has come of this worthy rhetoric on making big business more socially responsible. Nevertheless, the fact that May was prepared to argue for such a move provides some hope in a UK context.[35] Though she is not expected to win at the time of writing, the same goes in the USA for the 2020 Democrat presidential candidate Elizabeth Warren, who has made commitments to a package of "accountable capitalism" policies.

The point of involving employees in the running of your business is twofold. First, it makes business leaders at least partly accountable to those who will be most affected by their decisions; second, by acknowledging that we are all in this together, business included, it helps to increase social solidarity. This works both ways: shareholders need to hear from the real people whom their votes will affect, and employees benefit from the opportunity to see why decisions are made and by whom. One logical extension of this model is in employee-owned businesses, one of the most prominent being the British department store chain John Lewis. Interestingly, employee-owned companies well outperform most of the FTSE 100, suggesting that, even beyond the advantages for solidarity, there is also evidence that companies have little to fear from such moves in terms of undermining their profits.[36] Another logical conclusion of stakeholder capitalism is that we desperately need to restore some semblance of organized labour, particularly for vulnerable workers in the gig economy, who are too obviously at risk of exploitation.

However, business does not only need to interact better with its workers. If it is to become part of a socially responsible and connected community, it also needs to embrace its broader responsibility to its community. Too often the balance between local government seeking to encourage business and holding business to account weighs in favour of the former. The levels of pollution and environmental damage in parts of the American south are the direct and predictable consequence of local government's encouragement of dirty industries and inadequate efforts to police their environmental impact, in desperation over the local economy.[37] Of course it is a good thing that businesses are able to bring jobs and investment to Louisiana. It is self-evidently bad that corporate negligence has wiped out whole habitats— previously public spaces used for fishing and integral to people's quality of life. It is frankly appalling that air toxin rates along the Mississippi River are so high that the whole area between Baton Rouge and New Orleans is now known as "Cancer Alley".

Tougher responses to businesses with negative social impact will be essential for repairing public trust in the West. This includes on environmental damage—the Volkswagen emissions scandal is just one example among far too many of companies showing scant regard for the health of ordinary people—but the West also needs to crack down on broader corporate negligence. It cannot be right that those who were the most direct culprits of the financial crash have seen little or no consequences for actions that brought misery to millions of citizens, while it is the latter who have suffered the impact of austerity. Whether through redressing this injustice or through some other move, there is most certainly a need to prove to the majority of Westerners that executives and financiers have genuine skin in the game—that is, that they will pay for the consequences of their actions. If a bank in trouble will simply be saved by the state, then all the risk for its dodgy financial dealings is borne by the taxpayer—solidarity cannot thrive when such obvious injustice is woven into the fabric of Western society.

If the above solutions seems to stray into the old adage that the left will always call for further state intervention, it is worth noting that there is plenty of work that civil society can do to confront negative economic trends. One of the more interesting examples has been the astonishing success of the UK's living wage campaign. Started in 2001 as an initiative of the community organizing group Citizens UK, this movement identified that the statutory minimum wage (just £3.70 an hour at the time) was inadequate to live on in London, and sought to persuade local businesses to become "living wage employers" that took seriously the need to pay their employees not only legally, but adequately. The campaign gathered huge support from both other local groups and local government, and over 5,000 organizations have joined the campaign to date, gaining status as living wage employers, including over a third of FTSE 100 businesses. This remarkable victory for civil society is a perfect example of the mutually reinforcing cycle of solidarity: following a grassroots organization that identified local need and built a campaigning coalition, change was wrought in company policies, which in turn will help to lower the wage gap nationwide. This success will build the sense that companies care about employees, and that we are all in this together, which should in turn encourage further organization.

A culture of solidarity

Pope John Paul II captured the Catholic intellectual approach to the idea of solidarity perfectly when he stated that solidarity is "not a feeling of vague compassion or shallow distress at the misfortunes of so many people both near and far. On the contrary, it is a firm and persevering determination to commit oneself to the common good; that is to say the good of all and of each individual, because we are all really responsible for all".[38]

265

Often solidarity in public debate is reduced to a bland sympathy. For the necessary restoration of a sense of togetherness in the West, something much more will be required: a hard, concrete, and deep-felt sense of collective responsibility; a commitment to action on behalf of the whole.

The UK's living wage campaign is illustrative of the point of this chapter more broadly. It is perhaps no coincidence Citizens UK was in its origins majority faith-based—the founding chapter of what became Citizens UK, the East London Communities Organisation, was formed primarily of churches and parishes, church schools, and Christian associations. Their membership may be in serious decline across the West, but faith groups are among the rare organizations in civil society that still have genuine local presence and the ability to bring people together across different racial, economic, class and other divides. Putnam and Campbell's research on American Christianity found that American Christians were both more generous—in terms of volunteering and philanthropic giving—and more civically engaged than other Americans. They concluded that the biggest single factor in this phenomenon was the relational network created by faith groups.[39] Their presence in virtually every American community, and their propensity to create networks in communities, is crucial to their success. They also have a deep identity, critical to their members' sense of self, which motivates them to act for a purpose—the whole impetus missing from the wider West today. Specifically, the tenets of faith give citizens an imperative to work actively towards making a difference, rather than observing dispassionately.

This is not to claim that faith groups are unique in this respect, and indeed we know that organized religion is playing a lesser and lesser role in Western life. But if we are to restore solidarity, then we need to replicate more widely the success of faith groups, in partnership with others, in Citizens UK's campaigns.

If churches, mosques and so on, whose power is declining, can still make a mark on Western solidarity, then surely secular civil society groups should be able to accomplish even more. The reason the call for a living wage has been so effective is that it harnessed the energy and moral imperative inherent in a strong identity, and channelled it through a civil society body able to focus this energy on a specific societal problem. The triplet of powerful identity, civil society structure, and the pursuit of the common good should work to restore solidarity anywhere in the West. The campaign has also built on the identified need of local communities, and the use of local actors—in other words, valuing and strengthening relationships in our increasingly individualized and transient world. This takes us back to John Paul II's distinction between our willingness and ability simply to acknowledge the humanity of others, and our commitment to knowing them and working together with them. Similarly, the Catholic priest and former Czech dissident Tomáš Halík noted in his Templeton Prize acceptance speech that the contemporary West has mistaken Jesus' great commandment:

> Tolerance is the secular translation of the Gospel injunction to love one's enemies. But when religious concepts are translated into secular language and concepts something is usually lost. In order to tolerate an unpleasant neighbour I really don't need to love him in any sense. It is enough for me to ignore him, since I don't care about him. We each have our own life, our own style, our own truth. A certain model of "multiculturalism" based on the principle of tolerance resulted not in a community of citizens, or neighbours, but in a conglomeration of ghettoes.[40]

Transcending this Western hollowing of tolerance—a tolerance short of love—will be hard. But it is essential work. How else can we re-establish the true point of politics and economics, which is to serve society? How else can we make solidarity a genuine aim of public life and an essential value of the West? If we carry on practising solidarity—or purporting to practise solidarity—as we have been, then there is no reason why it should be restored from its current crisis. Without committing to a true culture of active solidarity, the myth of the West will be impossible to recover.

AFTERWORD

The crisis of the West, as argued throughout this book, is an introverted, existential crisis. If the West collapses, it will not be because of some external enemy, but because it has betrayed itself and abandoned the values that once defined it.

In place of a proactive, missional West, the political sphere has become increasingly dominated by a technocratic, managerial mindset. Propping up a struggling political and economic system has become more important than questioning whether that system is still the best vehicle to deliver on the West's essential values. Symptomatic of this trend has been the fate of the EU, which began as an ideological construction with a very clear sense of its own missions and values, but has morphed over time into an economic model that has come to undermine its own mission. The three key markers of the West—its sense of moral progress towards a better future, its commitment to the three republican values, and its universalism—have each independently come to be misused or forgotten.

The economic crash of the late 2000s broke this sleepwalking cycle to some extent, insofar as it shattered the West's sense of total confidence in the benevolence and efficacy of our economic system. However, while that economic shock caused some soul-searching, it has led to relatively little long-term systematic change. In fact, on the contrary, the response to the crisis has been to further empower the technocrats, who sought to repair (or at least limit) the damage as quickly as possible, regardless of other considerations. The EU's response in Greece and its other "debtor nations" has been to dispense almost entirely with the niceties of democracy or the concerns for working and living conditions that strongly characterized the early European project. The solutions were dictated from the centre, with seemingly no concern as to the long-term damage that that might do, or indeed to the European notion of subsidiarity.

Should we not instead have had a serious rethink as to the basis of the models that had enabled or caused the economic crisis? This question is certainly widely asked, but hardly acted on at all. In the decade since the 2008 crash, we have seen most Western governments return to the same business-as-usual practices and assumptions that underpinned the collapse, with only some additional technocratic measures and institutions now in place. We have continued our existential sleepwalking—in terms of who we are, whether these models can really deliver the future the West wishes to see, and what exactly that future is.

We got here by a combination of our own choices and our own complacency. Choices have included the economic and policy options leaving the young and the squeezed middle feeling excluded or abandoned. Complacency has centred on the assumption of inevitable progress towards a happy cosmopolitan future. The end-of-history narrative still too prevalent among the American liberal elite, and the inability of the EU to see coming (or do much to prevent) the autocratic turn of its newer member states, are just two examples of a poor assumption that Western values will prevail, in place of a concerted effort to ensure that they do. Our crisis is one of the West's own making: a creeping failure over successive decades to live out the values of the West, as we have lost sight of our moral mission.

AFTERWORD

It's true, of course, that the 1990s and 2000s were defined on Western terms, while there were very few opposing visions of the future. Perhaps now, as the second decade of the twenty-first century comes to a close, there are clearer signs that this may be changing. Some of the negative economic choices that have been made in the West are, of course, reflective of the West's attempts to keep up with rapid economic gains elsewhere, including advances in technology and manufacturing in Asia, largely driven by Western-led globalization. The re-emergence of Russia as a significant and real military threat, and the constant vigilance required to keep violent Islamism in check, are just two factors that have undermined the Western sense of security and self-confidence.

After years of annexing parts of neighbouring states without much concern for Western opposition—Abkhazia, South Ossetia, Crimea—Putin's Russia now poses a serious military threat. When Russia carries out assassinations on the streets of the West with impunity, as it did in poisoning Alexander Litvinenko in London in 2006, and Sergei and Yulia Skripal in Salisbury in 2018, this feeds the idea that the West is impotent in the face of blatant Russian aggression. Meanwhile, Russia's ideological and financial support for some of the West's more unpleasant ethno-nationalist parties (such as Jobbik in Hungary, Attack in Bulgaria and Golden Dawn in Greece) helps feed an embryonic but growing network of semi-authoritarian national-ist political parties in Europe. The Russian alternative is a dan-gerously appealing combination of socially conservative, high (ethno-nationalist) solidarity and capitalist economic gains—a trilogy of values that resonates with plenty of Westerners.

That said, we need to be careful to avoid over-generalizing. Poland's Law and Justice party is certainly nationalist, but also virulently anti-Russian; Orbán's Fidesz in Hungary has a hot-and-cold relationship of self-interest with Putin; and ethnonationalism, particularly in formerly communist states, is not the same thing as being part of a new Russian ideological bloc. Many of the parties that are more explicitly pro-Russian remain on the fringes of the political system. If the West's own vision can meet the same demands of solidarity that are so powerful in the world-view of Putin's Russia, it will be far less vulnerable to this assault from the right.

China—with far more economic clout than Russia, and a distinctive, non-Western ideological construction—is increasingly presenting a truly compelling alternative model. The authoritarian capitalist system has obvious appeal to any number of political elites in the developing world, for whom it represents the ability to maintain a political stranglehold while enjoying all the benefits of economic development. In truth, as the former Australian prime minister Kevin Rudd has noted, this is often little different in practice from Western efforts at development, which have preached freedoms at home, while turning a blind eye in the developing world.[1] There are any number of books and articles predicting that the twenty-first century will be dominated by China.[2] However, within the West at least, there seems little enthusiasm for a Chinese model. As discredited as democracy and liberalism have become, no one serious is calling for authoritarian capitalism as the alternative, no matter how impressive China's economic performance.

We cannot, therefore, pin our problems on an emerging non-Western superpower; we have ourselves to blame for the power of China and the idea of China. If the PRC presents a threat to the West, it is not because its politics truly appeals to Westerners. Rather, the danger lies in the West attempting to outperform the Chinese economy, and so beginning to sacrifice parts of itself and moving closer to the Chinese model. If, for example, the West continues to strip back the hard-won working rights and conditions of employees, in order to reduce the costs for companies and corporations, this might aid the performance of those companies, but would also undoubtedly add to the rampant inequality and prioritizing of business over people that has characterized all too much of Western policy in recent decades. In other words, the threat from China is that the West's response to it will be a continued complicity in its own unravelling.

This book has sought to explore how the West was lost, and it has not been a story of "Others" or enemies. The West has not needed any outside stimulus to forget what it is and what it values. We have done that ourselves, and so this book is a story of Westerners. The damage from this "narrative amnesia" and loss of identity has been enormous, and more diverse in its victims than many commentators have perhaps recognized, as we can see in the range of "lost Westerners" explored in Part Two. However, what this book has also hopefully shown is that there is still a chance to win back the West, and to open a new chapter in its story. The West is still more Western than anywhere else, and it still contains kernels of hope. There are projects and policies and principles already alive that show the way forward, if only we can apply them more deliberately and more widely. More importantly, the great underlying values that define what it is to be Western still resonate to some extent; they can still be found everywhere in constitutions and manifestos. The challenge is to rekindle those sparks, in the hope of a new and restored model for the future West. Now more than ever, if the West is to survive, it needs to rediscover a powerful myth of its own purpose.

NOTES

FOREWORD

1. Oswald Spengler, ed. Helmut Werner, trans. Charles Atkinson (1991), *The Decline of the West: An Abridged Edition*, Oxford: OUP.
2. See, for example, Paul Valéry (1919) *The Crisis of the Mind*; and Henri Massis (1927), *Defence of the West*.
3. Richard Koch and Chris Smith (2006), *Suicide of the West*, London: Continuum.
4. Douglas Murray (2017), *The Strange Death of Europe: Immigration, Identity, Islam*, London: Bloomsbury.
5. Afua Hirsch (2018), *Brit(ish): On Race, Identity and Belonging*, London: Jonathan Cape.
6. David Runciman (2018), *How Democracy Ends*, London: Profile Books.
7. Today, by way of contrast, the West struggles to raise any resistance worthy of the name to rather more rampant abuses in Hungary and Poland.

1. WHAT THE WEST IS

1. Benedict Anderson (2016) *Imagined Communities: Reflections on the Origin and Spread of Nationalism*, 2nd edition, London: Verso, pp. 11, 7.
2. Oswald Spengler, ed. Helmut Werner, trans. Charles Atkinson (1991) *The Decline of the West: An Abridged Edition*, Oxford: OUP, p. 3.

3. Bill Emmott (2018) *The Fate of the West: The Battle to Save the World's Most Successful Political Idea*, London: The Economist Books.

4. Isaiah Berlin (1958) *Two Concepts of Liberty*, Oxford: Clarendon.

5. Edward W. Said (1978) *Orientalism*, New York: Pantheon Books.

6. Samuel Huntington (1996) *The Clash of Civilizations and the Remaking of World Order*, New York: Simon and Schuster.

7. Spengler, *Decline of the West*, p. 19.

8. Ibid., p. 1.

9. Richard Nisbett (2003) *The Geography of Thought: How Asians and Westerners Think Differently—And Why*, New York: Simon and Schuster.

10. The Greek note is important because it shows the flaws of seeing the West as a geographical entity. Greece today is part of the West, and ancient Greek philosophy is part of the intellectual tradition that forged the West, but ancient Greece was not Western, because the West did not exist until much later. In the creation of the West, Greek philosophy and other threads were drawn together into a new intellectual space in the nineteenth century. Furthermore, we can call this heritage Christian rather than Judaeo-Christian, given the overwhelming dominance of Christian culture during that era.

11. Robert Pippin (1999) *Modernism as a Philosophical Problem*, Oxford: Blackwell, p. 26.

12. Jacques Derrida (1997) *Politics of Friendship*, New York: Verso.

13. Pippin, *Modernism as a Philosophical Problem*, p. 2.

14. Francis Fukuyama (1989) "The End of History?", *The National Interest* (16), pp. 3–18.

15. Dominic Lieven (1992) *The Aristocracy in Europe, 1815–1914 (Themes in Comparative History)*, Basingstoke: Palgrave Macmillan.

16. US Census 2017.

17. See, for example, the UK Office for National Statistics (ONS) report "Sexual Identity, UK: 2016", published October 2017. Available online (accessed 17/09/2018 09:13): https://www.ons.gov.uk/peoplepopulationandcommunity/culturalidentity/sexuality/bulletins/sexualidentityuk/2016

18. See James K. Harter et al. (2016) "The Relationship Between

Engagement at Work and Organizational Outcomes 2016 Q12 Meta-Analysis: Ninth Edition", Gallup, April 2016.

19. See, for example, F. Herzberg, B. Mausner & B. Snyderman (1959) *The Motivation to Work*, New York: Wiley.

20. Gallup (2013) "Americans Unsure if Best Times for U.S. are Past or to Come", 2 January 2013.

21. Richard Koch and Chris Smith (2006) *Suicide of the West*, London: Continuum, p. 23.

22. See, for example, Patrick J. Deneen (2018) *Why Liberalism Failed*, London: Yale University Press; Jan Zielonka (2018) *Counter-Revolution: Liberal Europe in Retreat*, Oxford: OUP; and Edward Luce (2017) *The Retreat of Western Liberalism*, London: Little Brown.

23. Yascha Mounk (2018) *The People vs Democracy: Why Our Freedom is in Danger and How to Save it*, London: Harvard University Press, p. 5.

24. Ibid., p. 105.

25. Ibid., p. 108.

26. Michael J. Abramowitz (2018) "Freedom in the World 2018: Democracy in Crisis", Freedom House, available online (accessed 17/09/2018 10:32): https://freedomhouse.org/report/freedom-world/freedom-world-2018

27. Understood here as deliberately falsified news pieces produced for commercial or political gain.

28. Larry Siedentop (2014) *Inventing the Individual: The Origins of Western Liberalism*, London: Allen Lane.

29. Deneen's *Why Liberalism Failed* is only one of the latest in a long history of books that embody this argument, going back to the nineteenth century.

30. David Goodhart (2017) *The Road to Somewhere: The Populist Revolt and the Future of Politics*, London: Hurst.

31. Amy Chua (2018) *Political Tribes: Group Instinct and the Fate of Nations*, London: Bloomsbury.

32. Afua Hirsch (2018) *Brit(ish): On Race, Identity and Belonging*, London: Jonathan Cape.

33. *Citizens United v. Federal Election Commission*, 558 U.S. 310 (2010).

34. *Burwell v. Hobby Lobby*, 573 U.S. (2014).

35. Michael Sandel (2013) *What Money Can't Buy: The Moral Limits of Markets*, London: Penguin.

36. See IFOP (November 2015) "Les Français et la laïcité. Sondage Ifop pour le Comité national d'action laïque", available online (accessed 09/05/2019 15:29): https://www.ifop.com/wp-content/uploads/2018/03/3232-1-study_file.pdf

37. Sasha Polakow-Suransky (2017) *Go Back to Where You Came From: The Backlash Against Immigration and the Fate of Western Democracy*, London: Hurst.

38. Douglas Murray (2017) *The Strange Death of Europe: Immigration, Identity, Islam*, London: Bloomsbury, p. 5.

39. Jean-François Lyotard, trans. Bill Readings and Kevin Paul German (1993) *Political Writings*, Minneapolis: University of Minnesota Press.

2. WHAT'S BEEN LOST

1. The exact number seems to be contested, but was much discussed in 2015 during a dispute over whether Italy was going to tax Church properties. Most commentators placed it somewhere between 8,000 and 14,000 educational facilities, and just under 5,000 hospitals.

2. According to a critical report from MergerWatch and the ACLU, the Catholic Church ran 10.1% of US hospitals in 2011, up from 8.2% in 2001. In total there were 381 hospitals in 2011 with a Catholic identity. See Uttley et al (2013) "Miscarriage of Medicine: the growth of Catholic healthcare and the threat to reproductive health care", for ACLU and MergerWatch.

3. See, for example, from a UK context, Dame Louise Casey DBE CB (2016) "The Casey Review: A review into opportunity and integration", December 2016, available online (accessed 10/05/2019 15:22): https://assets.publishing.service.gov.uk/government/uploads/system/uploads/attachment_data/file/575973/The_Casey_Review_Report.pdf

4. For a summary of the results, see ONS (2011) "Religion in England and Wales 2011", available online (accessed 10/05/2019 15:23): https://www.ons.gov.uk/peoplepopulationandcommunity/culturalidentity/religion/articles/religioninenglandandwales2011/2012-12-11

5. The Pew Forum put it at 8.8% in Pew Research Center (2017) "Europe's Growing Muslim Population", 29 November 2017.

6. According to Statistics Finland's PX-Web databases (n.d.) "11rx—Belonging to a religious community by age and sex, 2000–2018", available online (accessed 04/06/2019 18:00): http://pxnet2.stat.fi/PXWeb/pxweb/en/StatFin/StatFin__vrm__vaerak/statfin_vaerak_pxt_11rx.px/

7. Reported by Divya Talwar (2016) "UK attitudes towards Islam 'concerning' after survey of 2,000 people", BBC Newsbeat, 23 May 2016, available online (accessed 10/05/2019 15:27): http://www.bbc.co.uk/newsbeat/article/36346886/uk-attitudes-towards-islam-concerning-after-survey-of-2000-people

8. A 40-nation study by Ipsos MORI found persistent, often dramatic over-estimates from the public about how many Muslims lived in their country. See Ipsos MORI (2016) "Perils of Perception", available online (accessed 10/05/2019 15:29): https://www.ipsos.com/sites/default/files/2016–12/Perils-of-perception-2016.pdf

9. Peter Berger (1968) "A Bleak Outlook is Seen for Religion", *The New York Times*, 25 February 1968, p. 3.

10. These projections and data on global religious change are drawn from Pew Research Center (2017) "The Changing Global Religious Landscape", 5 April 2017, available online (accessed 10/05/2019 15:31): http://www.pewforum.org/2017/04/05/the-changing-global-religious-landscape/

11. See Pew Research Center (2011) "Global Christianity: A Report on the Size and Distribution of the World's Christian Population", December 2011, available online (accessed 10/05/2019, 15:32): http://www.pewforum.org/2011/12/19/global-christianity-exec/

12. See British Social Attitudes (2017) "Chapter 12: Religion. Losing Faith", *British Social Attitudes 28*, available online (accessed 10/05/2019, 15:33): http://www.bsa.natcen.ac.uk/latest-report/british-social-attitudes-28/religion.aspx

13. Peter Brierley (2011) *Major UK Religious Trends, 2010 to 2020*, Tonbridge: Brierley Consultancy.

14. Pew Research Center (2018) "10 key findings about religion in Western Europe", 29 May 2018, available online (accessed 10/05/2019, 15:34):

http://www.pewresearch.org/fact-tank/2018/05/29/10-key-findings-about-religion-in-western-europe/

15. Leila Marchand (2015) "Plus de la moitié des Français ne se réclament d'aucune religion", *Le Monde*, 7 May 2015, available online (accessed 10/05/2019 15:36): https://www.lemonde.fr/les-decodeurs/article/2015/05/07/une-grande-majorite-de-francais-ne-se-reclament-d-aucune-religion_4629612_4355770.html

16. From 270,000 in the 2011 census to 468,000 in 2016.

17. Aleksandra Sandstrom (2017) "Faith on the Hill: The religious composition of the 115th Congress", Pew Research Center, 3 January 2017, available online (accessed 10/05/2019, 15:38): http://www.pewforum.org/2017/01/03/faith-on-the-hill-115/

18. See Daniel Cox and Robert Jones (2017) "America's Changing Religious Identity: Findings from the 2016 American Values Atlas", PRRI, 6 September 2017, p. 11, available online (accessed 10/05/2019, 15:50): http://www.pewforum.org/2017/01/03/faith-on-the-hill-115/

19. Ibid., p. 7.

20. Grace Davie (2002) *Europe, the Exceptional Case: Parameters of Faith in the Modern World*, London: Darton, Longman & Todd Ltd.

21. World Values Survey (2014), "Wave 6: 2010–2014", V147 Religious Person, available online (accessed 10/05/2019, 15:51): http://www.worldvaluessurvey.org/WVSOnline.jsp

22. Theos (2013) *The Spirit of Things Unseen: Belief in Post-Religious Britain*, London: Theos, p. 12.

23. Gallup International (2015) "Losing Our Religion? Two Thirds of People Still Claim to Be Religious", available online (accessed 04/06/2019 18:07): http://gallup-international.bg/en/Publications/2015/223-Losing-Our-Religion-Two-Thirds-of-People-Still-Claim-to-Be-Religious

24. Pope Pius IX (1864) "Error 80", *Syllabus of Errors*.

25. Details of all the convention's discussions were recorded. On the specific debate over who backed the call for Christianity to be included in the constitution, see CONV 555/03 CONTRIB 244 "Contribution to the religious reference in the European Constitution" from Ms Hildegard Carola Puwak, Member of the Convention, European Convention Secretariat archives.

26. Peter Norman (2005) *The Accidental Constitution: The Making of Europe's Constitutional Treaty*, Brussels: Eurocomment, pp. 66–7.

27. Scott Thomas (2005) *The Global Resurgence of Religion and the Transformation of International Relations: The Struggle for the Soul of the Twenty-First Century*, New York: Palgrave Macmillan, p. 150.

28. Nicolas Sarkozy (2004) *La République, Les Religions, L'Espérance*, Paris: CERF, p. 155.

29. Speech delivered by Sarkozy on 20 December 2007 in Rome.

30. In a *Libération* article, December 2007—an accusation he would later repeat in Jean Baubérot (2010) "The Evolution of Secularism in France: Between two civil religions", in Linell E. Cady and Elizabeth Shakman Hurd (eds), *Comparative Secularisms in a Global Age*, Basingstoke: Palgrave Macmillan.

31. Quoted in Eugénie Bastié (2016) "Nicolas Sarkozy, le pape François, la laïcité et la religion catholique", *Le Figaro*, 21 March 2016, available online (10/05/2019, 16:00): http://www.lefigaro.fr/vox/societe/2016/03/21/31003–20160321ARTFIG00219-nicolas-sarkozy-le-pape-francois-la-laicite-et-la-religion-catholique.php

32. A motif Le Pen has used on several occasions, but perhaps most notably in a speech delivered to American conservatives, in which she declared, "France is in the process of passing from the eldest daughter of the Catholic Church to the little niece of Islam". Thursday 22 February 2018, CPAC event in National Harbor, Maryland.

33. Quoted by Emma Green (2017) "The Specter of Catholic Identity in Secular France", *The Atlantic*, 6 May 2017, itals in original. Available online (accessed 10/05/2019, 16:04): https://www.theatlantic.com/international/archive/2017/05/christian-identity-france/525558/

34. AfD (2016) "MANIFESTO FOR GERMANY: The Political Programme of the Alternative for Germany", approved at the Federal Party Conference held in Stuttgart, 30 April–1 May 2016.

35. See Nick Spencer (2017) "Donald Trump", in Nick Spencer (ed.), *The Mighty and the Almighty: How Political Leaders Do God*, London: Biteback.

36. Kai Arzheimer and Elisabeth Carter (2009) "Christian Religiosity and Voting for West European Radical Right Parties", *West European Politics*

(32:5), 985–1011; and Tim Immerzeel, Eva Jaspers & Marcel Lubbers (2013) "Religion as Catalyst or Restraint of Radical Right Voting?", *West European Politics* (36:5), 946–68

37. See Nadia Marzouki, Duncan McDonnell, & Olivier Roy (2016) *Saving the People: How Populists Hijack Religion*, London: Hurst.

38. Timothy Peace (2016) "Religion and Populism in Britain", in Marzouki, McDonnell & Roy (2016) *Saving the People*; Steven Woodbridge (2010) "Christian Credentials?: The Role of Religion in British National Party Ideology", *Journal for the Study of Radicalism* (4:1), 25–54.

39. Speech at the Downing Street Easter reception, April 2014.

40. Letter to *The Daily Telegraph* (2014) "David Cameron fosters division by calling Britain a 'Christian country'", 20 April 2014, available online (accessed 10/05/2019, 16:14): https://www.telegraph.co.uk/comment/ letters/10777417/David-Cameron-fosters-division-by-calling-Britain-a-Christian-country.html

41. Jean-Paul Sartre, trans. Carol Cosman (1991) *The Family Idiot*, Chicago: Chicago University Press, vol. 4, p. 346.

42. Friedrich Nietzsche, ed. Walter Kaufmann (1974) *The Gay Science* (1882, 1887), New York: Vintage, pp. 181–2, para. 125.

43. Emmanuel Levinas (1986) "The Bible and the Greeks", in Levinas, trans. Michael B. Smith, *In the Time of the Nations*, Bloomington and Indianapolis: Indiana University Press.

44. See Nick Spencer (2016) "The Religion of Christianity and the Religion of Human Rights", in Spencer, *The Evolution of the West*, London: SPCK.

45. Grace Davie (1994) *Religion in Britain Since 1945: Believing Without Belonging*, London: John Wiley & Sons.

46. John Gray (2018) "The rise of post-truth liberalism", *Unherd*, 5 September 2018, available online (accessed 18/09/2018 16:50): https://unherd.com/2018/09/the-rise-of-the-post-truth-liberals/

47. Lucy Kellaway (2015) "Hands up if you can say what your company values", *Financial Times*, 4 October 2015, available online (accessed 10/05/2019 16:22): https://www.ft.com/content/d508d08e-682d-11e5-a57f-21b88f7d973f

48. Maitland (2015) *The values most valued by UK plc*, report, London:

Maitland, available online (accessed 18/09/2018 16:57): http://www.maitland.co.uk/wp-content/uploads/2015/10/20151001-Maitland-Values-Report.pdf

49. See Wolfram Kaiser (2007) *Christian Democracy and the Origins of European Union*, Cambridge: Cambridge University Press.

50. Acceptance speech, EPP Congress, Dublin, 7 May 2015.

51. Originally said at a fundraising event on the 9th of September 2016 in New York

52. President Macron addressed Congress on Wednesday April 25th, 2018 with a speech that was widely reported as a rebuke to Trump and in defence of shared values.

3. THE FADING OF THE EUROPEAN PROJECT

1. Ivan Krastev (2017) *After Europe*, Philadelphia: University of Pennsylvania Press, p. 10.

2. See, for example, Ambrose Evans-Pritchard (2016) "The European Union always was a CIA project, as Brexiteers discover", *The Daily Telegraph*, 27 April 2016, available online (accessed 14/05/2019 15:33): https://www.telegraph.co.uk/business/2016/04/27/the-european-union-always-was-a-cia-project-as-brexiteers-discov/?icid=registration_eng_nba158433_personalised

3. Quoted in Mark Hewitson and Matthew D'Auria (2012) *Europe in Crisis: Intellectuals and the European Idea 1917–57*, New York: Berghahn Books, p. 11.

4. Monnet Memorandum to Schuman and Bidault, 4 May 1950, recorded in full in David Weigall and Peter Stirk (1992) *The Origins and Development of the European Community*, Leicester: Leicester University Press, pp. 57–8.

5. See, for example, telegrams from US Secretary of State Dean Acheson, 10 May 1950, in Weigall and Stirk (1992) pp. 63–4.

6. Wolfram Kaiser (2007) *Christian Democracy and the Origins of European Union*, Cambridge: Cambridge University Press.

7. "The Schuman Declaration", 9 May 1950.

8. Ibid.

9. Ibid.

10. Ibid.

11. Available online (accessed 18/09/18 17:40): https://eur-lex.europa.eu/summary/glossary/subsidiarity.html

12. Pius XI (1931) *Quadragesimo anno*, available online (accessed 14/05/2019 15:38) http://w2.vatican.va/content/pius-xi/en/encyclicals/documents/hf_p-xi_enc_19310515_quadragesimo-anno.html

13. Speech delivered in the Bundestag as Chancellor of the Federal Republic of Germany, 12 July 1952.

14. James Kirchick (2018) *The End of Europe: Dictators, Demagogues, and the Coming Dark Age*, London: Yale University Press, p. 225.

15. Scott Thomas (2005) *The Global Resurgence of Religion and the Transformation of International Relations*, London: Palgrave Macmillan, p. 167.

16. Mark Leonard (2005) *Why Europe Will Run the 21st Century*, London: HarperCollins.

17. Jeremy Rifkin (2004) *The European Dream: How Europe's Vision of the Future is Quietly Eclipsing the American Dream*, New York: Jeremy P. Tarcher.

18. Alan Milward (1992) *The European Saving of the Nation State*, Berkeley and Los Angeles: University of California Press.

19. Jan Zielonka (2014) *Is the EU Doomed?*, Cambridge: Polity Press.

20. EU-wide growth of 2%, and Eurozone growth of 2.2%.

21. Jürgen Habermas, trans. Ciaran Cronin (2015) *The Lure of Technocracy*, Cambridge: Polity Press, p. 3.

22. See Amy Chua, for example, who notes the extent to which democracy can galvanize, rather than resolve, group conflict: Amy Chua (2018) *Political Tribes: Group Instinct and the Fate of Nations*, London: Bloomsbury, p. 31; or Krastev (2017) *After Europe*, pp. 24–5, which notes the transition in European democracy from something favouring emancipation of minorities to something empowering majority prejudices.

23. Helena Smith (2015) "Fight to save the Greek pension takes centre stage in Brussels and Athens", *The Guardian*, 21 May 2015, available online (accessed 14/05/2019 13:05): https://www.theguardian.com/

world/2015/may/21/fight-save-greek-pension-centre-stage-brussels-athens

24. Mića Panić (2005) "The Euro and the Welfare State", in Eleanor Spaventa and Michael Dougan (eds), *Social Welfare and EU Law*, Oxford: Hart Publishing, pp. 25–30.

25. Ginger Hervey (2017) "The EU exodus: When doctors and nurses follow the money", *Politico*, 27 September 2017, available online (accessed 14/05/2019 15:42): https://www.politico.eu/article/doctors-nurses-migration-health-care-crisis-workers-follow-the-money-european-commission-data/

26. Krastev (2017) *After Europe*, p. 50.

27. The BSA34 survey noted that "Any suggestion that immigration was not at the heart of this vote [the Brexit referendum] runs counter to what we have found." Roger Harding (2017) "Key Findings: A kind-hearted but not soft-hearted country", *British Social Attitudes 34*, NatCen Social Research, p. 9, available online (accessed 05/06/2019 14:08): http://www.bsa.natcen.ac.uk/latest-report/british-social-attitudes-34/key-findings/context.aspx

28. YouGov Survey Results, 24–25 April 2018, available online (accessed 14/05/2019 15:46): https://d25d2506sfb94s.cloudfront.net/cumulus_uploads/document/dqjh8rbx2e/InternalResults_180425_Immigration.pdf

29. Jean-Claude Juncker (2014) "A new start for Europe", opening statement in the European Parliament plenary session, Strasbourg, 15 July 2014.

30. Olaf Cramme and Sara B. Hobolt (2015) "A European Union under Stress", in Cramme and Hobolt (eds), *Democratic Politics in a European Union under Stress*, Oxford: Oxford University Press, p. 3.

31. Larry Siedentop (2000) *Democracy in Europe*, London: Allen Lane, pp. 124–5.

32. The Lisbon Treaty, signed in 2007 and in effect from 2009, created the role of European Council president, established the Charter of Fundamental Rights as legally binding for all member states, increased the powers of the European Parliament, and removed the need for unanimity in Council of Ministers votes, instead requiring only a simple majority.

33. Alexis Tsipras (2013) "Foreword", in Slavoj Žižek and Srećko Horvat, *'What Does Europe Want?'*: *The Union and Its Discontents*, London: Istros Books, p. 14.
34. Speech in the Bundestag, outlining the line Germany would take at a G20 meeting, 14 June 2012.
35. Speech to the think tank Policy Exchange, 18 February 2018.
36. Habermas (2015) *The Lure of Technocracy*.
37. Address to the European Parliament, 7 October 2010. He re-iterated the point in an interview with the Parliament, 8 October 2010, available online (accessed 14/05/2019 15:50): http://www.europarl.europa.eu/news/en/headlines/eu-affairs/20101006STO85428/jacques-delors-europe-needs-a-soul
38. Krastev (2009) *After Europe*, p. 5.

4. BROKEN PROMISES AND SHATTERED DREAMS: HOW THE NEW WESTERNERS LOST FAITH

1. Timothy Garton Ash (2017) "Is Europe Disintegrating", *The New York Review of Books*, 19 January 2017.
2. Lecture at the London School of Economics, 16 May 2018.
3. Anne Applebaum (2013) "Does Eastern Europe Still Exist?", in LSE IDEAS, *The Crisis of EU Enlargement*, special report SR018, November 2013, p. 34.
4. Michal Kopeček (2019) "Sovereignty, 'Return to Europe' and Democratic Distrust in the East after 1989 in the Light of Brexit", *Contemporary European History* (28:1), February 2019, pp. 73–6.
5. Ibid.
6. See Cristina Blanco Sío-López (2013) "Reconditioning the 'Return to Europe': The Influence of Spanish Accession in Shaping the EU's Eastern Enlargement Process", in LSE IDEAS, *The Crisis of EU Enlargement*.
7. *Novi List* (2008) "Bye Bye Balkans", 5 March 2008.
8. Quoted in Srećko Horvat (2013) "Danke Deutschland!", in Slavoj Žižek and Srećko Horvat, *'What Does Europe Want?'*: *The Union and Its Discontents*, London: Istros, p. 30.
9. The prestigious *Foreign Affairs* journal, for example, was highly doubtful,

suggesting that the transition to capitalism would rapidly lead to "instability". See Abraham Brumberg (1989) "Poland, the Demise of Communism", *Foreign Affairs* (69:1).

10. Yascha Mounk (2018) *The People vs Democracy: Why Our Freedom is in Danger and How to Save it*, London: Harvard University Press, pp. 124–5.

11. Erich Follath and Jan Puhl, trans. Christopher Sultan (2012) "The Miracle Next Door: Poland Emerges as a Central European Powerhouse", *Der Spiegel* online, 25 May 2012.

12. James Kirchick (2018) *The End of Europe: Dictators, Demagogues and the Coming Dark Age*, London: Yale University Press, p. 226.

13. Zsolt Boda and Gergő Medve-Bálint (2012) "Institutional Trust in Central and Eastern European Countries: Is it Different from Western Europe?", presented at the European Political Science Association 2nd Annual Conference, Berlin.

14. Jan Zielonka (2018) *Counter-Revolution: Liberal Europe in Retreat*, Oxford: OUP, p. 26.

15. Ralf Dahrendorf (2005) *Reflections on the Revolution in Europe*, New Jersey: Transaction Publishers.

16. As of December 2018, the Czechs had the lowest unemployment rate in the EU; Hungary and Poland came third and fourth; and Latvia and Croatia were above the EU average. Eurostat (2019), "Unemployment rates, seasonally adjusted, March 2019", available online (17/02/2019 16:39): https://ec.europa.eu/eurostat/statistics-explained/index.php/ Unemployment_statistics

17. Bronisław Baczko (1994) *Wyobrażenia społeczne: Szkice o nadziei ipamięci zbiorowej*, Warsaw: Wydawnictwo Naukowe PWN.

18. See Ivan Krastev (2017) *After Europe*, Philadelphia: University of Pennsylvania Press, p. 48.

19. Freedom House (2018) "Freedom in the World 2018: Democracy in Crisis", January 2018.

20. He has used the term "illiberal democracy" in many speeches over the years since becoming prime minister, but his recent branding of his ideological programme has tended to focus more on "Christian democracy".

21. Paul Lendvai (2017) *Orbán: Europe's New Strongman*, London: Hurst, p. 53.

22. Ibid., pp. 150–5.

23. One report had Fidesz leaders enjoying 70% of the main TV channels' coverage of politicians, and 80% on Kossuth radio—hardly ever in a negative light.

24. OSCE/ODIHR (2014) "Limited Election Observation Mission Final Report: PARLIAMENTARY ELECTIONS 6 April 2014".

25. Bálint Magyar, trans. Bálint Bethlenfalvy, Ágnes Simon, Steven Nelson & Kata Paulin (2016) *The Post-Communist Mafia State*, Budapest: Central European Press.

26. The 19 British Conservative MEPs voted in September 2018 against invoking Article 7 against Hungary (see below). The Parliament as a whole supported the motion 448–197.

27. Quoted in Lendvai (2017) *Orbán*, p. 184.

28. Speech to the European Parliament, Strasbourg, 11 September 2018, available online (accessed 17/02/2019 17:34): https://visegradpost.com/en/2018/09/11/viktor-orban-denounces-the-blackmail-of-the-eu-full-speech/

29. Ceremonial speech on the 170th anniversary of the Hungarian Revolution of 1848, Budapest, 15 March 2018, available online (accessed 14/05/2019 18:00): https://www.kormany.hu/en/the-prime-minister/the-prime-minister-s-speeches/orban-viktor-s-ceremonial-speech-on-the-170th-anniversary-of-the-hungarian-revolution-of-1848

30. Quoted in Zielonka (2018) *Counter-Revolution*, p. 46.

31. See Mounk (2018) *The People vs Democracy*, pp. 126–7.

32. Quoted in Drew Hinshaw and Marcus Walker (2018) "Poland's New Nationalist Rulers Are Erasing Lech Walesa From History", *Wall Street Journal*, 22 January 2018, available online (accessed 15/05/2019 17:59): https://www.wsj.com/articles/polands-new-nationalist-rulers-are-erasing-lech-walesa-from-history-1516636420

33. European Commission for Democracy through Law (2016) "Draft Opinion on Amendments to the Act of 25 June 2015 on the Constitutional Tribunal of Poland", 26 February 2016.

34. Richard Wike, Bruce Stokes & Katie Simmons (2016) "Europeans Fear

Wave of Refugees Will Mean More Terrorism, Fewer Jobs", Pew Research Center, 11 July 2016, available online (accessed 15/05/2019 15:05): https://www.pewglobal.org/2016/07/11/europeans-fear-wave-of-refugees-will-mean-more-terrorism-fewer-jobs/

35. Katarzyna Markusz (2019) "Poland picks former hate group boss to police internet, says Jewish organization", *The Times of Israel*, 8 January 2019.

36. It is worth noting that things look very different in each of the Baltic states: though grouped together by geography and a shared history within the Soviet and Tsarist Russian empires, they are quite distinct in other respects. Lithuania, for example, does not have a significant Russian minority, unlike the others. Estonia has strong historic links with Finland, and often looks there for political and social models. Lithuania has deeper historic links with Poland.

37. Jasmin Mujanović (2018) *Hunger and Fury: The Crisis of Democracy in the Balkans*, London: Hurst, p. 131.

38. Krastev (2017) *After Europe*, p. 11.

39. Quoted in Mark Mazower (1998) *Dark Continent*, London: Allen Lane, p. 402.

40. Mujanović (2018) *Hunger and Fury*.

41. Quoted in Gerald Frost (2017) "Orbán's Hungary is haunted by its ghosts", *Standpoint*, November 2017.

42. Milan Kundera, trans. Edmund White (1984) "A Kidnapped West, or Culture Dies Out", *Granta* (*11*) *Greetings from Prague, Essays & Memoir*, 1 March 1984.

43. Gordon F. Sander (2018) "Latvia, a disappearing nation", *Politico* (101), 1 May 2018, available online (accessed 16/05/2019 10:59): https:///www.politico.eu/article/latvia-a-disappearing-nation-migration-population-decline/

44. Krastev (2017) *After Europe*, p. 50.

45. Matthew Engel "Romania: the land of no return", *New Statesman*, 30 January 2019.

46. Mujanović (2018) *Hunger and Fury*, p. 110.

5. AMERICA AFTER THE END OF HISTORY: FROM TRIUMPH TO TRUMP

1. Amy Chua (2018) *Political Tribes: Group Instinct and the Fate of Nations*, London: Bloomsbury, p. 12.
2. This is not the first time in US history that traumatic intervention has created a reluctance to engage abroad. There was a similar haemorrhaging of support for US international activities and a similar existential crisis during and after the Vietnam War. Confidence in foreign intervention had, however, largely been restored with the end of the Cold War.
3. Samuel Huntington (2004) *Who Are We? America's Great Debate*, New York: The Free Press.
4. See, for example, L. Huddy, S. Feldman and E. Cassese (2007) "On the distinct political effects of anxiety and anger", in W.R. Neuman, G.E. Marcus, A.N. Crigler & M. MacKuen (eds), *The Affect Effect*, Chicago: University of Chicago Press, pp. 202–30.
5. Shafik Mandhai (2018) "Two in five Americans say Islam 'is incompatible with US values'", Al Jazeera, 1 November 2018, available online (accessed 17/05/2019 11:11): https://www.aljazeera.com/news/2018/11/americans-islam-incompatible-values-181101185805274.html
6. Michael Lipka (2017) "Muslims and Islam: Key findings in the U.S. and around the world", Pew Research Centre, 9 August 2017, available online (accessed 17/05/2019 11:12): https://www.pewresearch.org/fact-tank/2017/08/09/muslims-and-islam-key-findings-in-the-u-s-and-around-the-world/
7. Danielle Kaeble and Mary Cowhig (2018) "Correctional Populations in the United States, 2016", Bureau of Justice Statistics, US Department of Justice, April 2018, available online (accessed 17/05/2019 11:13): https://www.bjs.gov/index.cfm?ty=pbdetail&iid=6226
8. Roy Walmsley (2018) "World Prison Population List", World Prison Brief 12th edition, Institute for Criminal Policy Research. According to this list, there were 10.7 million prisoners in the world in 2018, over 2.1 of whom were in the USA.
9. *The Economist* (2015) "How America's police became so heavily armed", 18 May 2015, available online (accessed 17/05/2019 11:13): https://

www.economist.com/the-economist-explains/2015/05/18/how-americas-police-became-so-heavily-armed

10. Jonathon Mummulo (2018) "Militarization fails to enhance police safety or reduce crime but may harm police reputation", *Proceedings of the National Academy of Sciences*, 11 September 2018 (115.37), 9181–6.

11. *The Economist* (2014) "Don't Shoot", 11 December 2014, available online (accessed 17/05/2019 11:15): https://www.economist.com/united-states/2014/12/11/dont-shoot

12. Patrick J. Deneen (2018) *Why Liberalism Failed*, London: Yale University Press.

13. Ibid., p. 3.

14. Chua (2018) *Political Tribes*, p. 3.

15. Milton Friedman (1962) *Capitalism and Freedom*, 40th Anniversary Edition (2002), London: University of Chicago Press.

16. Adam Smith (1776) *Wealth of Nations*.

17. The Heritage Foundation (2019) "2019 Index of Economic Freedom", available online (accessed 17/05/2019 11:18): https://www.heritage.org/index/

18. Arlie Russell Hochschild (2018) *Strangers in Their Own Land*, New York: The New Press.

19. Bradley Jones (2018) "Most Americans want to limit campaign spending, say big donors have greater political influence", Pew Research Center, 8 May 2018, available online (accessed 05/06/2019 15:18): https://www.pewresearch.org/fact-tank/2018/05/08/most-americans-want-to-limit-campaign-spending-say-big-donors-have-greater-political-influence/

20. Naomi Klein (2017) *No Is Not Enough*, London: Allen Lane, p. 70.

21. Greenpeace (2016) "Hillary Clinton's Connections to the Oil and Gas Industry", 21 April 2016, available online (accessed 21/12/2018): https://www.greenpeace.org/usa/campaign-updates/hillary-clintons-connection-oil-gas-industry/

22. Naomi Klein (2016) "The Problem With Hillary Clinton Isn't Just Her Corporate Cash. It's Her Corporate Worldview.", *The Nation*, 6 April 2016.

23. Michael Leachman, Kathleen Masterson and Eric Figueroa (2017) "A

Punishing Decade for School Funding", Center on Budget and Policy Priorities, 29 November 2017.

24. For the damage wrought in just one state, see Valerie Strauss (2016) "North Carolina's assault on public education just got worse", *The Washington Post*, 17 December 2016, available online (accessed 17/05/2019 11:22): https://www.washingtonpost.com/news/answer-sheet/wp/2016/12/17/north-carolinas-assault-on-public-education-just-got-worse/?utm_term=.e2c101fc537b

25. Bill Emmott (2018) *The Fate of the West: The Battle to Save the World's Most Successful Political Idea*, London: The Economist Books, p. 39.

26. Office of the Inspector General, US Department of Justice (2016) "Review of the Federal Bureau of Prisons, Monitoring of Contract Prisons", August 2016, available online (17/05/2019 11:31): https://oig.justice.gov/reports/2016/e1606.pdf

27. Sally Yates (2016) "Reducing Our Use of Private Prisons", Memorandum for the Acting Director Federal Bureau of Prisons, 18 August 2016, available online (accessed 17/05/2019 11:32): https://www.justice.gov/archives/opa/file/886311/download

28. Liberty Vittert (2018) "The cold hard facts about America's private prison system", Fox News online, 19 December 2018, available online (accessed 17/05/2019 11:32): https://www.foxnews.com/opinion/the-cold-hard-facts-about-americas-private-prison-system

29. Jimmy Tobias (2018) "The Zinke effect: how the US interior department became a tool of big business", *The Guardian*, 12 November 2018, available online (accessed 17/05/2019 11:33): https://www.theguardian.com/us-news/2018/nov/12/the-zinke-effect-how-the-us-interior-department-became-a-tool-of-industry

30. Michael Sandel (2013) *What Money Can't Buy: The Moral Limits of Markets*, London: Penguin.

31. Jon Swaine, Oliver Laughland, Jamiles Lartey and Ciara McCarthy (2015) "Young black men killed by US police at highest rate in year of 1,134 deaths", *The Guardian*, 31 December 2015, available online (accessed 21/12/2018 18:18): https://www.theguardian.com/us-news/ng-interactive/2015/jun/01/the-counted-police-killings-us-database

32. Roland G. Fryer, Jr (2018) "An Empirical Analysis of Racial Differences

in Police Use of Force" NBER Working Paper No. 22399, first issued in July 2016, revised in January 2018, available online (accessed 17/05/2019 11:34): https://www.nber.org/papers/w22399

33. NAACP (n.d.) "Criminal Justice Fact Sheet", available online (accessed 21/12/18 18:19): https://www.naacp.org/criminal-justice-fact-sheet/

34. Chua (2018) *Political Tribes*, p. 174.

35. Ibid., p. 8.

36. Ibid.

37. John Gramlich (2017) "10 things we learned about gender issues in the U.S. in 2017", Pew Research Center, 28 December 2017, available online (accessed 17/05/2019 11:36): http://www.pewresearch.org/fact-tank/2017/12/28/10-things-we-learned-about-gender-issues-in-the-u-s-in-2017/

38. CBS news (2017) "More than 12M 'Me Too' Facebook posts, comments, reactions in 24 hours", 17 October 2017, available online (accessed 17/05/2019 11:37): https://www.cbsnews.com/news/metoo-more-than-12-million-facebook-posts-comments-reactions-24-hours/

39. Justin Wolfers (2015) "Fewer Women Run Big Companies Than Men Named John", *The New York Times*, Glass Ceiling Index, available online (accessed 30/03/19 10:03): https://www.nytimes.com/2015/03/03/upshot/fewer-women-run-big-companies-than-men-named-john.html; Claire Cain Miller, Kevin Quealy and Margot Sanger-Katz (2018) "The Top Jobs Where Women Are Outnumbered by Men Named John", *The New York Times*, 24 April 2018, available (accessed 05/06/2019 16:16): https://www.nytimes.com/interactive/2018/04/24/upshot/women-and-men-named-john.html

40. Melissa Kearney (2014) "Testimony before the Joint Economic Committee: 'Income Inequality in the United States'", 16 January 2014, available online (accessed 17/05/2019 11:38): https://www.brookings.edu/wp-content/uploads/2016/06/16-income-inequality-in-america-kearney-1.pdf

41. Hochschild (2018) *Strangers in Their Own Land*, p. 125.

42. Economic Policy Institute (2011) "More compensation heading to the very top: Ratio of average CEO total direct compensation to average production worker compensation, 1965–2009", 16 May 2011.

43. Thomas Piketty (2019) "Wealth Tax in America", *Le Monde*, 12 February 2019, available online (accessed 17/05/2019 11:40): http://piketty.blog.lemonde.fr/2019/02/12/wealth-tax-in-america/

44. Jeffrey Jones (2015) "In U.S., Confidence in Police Lowest in 22 Years", Gallup, 19 June 2015, available online (accessed 17/05/2019 11:41): https://news.gallup.com/poll/183704/confidence-police-lowest-years.aspx

45. Gallup Podcast (2018) "Why is Climate Change so Politically Polarizing?", 4 April 2018, available online (accessed 17/05/2019 11:41): https://news.gallup.com/podcast/232070/why-climate-change-politically-polarizing.aspx

46. Quoted in Hochschild (2018) *Strangers in Their Own Land*, p. 6.

47. Madison Feller (2018) "Do Trump Supporters Need Their Own Dating App?", *Elle*, 18 December 2018, available online (accessed 17/05/2019 11:42): https://www.elle.com/culture/career-politics/a25605974/donald-daters-app-emily-moreno-interview/

48. Cited in J.D. Vance (2016) *Hillbilly Elegy: A Memoir of a Family and a Culture in Crisis*, London: William Collins, p. 190.

49. Yascha Mounk (2018) "The Rise of McPolitics", *The New Yorker*, 2 July 2018.

50. Chua (2018) *Political Tribes*.

51. Jonah Goldberg (2018) *Suicide of the West*, New York: Crown Forum, p. 298.

52. Yascha Mounk (2018) *The People vs Democracy: Why Our Freedom is in Danger and How to Save it*, London: Harvard University Press, p. 100.

53. Robert D. Putnam (2000) *Bowling Alone: The Collapse and Revival of American Community*, New York: Simon & Schuster.

54. Robert D. Putnam and David E. Campbell (2010) *American Grace: How Religion Divides and Unites Us*, New York: Simon & Schuster.

55. Jonathan Haidt (2012) *The Righteous Mind: Why Good People Are Divided by Politics and Religion*, New York: Knopf Doubleday.

56. Vance (2016) *Hillbilly Elegy*, p. 93.

57. Robert Jones and Daniel Cox (2017) "America's Changing Religious Identity: Findings from the 2016 American Values Atlas", Public

Religion Research Institute, p. 11, available online (accessed 17/05/2019 11:44): https://www.prri.org/research/american-religious-landscape-christian-religiously-unaffiliated/

58. Vance (2016) *Hillbilly Elegy*, p. 4.

59. Ibid. Kentucky is 89% white, with a median household income over the period 2009–13 that was $20,000 lower than Virginia's, according to the 2010 census.

60. Eric Kaufmann (2018) *Whiteshift: Populism, Immigration and the Future of White Majorities*, London: Allen Lane, p. 67.

61. Chua (2018) *Political Tribes*, p. 170.

62. Kaufmann (2018) *Whiteshift*, p. 10.

63. Mark Lilla (2017) *The Once and Future Liberal*, New York: HarperCollins; Vance (2016) *Hillbilly Elegy*; Shadi Hamid (2016) "There's no 'good' or 'bad' America", *The Washington Post*, 18 November 2016; Goldberg (2018) *Suicide of the West*; Kaufmann (2018) *Whiteshift*; Chua (2018) *Political Tribes*.

64. Aaron Blake (2016) "The first Trump-Clinton presidential debate transcript, annotated", *The Washington Post*, 26 September 2016, available online (accessed 17/05/2019 11:48): https://www.washingtonpost.com/news/the-fix/wp/2016/09/26/the-first-trump-clinton-presidential-debate-transcript-annotated/?utm_term=.d201669cedc9

65. Goldberg (2018) *Suicide of the West*, p. 289.

6. THE LOST CLASS

1. Matthijs Rooduijn (2018) "What unites the voter bases of populist parties? Comparing the electorates of 15 populist parties", *European Political Science Review* (10:3), 351–68.

2. Nicholas Carnes and Noam Lupu (2017) "It's time to bust the myth: Most Trump voters were not working class", *The Washington Post*, 5 June 2017 (accessed 17/05/2019 12:18): https://www.washingtonpost.com/news/monkey-cage/wp/2017/06/05/its-time-to-bust-the-myth-most-trump-voters-were-not-working-class/?utm_term=.806678a1f018

3. Nate Silver (2016) "The Mythology of Trump's 'Working Class' Support", *FiveThirtyEight*, 3 May 2016.

4. Philip Bump (2017) "Places that backed Trump skewed poor; voters who backed Trump skewed wealthier", *The Washington Post*, 19 December 2017.

5. Jonathan T. Rothwell and Pablo Diego-Rosell (2016) "Explaining Nationalist Political Views: The Case of Donald Trump", *Social Science Research Network* (88).

6. Lorenza Antonucci, Laszlo Horvath & André Krouwel (2017) "Brexit was not the voice of the working class nor of the uneducated—it was of the squeezed middle", *LSE British Politics and Policy* blog, 13 October 2017, available online (accessed 21/05/2019 12:26): https://blogs.lse.ac.uk/politicsandpolicy/brexit-and-the-squeezed-middle/

7. Ronald Inglehart and Pippa Norris (2016) "Trump, Brexit, and the Rise of Populism: Economic Have-Nots and Cultural Backlash", Harvard Kennedy School Faculty Research Working Paper Series RWP16–026, August 2016.

8. Naomi Klein (2017) *No Is Not Enough*, London: Allen Lane, p. 88.

9. Éric Grenier (2019) "Leader Meter", CBC News, last updated 6 May 2019, available online (accessed 20/05/2019 12:37): https://www.cbc.ca/news2/interactives/leadermeter/index.html#hilo

10. Nanos (2019) "Conservatives 36, Liberals 31, NDP 14, Green 11, People's 1 in latest Nanos federal tracking", Nanos Weekly Tracking, ending 17 May 2019, available online (accessed 06/06/2019 12:56): https://www.nanos.co/wp-content/uploads/2019/05/Political-Package-2019–05–17-FR.pdf

11. Thomas Piketty (2018) "Brahmin Left vs Merchant Right: Rising Inequality and the Changing Structure of Political Conflict", World Inequality Database working paper series N° 2018/7.

12. Ibid., p. 3.

13. Chris Curtis (2017) "How Britain voted at the 2017 general election", YouGov, 13 June 2017, available online (accessed 21/05/2019 12:44): https://yougov.co.uk/topics/politics/articles-reports/2017/06/13/how-britain-voted-2017-general-election

14. Mark Lilla (2017) *The Once and Future Liberal*, New York: HarperCollins; Francis Fukuyama (2018) *Identity*, London: Profile; David Goodhart (2017) *The Road to Somewhere: The Populist Revolt and the Future of Politics*, London: Hurst.

15. Based on exit polls conducted by Edison Research for the National Election Pool, reported and collected by CNN, available online (accessed 21/05/2019 12:46): https://edition.cnn.com/election/2018/exit-polls

16. Naomi Klein (2017) *No Is Not Enough*, London: Allen Lane, p. 88; Eric Kaufmann (2018) *Whiteshift: Populism, Immigration and the Future of White Majorities*, London: Allen Lane, p. 67.

17. Goodhart (2017), *The Road to Somewhere*, p. 72.

18. Glenn Gottfried, Guy Lodge & Sarah Birch (2013) "Divided Democracy: Political inequality in the UK and why it matters", Institute for Public Policy Research, 10 November 2013.

19. Stephen L. Morgan and Jiwon Lee (2017) "The White Working Class and Voter Turnout in U.S. Presidential Elections, 2004 to 2016", *Sociological Science* (4), 656–85.

20. Eric Groenendyk (2018) "Competing Motives in a Polarized Electorate: Political Responsiveness, Identity Defensiveness, and the Rise of Partisan Antipathy", *Political Psychology* (39), 159–71.

21. Jane Green and Christopher Prosser (2016) "Party system fragmentation and single-party government: the British general election of 2015", *Western European Politics* (39.6), 1299–1310.

22. Thomas Piketty, trans. Arthur Goldhammer (2014) *Capital in the Twenty-First Century*, Cambridge MA: Harvard University Press.

23. Philip Booth (2014) "Does Inequality Matter?", Institute of Economic Affairs blog, 8 August 2014, available online (accessed 12/02/2019 15:16): https://iea.org.uk/blog/does-inequality-matter

24. Office of the UN High Commissioner for Human Rights (2018) "Statement on Visit to the United Kingdom, by Professor Philip Alston, United Nations Special Rapporteur on extreme poverty and human rights", London, 16 November 2018.

25. Richard Wilkinson and Kate Pickett (2009) *The Spirit Level: Why Equality is Better for Everyone*, London: Allen Lane. See also their follow-up (2018) *The Inner Level: How More Equal Societies Reduce Stress, Restore Sanity and Improve Everybody's Wellbeing*, London: Penguin.

26. Theos (2018) "'They are dying of hopelessness': how inequality affects our mental health", interview with Richard Wilkinson and Kate Pickett, 13 June 2018, available online (accessed 12/01/2019 16:18): https://

www.theosthinktank.co.uk/comment/2018/06/13/they-are-dying-of-hopelessness-how-inequality-affects-our-mental-health

27. Sarah Kessler (2018) *Gigged: The Gig Economy, the End of the Job and the Future of Work*, London: Penguin Random House.

28. Ibid., p. 9.

29. Deborah Hargraves (2019) *Are Chief Executives Overpaid?*, Cambridge: Polity, p. 6.

30. Quoted in ibid., p. 37.

31. Paul Collier (2018) *The Future of Capitalism: Facing the New Anxieties*, London: Allen Lane, p. 95.

32. Hargraves (2018), *Are Chief Executives Overpaid?*, p. 71.

33. Patricia Kotnik, Mustafa Erdem Sakinç, Alenka Slavec & Dejan Guduraš (2017) "Executive compensation in Europe: Realized gains from stock-based pay", ISI Growth working paper, 7 May 2017, available online (accessed 20/05/2019 17:56): http://www.isigrowth.eu/wp-content/uploads/2017/06/working_paper_2017_07.pdf

34. Klein (2017) *No Is Not Enough*.

35. Walter Scheidel (2017) *The Great Leveler: Violence and the History of Inequality from the Stone Age to the Twenty-First Century*, Princeton: Princeton University Press.

36. Dunja Mijatović (2018) "Report of the Commissioner For Human Rights of the Council of Europe Following Her Visit to Greece From 25 to 29 of June 2018", Council of Europe CommDH(2018)24, Strasbourg, 6 November 2018.

37. It is interesting to note that Podemos is also explicitly committed to promoting the Western values of freedom, equality and fraternity.

38. British Social Attitudes (2015) "Benefits and Welfare", *British Social Attitudes 32*, available online (accessed 22/01/2019 17:09): http://www.bsa.natcen.ac.uk/latest-report/british-social-attitudes-32/welfare.aspx

39. Ipsos MORI (2018) "Two in three want the government to increase spending on public services", *Ipsos MORI October 2018 Political Monitor*, 29 October 2018, available online (accessed 23/01/2019 09:56): https://www.ipsos.com/ipsos-mori/en-uk/two-three-want-government-increase-spending-public-services

40. British Social Attitudes (2017) "Work and welfare", *British Social*

Attitudes 35, available online (accessed 06/06/2019 13:08): http://www.bsa.natcen.ac.uk/media/39254/bsa35_work.pdf

41. Ipsos MORI (2013) "Perceptions are not reality" 9 July 2013, available online (accessed 21/05/2019 11:55): https://www.ipsos.com/ipsos-mori/en-uk/perceptions-are-not-reality

42. Anthony Heath and Lindsay Richards (2016) "Attitudes towards Immigration and their Antecedents: Topline Results from Round 7 of the European Social Survey", *European Social Survey Topline Results* (7), November 2016.

43. Special Eurobarometer 469 (2018) "Integration of Immigrants in the European Union", April 2018, p. 5.

44. Christian Dustmann, Tommasso Frattini & Ian Preston (2012) "The Effect of Immigration along the Distribution of Wages", *Review of Economic Studies* (80:1), 145–73.

45. For a full account, see Sasha Polakow-Suransky (2017) *Go Back To Where You Came From*, London: Hurst, pp. 179–80.

46. Matthew Stewart (2018) "The 9.9 Percent Is the New American Aristocracy", *The Atlantic*, June 2018.

47. Collier (2018) *The Future of Capitalism*, p. 192.

48. Chantal Mouffe (2016) "The Populist Moment", *Open Democracy*, 21 November 2016.

49. *The Economist* (2018) "Are liberals and populists just searching for a new master? An interview with Slavoj Žižek , author of 'Like a Thief in Broad Daylight'", 18 October 2018.

7. THE LOST GENERATION

1. Yascha Mounk (2018) *The People vs Democracy: Why Our Freedom Is in Danger and How to Save It*, London: Harvard University Press.

2. For the US context, see Robert D. Putnam (2015) *Our Kids: The American Dream in Crisis*, New York: Simon & Schuster.

3. Ivan Krastev (2017) *After Europe*, Philadelphia: University of Pennsylvania Press, p. 14.

4. British Election Study data, available online at https://www.britishelectionstudy.com/

5. Daniela Melo and Daniel Stockemer (2014) "Age and Political Participation in Germany, France and the U.K.: A Comparative Analysis", *Comparative European Politics* (12:1), 33–53.

6. Mounk (2018) *The People vs Democracy*, p. 105.

7. Ibid.

8. Roberto Stefan Foa and Yascha Mounk (2016) "The Democratic Disconnect", *Journal of Democracy* (27), 5–17.

9. Mounk (2018) *The People vs Democracy*, p. 109.

10. Cas Mudde (2018) "Democrats are losing the millennial vote and need to change message", *The Guardian*, 24 June 2018.

11. Reuters and Ipsos (2018), polls conducted in Jan–March 2016 and Jan–March 2018.

12. Torsten Bell (2018) "Demography is the new class war", Resolution Foundation, 21 September 2018, available online (accessed 28/12/18 13:54): https://www.resolutionfoundation.org/media/blog/why-demographers-are-the-new-class-warriors-in-british-politics

13. Ronald Inglehart and Pippa Norris (2016) "Trump, Brexit, and the Rise of Populism: Economic Have-Nots and Cultural Backlash", Harvard Kennedy School, Faculty Research Working Paper Series.

14. Polls varied slightly, but Ipsos MORI's final estimate for 18–24-year-olds was 75%; YouGov put it at 71%, Lord Ashcroft at 73%.

15. Ipsos (2017) "1er tour présidentielle 2017: sociologie de l'électorat", 23 April 2017, available online (accessed 06/06/2019 13:36): https://www.ipsos.com/fr-fr/1er-tour-presidentielle-2017-sociologie-de-lelectorat

16. According to Quorum/YouTrend, cited by Emily Schultheis (2018) "How Italy's Five-Star Movement Is Winning the Youth Vote", *The Atlantic*, 2 March 2018.

17. Peter Coy (2018) "Italy's Young Populists Are Coddling the Old—and Holding the Country Back", *Bloomberg*, 7 June 2018, available online (accessed 23/05/2019 11:22): https://www.bloomberg.com/news/articles/2018–06–07/italy-s-young-populists-are-coddling-the-old-and-holding-the-country-back

18. Ipsos MORI (2018) "Political Elections in Italy, 2018: Post-vote analysis", available online (accessed 28/12/18 14:15): https://www.ipsos.

com/sites/default/files/ct/news/documents/2018–03/Italy-Political_Elections_2018.pdf; Donatienne Ruy (2018) "Italian Election Results", Center for Strategic & International Studies, 7 March 2018, available online (accessed 23/05/2019 11:23): https://www.csis.org/blogs/european-election-watch/italian-elections-results

19. Sveriges Radio (2018) "Grafik: Valu 2018—årets vallokalsundersökning", 9 September 2018, available online (accessed 28/12/18 14:32): https://sverigesradio.se/sida/artikel.aspx?programid=83&artikel=7039360

20. Stefan Wagstyl (2017) "Germany's young voters back 'grandmother' Merkel", *Financial Times*, 9 August 2017, available online (accessed 06/06/2019 13:39): https://www.ft.com/content/b81e1828–7b70–11e7–9108-edda0bcbc928

21. Lili Bayer (2016) "Why Central Europe's youth roll right", *Politico*, 18 November 2016, available online (accessed 23/05/2019 11:27): http://www.politico.eu/article/why-central-europes-youth-roll-right-voting-politics-visegard/

22. See, for example, Eric Kaufmann (2018) *Whiteshift: Populism, Immigration and the Future of White Majorities*, London: Allen Lane.

23. *The Economist* (2017) "Eastern Europe's workers are emigrating, but its pensioners are staying", 19 January 2017, available online (accessed 06/06/2019 14:58): https://www.economist.com/europe/2017/01/19/eastern-europes-workers-are-emigrating-but-its-pensioners-are-staying

24. Ibid., p. 52.

25. Coy (2018) "Italy's Young Populists Are Coddling the Old".

26. Patrick J. Deneen (2018) *Why Liberalism Failed*, London: Yale University Press, p. 132.

27. Ed Husain (2018) *The House of Islam: A Global History*, London: Bloomsbury.

28. David Runciman (2018) *How Democracy Ends*, London: Profile.

29. One good example is Tony Cliff's International Socialists group (later the Socialist Workers Party), which split from the Labour Party in the mid-60s and went on the launch the *Socialist Worker* newspaper. It was largely made up of students, but peaked at about 4,000 members

in the mid-70s. The far-left youth had a national impact and public profile that far outstripped the size of its membership. See Jeremy Tranmer (2017) "A Force to be Reckoned with? The Radical Left in the 1970s.", *French Journal of British Studies* (special edition XXII, *The United Kingdom and the Crisis in the 1970s*).

30. Bell (2018) "Demography is the new class war".

31. Robert Colvile (2016) *The Great Acceleration: How the World is Getting Faster, Faster*, London: Bloomsbury.

32. Monica Anderson and Jingjing Jiang (2018) "Teens, Social Media & Technology 2018", Pew Research Center, 31 May 2018, available online (accessed 23/05/2019 11:31): https://www.pewinternet.org/2018/05/31/teens-social-media-technology-2018/

33. Bill Emmott (2018) *The Fate of the West: The Battle to Save the World's Most Successful Political Idea*, London: The Economist Books, p. 168.

34. Ed Howker and Shiv Malik (2010) *Jilted Generation: How Britain Has Bankrupted Its Youth*, London: Icon Books, p. 6.

35. ONS (2017) "National Population Projections: 2016-based statistical bulletin", 26 October 2017, available online (accessed 06/06/2019 15:08): https://www.ons.gov.uk/peoplepopulationandcommunity/populationandmigration/populationprojections/bulletins/nationalpopulationprojections/2016basedstatisticalbulletin

36. As discussed on David Runciman (2018) "Talking Politics" podcast 129, 5 December 2018, available online (accessed 23/05/2019 11:32): https://www.talkingpoliticspodcast.com/blog/2018/129-democracy-for-young-people

37. This basic observation informs, for example, the Overlapping Generations (OLG) Model made famous by the Nobel Prize-winning economist Paul Samuelson in the 1950s and 1960s.

38. Howker and Malik (2010) *Jilted Generation: How Britain Has Bankrupted Its Youth*, p. 78.

39. Data gathered by the Institute for Fiscal Studies and summarized by Andrew Hood (2017) "Seven Reasons It Helps to Have Rich Parents", BBC News, 23 April 2017.

40. Cited in Coy (2018) "Italy's Young Populists Are Coddling the Old".

41. Eurostat (2019) "Unemployment statistics", data up to April 2019,

available online (accessed 06/06/2019 15:13): https://ec.europa.eu/eurostat/statistics-explained/index.php?title=Unemployment_statistics#Youth_unemployment

42. See, for example, discussions of this trend in David Willetts (2010) *The Pinch: How the Baby Boomers Took Their Children's Future—And Why They Should Give It Back*, London: Atlantic Books.

43. See, for example, OECD (2014) "OECD's Gurría congratulates Italy on new Jobs Act bill", statement, 9 October 2014.

44. One summary among many is provided by Crispian Balmer (2016) "Renzi's reforms leave Italian economy and voters flat", *Reuters*, 28 September 2016.

45. Outside of Eastern Europe, where they are ageing, but not growing.

46. Willetts (2010) *The Pinch*, p. 77.

47. Lianna Brinded (2015) "The 11 Most Expensive Countries for a University Education", *Business Insider*, 28 December 2015.

48. Briana Boyington (2018) See "20 Years of Tuition Growth at National Universities", *US News*, 13 September 2018. In addition to tuition fees, US colleges also charge for administrative costs, e.g. campus fees, orientation fees.

49. Zack Friedman (2018) "Student Loan Debt Statistics In 2018: A $1.5 Trillion Crisis", *Forbes*, 13 June 2018.

50. Institute for Fiscal Studies and the Department for Education (2018) "The impact of undergraduate degrees on early-career earnings", research report, November 2018.

51. Nick Hillman (2015) "Students and the 2015 general election: Did they make a difference?", Higher Education Price Index Report 78, October 2015, available online (accessed 23/05/2019 11:37): https://www.hepi.ac.uk/wp-content/uploads/2015/10/Students-and-the-2015-general-election.pdf

52. Cary Funk and Meg Hefferon (2018) "Many Republican Millennials differ with older party members on climate change and energy issues", Pew Research Center, 14 May 2018, polling conducted between March and April 2018, available online (accessed 28/12/2018 15:54): http://www.pewresearch.org/fact-tank/2018/05/14/many-republican-millennials-differ-with-older-party-members-on-climate-change-and-energy-issues/

53. Joni Hersch and W. Kip Viscusi (2006) "The Generational Divide in Support for Environmental Policies: European Evidence", *Climatic Change* (77:1/2), 121–36.

54. IPCC Special Report (2018) "Global Warming of 1.5°C", IPCC

55. Michael Le Page "Was Kyoto climate deal a success? Figures reveal mixed results", *New Scientist*, 14 June 2016

56. David G. Victor, Keigo Akimoto, Yoichi Kaya, Mitsutsune Yamaguchi, Danny Cullenward & Cameron Hepburn (2017) "Prove Paris was more than paper promises", *Nature*, 1 August 2017.

57. Eurostat (2018) "Bye bye parents: when do young Europeans flee the nest?", 15 May 2018, available online (accessed 28/12/18 16:07): https://ec.europa.eu/eurostat/web/products-eurostat-news/-/EDN-20180515–1?inheritRedirect=true

58. Willetts (2010) *The Pinch*.

8. MIGRANTS, ISLAM AND WESTERN VALUES

1. See Ben Ryan, ed. (2018) *Fortress Britain? Ethical Approaches to Immigration for a Post-Brexit Britain*, London: JKP.

2. Charles Hawley (2006) "A German State Quizes [sic] Muslim Immigrants on Jews, Gays and Swim Lessons", *Der Spiegel*, 31 January 2006, available online (accessed 24/03/2019 22:46): http://www.spiegel.de/international/muslim-profiling-a-german-state-quizes-muslim-immigrants-on-jews-gays-and-swim-lessons-a-397482.html

3. "Meeting with the world of labour", address at Bachilleres College, State of Chihuahua, during the apostolic journey of Pope Francis to Mexico, 17 February 2016.

4. Besheer Mohamed (2018) "New estimates show U.S. Muslim population continues to grow", Pew Research Center, 3 January 2018, available online (23/05/2019 17:41): http://www.pewresearch.org/fact-tank/2018/01/03/new-estimates-show-u-s-muslim-population-continues-to-grow/

5. Ipsos MORI (2016) "Perceptions are not reality: what the world gets wrong", Ipsos 2016 Perils of Perception survey, 14 December 2016,

available online (23/05/2019 17:42): https://www.ipsos.com/ipsos-mori/en-uk/perceptions-are-not-reality-what-world-gets-wrong

6. BBC News (2019) "How many IS foreign fighters are left in Iraq and Syria?", 20 February 2019, available online (23/05/2019 17:42): https://www.bbc.co.uk/news/world-middle-east-47286935

7. *Le Point* (2018) "56 % des Français jugent l'islam compatible avec les valeurs françaises", 11 February 2018, available online (accessed 12/03/2019 22:15): https://www.lepoint.fr/societe/56-des-francais-jugent-l-islam-compatible-avec-les-valeurs-francaises-11-02-2018-2193999_23.php

8. Douglas Murray (2017) *The Strange Death of Europe: Immigration, Identity, Islam*, London: Bloomsbury, p. 194.

9. Kerry Moore, Paul Mason and Justin Lewis (2008) "Images of Islam in the UK: the representation of British Muslims in the national print news media 2000–2008", Cardiff University working paper, 7 July 2008.

10. Andy Ngo (2018) "A Visit to Islamic England", *Wall Street Journal*, 29 August 2018.

11. Pew Research Center (2015) "U.S. Public Becoming Less Religious", 3 November 2015.

12. Miroslav Volf (2012) *Allah: A Christian Response*, New York: HarperCollins, p. 203.

13. Hawley (2006) "A German State Quizes [sic] Muslim Immigrants"; Ray Furlong (2006) "German 'Muslim test' stirs anger", BBC News, 10 February 2006, available online (accessed 23/05/2019 14:50): http://news.bbc.co.uk/1/hi/world/europe/4655240.stm

14. Melanie Phillips (2006) *Londonistan: How Britain Created a Terror State Within*, New York: Encounter.

15. Andrew Bolt (2019) "Tidal wave of new tribes dividing us", *Herald Sun*, 3 August 2019.

16. Istituto Nazionale di Statistica (2018) "Birth and Fertility of the Resident Population", 30 November 2018, available online (retrieved 23/05/2019 17:48): https://www.istat.it/en/archivio/224594

17. Daniel Tilles "Poland's 'anti-immigration' government is overseeing one of Europe's biggest waves of immigration—but doesn't want to admit it", *Notes From Poland*, 3 October 2018, available online (accessed

23/05/2019 17:49): https://notesfrompoland.com/2018/10/03/polands-anti-immigration-government-is-overseeing-one-of-europes-biggest-waves-of-immigration-but-doesnt-want-to-admit-it/

18. Eric Kaufmann (2018) *Whiteshift: Populism, Immigration and the Future of White Majorities*, London: Allen Lane.

19. Colin Woodard (2011) *American Nations: A History of the Eleven Rival Regional Cultures of North America*, London: Penguin.

20. See, for example, Lawrence D. Bobo et al. (2012) "The *Real* Record on Racial Attitudes", in Peter V. Marsden (ed.), *Social Trends in American Life: Findings from the General Social Survey since 1972*, Princeton: Princeton University Press, 2012, pp. 38–83.

21. Tessa E.S. Charlesworth and Mahzarin R. Banaji (2019) "Patterns of Implicit and Explicit Attitudes: I. Long-Term Change and Stability From 2007 to 2016", *Psychological Science* (30:2), 174–92.

22. From an interview with Sylvain Bourmeau (2015) "Scare Tactics: Michel Houellebecq Defends His Controversial New Book", *The Paris Review*, 2 January 2015.

23. Open Society Justice Initiative (2018) "Restrictions on Muslim women's dress in the 28 EU Member States: Current law, recent legal developments, and the state of play", briefing paper, updated July 2018, available online (accessed 06/06/2019 15:36): https://www.justiceinitiative.org/uploads/dffdb416–5d63–4001–911b-d3f46e159acc/restrictions-on-muslim-womens-dress-in-28-eu-member-states-20180709.pdf

24. See, for example, Wilders' speech at the 10-year memorial conference for Theo van Gogh arranged by the Danish Free Press Society in Copenhagen, 2 November 2014.

25. Pew Research Center (2018) "Global Uptick in Government Restrictions on Religion in 2016", 21 June 2018, available online (retrieved 25/03/2019 09:18): https://www.pewforum.org/2018/06/21/global-uptick-in-government-restrictions-on-religion-in-2016/

26. StatCan (2018) "Police-reported hate crime, 2017", 29 November 2018, available online (retrieved 25/03/2019 09:20): https://www150.statcan.gc.ca/n1/daily-quotidien/181129/dq181129a-eng.htm?HPA=1

27. Zac Goldsmith (2016) "On Thursday, are we really going to hand the

world's greatest city to a Labour party that thinks terrorists is [sic] its friends? A passionate plea from ZAC GOLDSMITH four days before Mayoral election", *Mail on Sunday*, 1 May 2016.

28. Peter Oborne (2016) "How Zac Goldsmith imported Donald Trump's politics into Britain", *Middle East Eye*, 21 April 2016.

29. Jonathan Sacks (2009) *The Home We Build Together: Recreating Society*, London: Continuum.

30. Paul M. Sniderman and Louk Hagendoorn (2007) *When Ways of Life Collide: Multiculturalism and Its discontents in the Netherlands*, Princeton: Princeton University Press.

31. Lori G. Beaman, Jennifer A. Selby & Amélie Barras (2017) "No Mosque, No Refugees: Some Reflections on Syrian Refugees and the Construction of Religion in Canada", in Luca Mavelli and Erin Wilson (eds), *The Refugee Crisis and Religion: Secularism, Security and Hospitality in Question*, London: Rowman and Littlefield.

32. For more details, and to see the original letter, see their website https://www.acommonword.com/

33. ComRes (2016) "Ahmadi Muslims: Perceptions of the Caliphate Polling", 23 May 2016, available online (accessed 25/03/2019 09:49): https://www.comresglobal.com/polls/ahmadiyya-perceptions-of-the-caliphate-polling/

34. For discussion on this, see David Barclay (2013) *Making Multiculturalism Work*, London: Theos.

9. RESTORING THE MYTH

1. Jürgen Habermas, trans. Ciaran Cronin (2015) *The Lure of Technocracy*, Cambridge: Polity Press.

2. See, for example, Jürgen Habermas, trans. Thomas McCarthy (1975) *Legitimation Crisis*, Boston: Beacon Press; and Claus Offe (1974) "Structural Problems of the Capitalist State: Class Rule and the Political System. On the Selectiveness of Political Institutions", *German Political Studies* (1), 31–57.

3. The Independent Group (2019) "Statement of Independence", quoted in Kat Hopps (2019) "Labour split: Chuka Umunna's new Independent

party's core beliefs revealed", *The Express*, 18 February 2019, available online (accessed 30/05/2019 16:14): https://www.express.co.uk/news/politics/1088834/labour-split-chuka-umunna-the-independent-group-party-core-beliefs

4. Naomi Klein (2017) *No Is Not Enough*, London: Allen Lane, p. 240.

5. IFOP have 69% of the French disapproving of Macron's performance in April 2019, and only 29% approving. IFOP and *Le Journal du Dimanche* (2019) "Les indices de popularité—avril 2019", 23 April 2019, available online (accessed 31/05/2019 16:30): https://www.ifop.com/publication/les-indices-de-popularite-avril-2019/

6. Matt Ridley (2011) *The Rational Optimist: How Prosperity Evolves*, London: Fourth Estate.

7. John Paul II (2003) *Ecclesia in Europa*, post-synodal apostolic exhortation, available online (accessed 06/06/2019 15:49): http://w2.vatican.va/content/john-paul-ii/en/apost_exhortations/documents/hf_jp-ii_exh_20030628_ecclesia-in-europa.html

8. Nicky Ison (2019) "Australia could hit 100% renewables sooner than most people think", *The Guardian*, 13 January 2019.

9. See Arlie Russell Hochschild (2018) *Strangers in Their Own Land*, New York: The New Press.

10. Figure cited by Miguel Arias Canete, the EU climate and energy commissioner, in Nikos Chrysoloras, Jonathan Stearns & Ewa Krukowska (2017) "EU steps up electric car push to close 'huge gap' on China", *The Independent*, 8 November 2017.

11. Lefteris Karagiannopoulos and Terje Solsvik (2019) "Tesla boom lifts Norway's electric car sales to record market share", Reuters, 1 April 2019.

12. Abel Gustafson et al. (2018) "The Green New Deal has Strong Bipartisan Support", Yale Program on Climate Change Communication, 14 December 2018.

13. Global Impact Investing Network (2018) "Annual Impact Investor Survey 2018", June 2018, available online (31/05/2019 16:33): https://thegiin.org/assets/2018_GIIN_Annual_Impact_Investor_Survey_web-file.pdf

14. Sarah Murray (2018) "Giving the green light to impact investing in environmental projects", *Financial Times*, 24 September 2018.

15. *24/7 Wall St* (2010) "America's Biggest Companies, Then and Now (1955 to 2010)", 21 September 2010, available online (accessed 07/06/2019): https://247wallst.com/investing/2010/09/21/americas-biggest-companies-then-and-now-1955-to-2010/; Mark J. Perry (2017) "Fortune 500 firms 1955 v. 2017: Only 60 remain, thanks to the creative destruction that fuels economic prosperity", American Enterprise Institute, 20 October 2017, available online (accessed 06/06/2019 16:15): http://www.aei.org/publication/fortune-500-firms-1955-v-2017-only-12-remain-thanks-to-the-creative-destruction-that-fuels-economic-prosperity/

16. Jillian D'Onfro (2019) "Google Parent Alphabet Reports Surge In Spending And Hiring, Hitting Nearly 100,000 Employees", *Forbes*, 4 February 2019, available online (accessed 06/06/2019 16:18): https://www.forbes.com/sites/jilliandonfro/2019/02/04/google-parent-alpha-bet-reports-surge-in-spending-and-hiring-hitting-near-ly-100000-employees/#3e7e1ca772e8; CNN Money (n.d.) "Fortune 500: A database of 50 years of FORTUNE's list of America's largest corporations", available online (accessed 06/06/2019 18:22): https://money.cnn.com/magazines/fortune/fortune500_archive/snap-shots/1955/563.html; Mitra Toossi (2002) "A century of change: the U.S. labor force, 1950–2050", *Monthly Labor Review* (125.5), pp. 15–28.

17. See, for example, Richard C. Longworth (2008) *Caught in the Middle: America's Heartland in the Age of Globalism*, New York: Bloomsbury.

18. Jasmin Mujanović (2018) *Hunger and Fury: The Crisis of Democracy in the Balkans*, London: Hurst, p. 149.

19. Dambisa Moyo (2009) *Dead Aid: Why Aid Is Not Working and How There Is Another Way for Africa*, London: Penguin.

20. Paul Collier (2007) *The Bottom Billion: Why the Poorest Countries are Failing and What Can Be Done About It*, Oxford: OUP.

21. Fekitamoeloa 'Utoikamanu (2018) "Closing the Technology Gap in Least Developed Countries", *UN Chronicle* (LV.3–4), available online (accessed 03/05/2019 09:21): https://unchronicle.un.org/issue/new-technologies-where

22. Nick Spencer (2016) *The Evolution of the West: How Christianity Has Shaped Our Values*, London: SPCK, pp. 125–38.

23. Amnesty International "100 Threats to Human Rights—And How We're Fighting Back", 27 April 2017, available online (accessed 31/05/2019 16:35): https://www.amnesty.ie/100-threats-human-rights-fighting-back/

24. US State Department (2017) "Turkey 2017 Human Rights Report", Country Reports on Human Rights Practices for 2017, United States Department of State Bureau of Democracy, Human Rights and Labor.

25. United Nations (2016) "International Migration Report 2015".

26. Anna Rowlands (2018) "On the Promise and Limits of Politics: Faith-Based Responses to Asylum Seeking", in Ben Ryan, *Fortress Britain?*, London: JKP.

27. See, for example, Virginia Harrison (2018) "Nauru refugees: The island where children have given up on life", BBC News, 1 September 2018.

28. All these data are from Eurostat (2018) "EU Member States granted protection to more than half a million asylum seekers in 2017", 19 April 2018.

29. Pew Research Center (2018) "Spring 2018 Global Attitudes Survey", available online (accessed 31/05/2019 16:38): https://assets.pewresearch.org/wp-content/uploads/sites/1/2018/09/18141059/FT_18.09.19_AttitudesRefugees_Topline.pdf

30. Yekaterina Chzhen et al. (2018) "An Unfair Start: Inequality in Children's Education in Rich Countries", Innocenti Report Card 15, UNICEF Office of Research—Innocenti, Florence.

31. UN Global Goals for Sustainable Development, 2015, Goal 4.1.

32. Eurostat (2019) "Children at risk of poverty or social exclusion", January 2019, available online (accessed 30/03/19 18:14): https://ec.europa.eu/eurostat/statistics-explained/index.php/Children_at_risk_of_poverty_or_social_exclusion#General_overview

33. Trades Union Congress (2019) "Unsecured debt hits new peak of £15,400 per household—new TUC analysis", 7 January 2019, available online (accessed 30/03/19 18:18): https://www.tuc.org.uk/news/unsecured-debt-hits-new-peak-%C2%A315400-household-%E2%80%93-new-tuc-analysis

34. Theresa May (2016) "Britain, the great meritocracy: Prime Minister's speech", 9 September 2016, available online (accessed 30/03/19 18:20):

https://www.gov.uk/government/speeches/britain-the-great-meritoc-racy-prime-ministers-speech

10. RESTORING SOLIDARITY

1. Robert D. Putnam (2000) *Bowling Alone: The Collapse and Revival of American Community*, New York: Simon & Schuster.
2. Kwame Anthony Appiah (2018) *The Lies That Bind*, London: Profile.
3. Francis Fukuyama (2018) *Identity: The Demand for Dignity and the Politics of Resentment*, London: Profile, p. 9.
4. Yascha Mounk (2018) *The People vs Democracy: Why Our Freedom Is in Danger and How to Save It*, London: Harvard University Press, p. 121.
5. *Le Point* (2018) "56 % des Français jugent l'islam compatible avec les valeurs françaises", 11 February 2018, available online (accessed 12/03/2019 22:15): https://www.lepoint.fr/societe/56-des-francais-jugent-l-islam-compatible-avec-les-valeurs-francaises-11-02-2018-2193999_23.php
6. For a fuller discussion of this trend, see Amy Chua (2018) *Political Tribes: Group Instinct and the Fate of Nations*, London: Bloomsbury.
7. James Walters (2019) *Loving Your Neighbour in an Age of Religious Conflict: A New Agenda for Interfaith Relations*, London: Jessica Kingsley, p. 121.
8. See Rodney Stark and Roger Finke (1988) "American Religion in 1776: A Statistical Portrait", *Sociological Analysis* (49.1), 39–51.
9. For discussion on this theme, see, for example, John Gray (2013) *The Silence of Animals: On Progress and Other Modern Myths*, London: Penguin.
10. Quoted in Jill Lepore (2019) "A New Americanism: Why a Nation Needs a National Story", *Foreign Affairs*, 5 February 2019, available online (accessed 04/06/2019 17:15): https://www.foreignaffairs.com/articles/united-states/2019–02–05/new-americanism-nationalism-jill-lepore
11. Timothy P. Carney (2019) *Alienated America: Why Some Places Thrive While Others Collapse*, New York: HarperCollins, p. 11.

12. R.C. Inglehart et al., eds (2014) "World Values Survey: Round Six—Country-Polled Datafile Version", cross-reference of questions V103 and V238, available online (accessed 06/06/2019 16:57): http://www.worldvaluessurvey.org/WVSDocumentationWV6.jsp

13. Ibid., cross-reference of V24 and Social Class.

14. Oliver Nachtwey, trans. Loren Balhorn & David Fernbach (2018) *Germany's Hidden Crisis: Social Decline in the Heart of Europe*, London: Verso.

15. Civil Societies Futures (2018) "The Story of Our Times: Shifting power, bridging divides, transforming society", final report, November 2018, p. 11.

16. Knight Foundation (2018) "Indicators of News Media Trust", 11 September 2018, available online (accessed 12/03/2019 22:55): https://www.knightfoundation.org/reports/indicators-of-news-media-trust

17. Raghuram Rajan (2019) *The Third Pillar: The Revival of Community in a Polarised World*, London: William Collins, p. 289.

18. One exploration of this can be found in Bruce Katz and Jeremy Nowak (2017) *The New Localism: How Cities Can Thrive in the Age of Populism*, Washington DC: Brookings Institution, which explores the effectiveness of cities and local communities in breaking through policy gridlocks and delivering change at a local level.

19. P.W. Speer, N.A. Peterson, A. Zippay & B.D. Christens (2010) "Participation in Congregation-Based Organizing: A Mixed-Method Study of Civic Engagement", in Maria Roberts-DeGennaro & Sondra J. Fogel (eds), *Using Evidence to Inform Practice for Community and Organizational Change*, Chicago: Lyceum, pp. 200–17.

20. Brian D. Christens and Paul W. Speer (2011) "Contextual influences on participation in community organizing: A multilevel longitudinal study", *American Journal of Community Psychology* (47.3–4), 253–63.

21. J. Hughey, N.A. Peterson, J.B. Lowe and F. Oprescu (2008) "Empowerment and sense of community: clarifying their relationship in community organizations", *Health Education & Behavior* (35.5), 651–63.

22. See, for example, Matteo Antonini, Michael A. Hogg, Lucia Mannetti,

Barbara Barbieri, and Joseph A. Wagoner (2015) "Motivating citizens to participate in public policymaking: Identification, trust and cost-benefit analyses", *Journal of Social and Political Psychology* (3.2), 131–47.

23. Shana Cohen, Sughra Ahmed & Alice Sandham (2013) "Near Neighbours Report", Woolf Institute, October 2013, available online (accessed 04/06/2019 17:20): https://www.woolf.cam.ac.uk/research/publications/reports/near-neighbours

24. See, for example, the report of the Joseph Rowntree Foundation on austerity's impact on charities and local government: Annette Hastings, Nick Bailey, Glen Bramley, Maria Gannon & David Watkins (2015) "The Cost of Cuts: The Impact on Local Government and Poorer Communities", Joseph Rowntree Foundation, 10 March 2015.

25. Colin Crouch (2004) *Post-Democracy*, Oxford: Polity.

26. Ank Michels and Harmen Binnema (2019) "Assessing the Impact of Deliberative Democratic Initiatives at the Local Level: A Framework for Analysis", *Administration & Society* (51.5), 749–69.

27. Ibid.

28. Richard Wilkinson and Kate Pickett (2009) *The Spirit Level: Why Equality is Better for Everyone*, London: Allen Lane.

29. Walter Scheidel (2017) *The Great Leveler: Violence and the History of Inequality from the Stone Age to the Twenty-First Century*, Princeton: Princeton University Press.

30. See Oxfam's "Commitment to Reducing Inequality" Index 2018, available online (accessed 04/06/2019 17:23): http://www.inequality-index.com

31. Nick Spencer (2016) *The Evolution of the West: How Christianity Has Shaped Our Values, Localism*, p. 166.

32. Paul Collier (2018) *The Future of Capitalism: Facing the New Anxieties*, London: Allen Lane, p. 69.

33. Felix Hörisch (2012) "The Macro-Economic Effect of Codetermination on Income Equality", *SSRN Electronic Journal, Arbeitspapiere*–Working Papers (147); Susan R. Holmberg (2017) "Fighting Short-Termism with Worker Power: Can Germany's Co-Determination System Fix American Corporate Governance?", Roosevelt Institute, October 2017.

34. Rowena Mason (2016) "May promises social reform in centrist leadership pitch", *The Guardian*, 11 July 2016, available online (accessed 04/06/2019): https://www.theguardian.com/politics/2016/jul/11/theresa-may-tory-leadership-pitch-andrea-leadsom

35. There has also been sporadic left-wing enthusiasm for such moves in recent years in the UK, most notably in the work of the economist Will Hutton.

36. William Davies (2009) *Reinventing the Firm*, London: Demos, p. 69.

37. Arlie Russell Hochschild (2018) *Strangers in Their Own Land*, New York: The New Press.

38. Pope John Paul II (1987) *Sollicitudo rei socialis*, papal encyclical, 30 December 1987, §38.

39. Robert D. Putnam and David E. Campbell (2010) *American Grace: How Religion Divides and Unites Us*, New York: Simon & Schuster, pp. 443–79.

40. Tomáš Halík (2014) "Templeton Prize Lecture", June 2014, text available online (accessed 13/03/2019 10:45): http://standpointmag.co.uk/templeton-prize-lecture-professor-tomas-halik

AFTERWORD

1. Kevin Rudd (2018) "The Rise of Authoritarian Capitalism", *The New York Times*, 16 September 2018.

2. See for example, Parag Khanna (2019) *The Future Is Asian: Global Order in the Twenty-First Century*, London: Orion; and Bruno Maçães (2018) *Belt and Road: A Chinese World Order*, London: Hurst.

INDEX

INDEX

INDEX

existential crisis, x, 6, 77, 106, 206, 250, 269

existentialism, ix

Facebook scandal, 217

Faith and Belief Forum, 204

"fake news", 20, 277n27

Fallwell Jr, Jerry, 42

Farron, Tim, case, 205

Fascism, 16–7
fall of, 18, 92

Female genital mutilation (FGM), 191, 192

FGM. See, Female genital mutilation (FGM)

financial crisis, Western, xiii, 74
Euro, 70, 75

Financial Times, 49, 221

Finkielkraut, Alain, 27

Five Star Movement (M5S), 10, 165

foreign aid, 226
experts to build political leadership, 227
military intervention, 227
poverty traps, 227

foreign intervention, 233

foreign policy (US), 225

fossil fuel industry, 116

FPÖ. *See*, Freedom Party of Austria

France, 5, 27, 32, 34, 35, 37, 39, 40, 43, 51, 59–61, 65, 74, 84, 139, 149, 156, 162, 165, 170, 173, 177, 179, 190, 192, 198, 199, 231, 233, 239, 243

Franco's dictatorship (1939–75), 7

Francoism, 7, 17

free market economics, 149

Freedom House, 88–89
annual report, 19
authoritarian slide in Hungary, 89

Freedom Party of Austria (FPÖ), xii, 96

"freeloader", 152

French Revolution, slogans, 14

Freud, Sigmund, 9

Fridays For Future, (November 2018), 184

Friedman, Milton, 24, 113
Freedom and Capitalism, 24, 113

Fukuyama, Francis, 11, 18, 140, 242
"end of history", 18, 81, 85, 106, 270

G1000 experiments, 256–7

Garton Ash, Timothy, 79
New York Review of Books, 79

Gasperi, Alcide De, 60

Gay Science, The, 46

Gazeta Polska (magazine)
Sakiewicz, Tomasz, 94

GDP, 70, 83, 91, 168

Geneva Circle of Christian Democrats, 59, 60

Genocides, 103, 224

Germany, 17

"gig economy", 146

INDEX

INDEX

INDEX

INDEX